I0123734

Gloom to Glory

Gloom to Glory

Indira Dutta
Meera Lal

ALLIED PUBLISHERS PVT. LTD.

New Delhi • Mumbai • Kolkata • Lucknow • Chennai
Nagpur • Bangalore • Hyderabad • Ahmedabad

ALLIED PUBLISHERS PRIVATE LIMITED

1/13-14 Asaf Ali Road, **New Delhi**–110002
Ph.: 011-23239001 • E-mail: delhi.books@alliedpublishers.com

87/4, Chander Nagar, Alambagh, **Lucknow**–226005
Ph.: 0522-4012850 • E-mail: appltdlko9@gmail.com

17 Chittaranjan Avenue, **Kolkata**–700072
Ph.: 033-22129618 • E-mail: cal.books@alliedpublishers.com

15 J.N. Heredia Marg, Ballard Estate, **Mumbai**–400001
Ph.: 022-42126969 • E-mail: mumbai.books@alliedpublishers.com

60 Shiv Sunder Apartments (Ground Floor), Central Bazar Road,
Bajaj Nagar, **Nagpur**–440010
Ph.: 0712-2234210 • E-mail: ngp.books@alliedpublishers.com

F-1 Sun House (First Floor), C.G. Road, Navrangpura,
Ellisbridge P.O., **Ahmedabad**–380006
Ph.: 079-26465916 • E-mail: ahmbd.books@alliedpublishers.com

751 Anna Salai, **Chennai**–600002
Ph.: 044-28523938 • E-mail: chennai.books@alliedpublishers.com

The Hebbar Sreevaishnava Sabha, Sudarshan Complex–2
No. 22, Seshadri Road, **Bangalore**–560009
Ph.: 080-22262081 • E-Mail: bngl.books@alliedpublishers.com

3-2-844/6 & 7 Kachiguda Station Road, **Hyderabad**–500027
Ph.: 040-24619079 • E-mail: hyd.books@alliedpublishers.com

Website: www.alliedpublishers.com

© 2016, Authors

First Edition: 2016

No part of the material protected by this copyright notice may be reproduced or utilized in any form or by any means, electronic or mechanical including photocopying, recording or by any information storage and retrieval system, without prior written permission from the copyright owners. The views expressed in this volume are of the individual contributors, editor or author and do not represent the view point of the Centre.

ISBN: 978-93-85926-07-5

Published by Sunil Sachdev and printed by Ravi Sachdev at Allied Publishers Pvt. Ltd., (Printing Division), A-104 Mayapuri Phase II, New Delhi-110064

Preface

India believes in people centred development. The government has tried its level best to enhance human rights, freedom, capabilities and opportunities for every citizen but when we look towards tribal India, majority of them live a life of disgrace where poverty, disease and hunger all are the order of the day. The problems of the tribal people cannot be dealt in a holistic way as each state has its own socio-economic problems. The journey in Andhra Pradesh and Gujarat tells us that even though both the states have seen prosperity in many terms but when we look towards tribal development, it presents a sorry spectacle. There are several tribal development policies in both the states but the state of Gujarat has fared far better than its counterpart. As we are moving from Millennium Development Goals to Sustainable Development Goals it is a fact that sustainable work for the tribes is must to promote their sustainable human development. History has witnessed many revolutions but if we want to bring a revolutionary change among tribes we have to break the vicious circle of poverty they are trapped in.

It is estimated that some 50 million persons have been displaced since 1950 on account of various development projects, of which more than 40 per cent are tribes. These projects include large irrigation dams, hydroelectric projects, open cast and underground coal mines, super thermal power plants and mineral-based industrial units. In the name of development, tribes are displaced from their traditional habitats and livelihoods with little or no rehabilitation, and are rendered destitute, bewildered and pauperised by the development process. They are pushed into a vortex of increasing assetlessness, unemployment, debt bondage and hunger due to loss of access to traditional sources of livelihood viz., land, forests, rivers, pastures, cattle etc. In these large development projects, tribes lose their land not only to the project authorities, but even to non-tribal outsiders who converge into these areas and corner both the land and the new economic opportunities in commerce and petty industry. Even wage employment to local tribes is rare.

As tribal people in India perilously, sometimes hopelessly, grapple with these tragic consequences, the small clutch of bureaucratic programmes have done little to assist the precipitous poverty stricken, exploitation and disintegration of tribal communities. Tribal people respond occasionally with anger and assertion, often in anomie and despair. This takes the shape of '*Maoist attacks*' and militancy. However, these incidents are branded as a typical '*law and order*' problem, ignoring its socio-economic dimensions. One such discrimination occurred in Nellore in Andhra Pradesh recently when tribes were injured and beaten up by Vanniyars (pallikapu) dominant caste and (local landlords). This happened when the tribal villagers wanted to celebrate the 'jathara' of the local goddess.

Thus, when we look at tribes in general, all over India, they have not made much progress in all these years. Almost 91 percent of tribal population lives below poverty line and are mostly indebted. Hence, as far as food security, inclusive growth or financial inclusion is concerned it is a distant dream. It is unfortunate that the Ministry of Tribal Affairs created in 2000 does not give sufficient attention to these issues on the plea that many of such subjects have not been allotted to them. Still as compared to Andhra Pradesh, Gujarat has shown little progress in tribal development. The efforts of the government in both the states have shown positive outcomes over the past decade. We anticipate that in the near future the tribal population will see a new dawn where they could march from 'gloom to glory'.

We express our heartfelt gratitude to Professor S.A. Bari, Vice Chancellor, Central University of Gujarat and Prof. V.S. Rao, Director BITS-Pilani, Hyderabad Campus for their constant support and guidance. We are equally grateful to Professor N. Rajaram, Dean of the School of Social Sciences, Central University of Gujarat for his constant encouragement. Last but not the least we thank Balraj and Sridhar from Hyderabad and Ruchi and Stuti from Central University of Gujarat for giving their valuable time in various ways.

I express my sincere thanks to Allied Publishers Pvt. Ltd. for bringing out the book in such as good form.

Contents

Abbreviations

AIDS	Acquired Immune Deficiency Syndrome
AIE	Alternative and Innovative Education
AITPN	Asian Indigenous and Tribal Peoples Network
AP	Andhra Pradesh
APFDC	Andhra Pradesh Forest Development Corporation
APSALTR	Andhra Pradesh Scheduled Areas Land Transfer Regulation
ASSAV	Adivasi Abhivrudhi Samskrithika Sangham
BCG	Bacillus Calmette–Guérin
BIA	Bureau of India Affairs
BPL	Below Poverty Line
CCD	Conservation-Cum-Development
CDP	Community Development Project
CDS	Combined Defence Services
CFM	Community Forest Management
CMP	Common Minimum Programme
CRSP	Central Rural Sanitation Programme
DESA	District Education Support Agency
DPAP	Drought Prone Area Programme
DPEP	District Primary Education Programme
DPT	Diphtheria, Pertussis (Whooping Cough) and Tetanus
DRDA	District Rural Development Agency
EAS	Employment Assurance Scheme
EGS	Education Guarantee Scheme
FDA	Forest Development Agency
GCC	Girijana Cooperative Corporation
GOI	Government of India
GUJCOST	Gujarat Council on Science and Technology

GVVKs	Girijana Vidya Vikas Kendras
GWRDC	Gujarat Water Resources Development Corporation
HDI	Human Development Index
IADP	Integrated Area Development Programme
IAS	Indian Administrative Service
IAY	Indira Awas Yojana
IFAD	International Fund for Agricultural Development
IHS	Indian Health Service
IKP	Indira Kranthi Patham
IPR	Intellectual Property Rights
IPS	Indian Police Service
IRDP	Integrated Rural Development Programme
ITDA	Integrated Tribal Development Agencies
ITDP	Integrated Tribal Development Projects
ITI	Industrial Training Institute
JFMC	Joint Forest Management Committees
JGSY	Jawahar Gram Samrudhi Yojana
JPC	Joint Parliamentary Committee
JRY	Jawahar Rozgar Yojana
LAMPS	Large Sized Multi-Purpose Societies
LIC	Life Insurance Corporation
MADA	Modified Area Development Approach
MCH	Maternal and Child Health
MDGs	Millennium Development Goals
MFAL	Marginal Farmers Agricultural Labourers Development Agencies
MFI	Micro-Finance Institution
MFP	Minor Forest Produce
MKSS	Mazdoor Kisan Shakti Sangathan
MLA	Member of the Legislative Assembly
MP	Member of Parliament
NABARD	National Bank for Agriculture and Rural Development

NAC	National Advisory Council
NDA	National Defence Academy
NES	National Extension Schemes
NGO	Non-Governmental Organization
NMBS	National Maternity Benefit Scheme
NPE	National Policy on Education
NREGA	National Rural Employment Guarantee Act
NREP	National Rural Employment Programme
NSTFDC	National Scheduled Tribes Finance and Development Corporation
NTFP	Non Timber Forest Produce
OMB	Office of Management and Budget
PDS	Public Distribution System
PESA	Panchayat Extension to the Scheduled Areas
PHC	Primary Health Centre
PMRY	Prime Minister's Rozgar Yojana
POA	Programme of Action
PPP	Public Private Partnership
PTG	Primitive Tribal Group
RAEOs	Rural Agriculture Extension Officers
RRB	Regional Rural Bank
SAP	Surplus Agriculture Produce
SC	Scheduled Caste
SCA	Special Central Assistance
SERP	Society for Elimination of Rural Poverty
SFDA	Small Farmers Development Agencies
SGSY	Swarnajayanti Gram Swarojgar Yojana
SHGs	Self Help Groups
SJSRY	Swarna Jayanthi Shahri Rozgar Yojana
SMC	School Management Committee
SMPT	Special Multi-Purpose Tribal Blocks
SPAY	Sardar Patel Awas Yojana

SSA   Sarva Shiksha Abhiyan
SSC   Staff Selection Commission
SSTD   Sub-Plan Scheme for Tribal Development
ST   Scheduled Tribe
STD   Sexually Transmitted Diseases
STDCC   State Tribal Development Cooperative
           Corporation
STMU   State Tribal Management Units
SWC   Soil and Water Conservation
TASP   Tribal Area Sub Plan
TB   Tuberculosis
TCPC   Training cum Production Centres
TDA   Tribal Development Agencies
TDB   Tribal Development Block
TDCC   Tribal Development Cooperative Corporation
THP   Tribal Health Plan
TLM   Teaching Learning Material
TPMU   Tribal Project Management Unit
TRIFED   Tribal Cooperative Marketing Development
           Federation of India
TRIPCO   Tribal Power Company Limited
TRYSEM   Training Rural Youth for Self Employment
TSC   Total Sanitation Campaign
TSP   Tribal Sub Plan
UPSE   Union Public Service Commission Exams
UPSC   Union Public Service Commission
UT   Union Territory
VA   Voluntary Agencies
VEC   Village Education Committees
VKY   Vanbandhu Kalyan Yojana
WDR   World Development Report

Scheduled Tribes in India
An Overview

INTRODUCTION

In the 21st century when the entire world desires for a sustainable and glorious future there is no scope for us to leave behind the marginalized and vulnerable sections of the society. A lot have been achieved in the past under the Millennium Development Goals and now we are marching towards the Sustainable Development Goals at a rapid pace. When we talk about 'Sustainable Development' we cannot turn a cold shoulder towards the social and economic empowerment of the Scheduled Tribes (STs). India is a land of harmony and diverse cultures. It is home to 104.3 million tribal people. There are twenty countries in the world with substantial tribal population. India has the largest tribal population in the world. We have arrived on the twelfth five year plan which focuses on 'inclusive growth'. Hence rampant measures are needed to be taken for raising the educational and living standards of the STs, if we dream of an all square development scenario in the nation. Several programmes are being implemented through states, government's apex corporations, and NGOs for the upliftment of disadvantaged and marginalized sections of society.

The 2011 census of India had recorded the tribal population to constitute 8.6 percent of the national population. Tribal groups are very heterogeneous. Article 366(25) refers to Scheduled Tribes as those communities who are scheduled in accordance with Article 342 of the Constitution. According to Article 342 of the Constitution, the Scheduled Tribes are the tribes or tribal communities or part of or groups within these tribes and tribal communities which have been declared as such by the President through a public notification. Scheduled Tribes are spread across the country mainly in forest and hilly regions.

Primitive, geographically isolated, shy and socially, education-ally and economically backward these are the traits that distinguish Scheduled Tribes of our country from other communities. Tribal communities live in about 15% of the country's areas in various ecological and geo-climatic conditions ranging from plains to forests, hills and inaccessible areas. Tribal groups are at different stages of social, economic and educational development. While some tribal communities have adopted a mainstream way of life at one end of the spectrum, there are 75 Primitive Tribal Groups (PTGs), at the other, who are characterized by: a pre-agriculture level of technology; a stagnant or declining population; extremely low literacy and subsistence level of economy.

The Ministry of Tribal Affairs has sanctioned proposals of State Governments and NGOs covering about 62 PTGs. The proposals covering mainly the activities relating to food, security, promotion of primary education and extending basic minimum health services to the primitive tribes were approved and Primitive tribal groups are tribal communities among the STs who live in near isolation in inaccessible habitats.

There are over 500 tribes (with many overlapping communities in more than one State) as notified under article 342 of the Constitution of India, spread over different States and Union Territories of the country, the largest number of tribal communities being in the State of Orissa. The main concentration of tribal population is in Central India and in the North-Eastern States. However, they have their presence in all States and Union Territories except Haryana, Punjab, Delhi, Pondicherry and Chandigarh. The predominantly tribal populated States of the country (tribal population more than 50% of the total population) are Arunachal Pradesh, Meghalaya, Mizoram, Nagaland, Union Territories of Dadra and Nagar Haveli and Lakshadweep. States with sizeable tribal population and having areas of large tribal concentration are Andhra Pradesh, Assam, Chhattisgarh, Gujarat, Himachal Pradesh, Madhya Pradesh, Maharashtra, Odisha and Rajasthan.

The 2011 Census figures reveal that an overwhelming proportion of the main workers from these communities are engaged in primary sector activities. The literacy rate of Scheduled Tribes is around quite low, as against the national average. More than three-quarters of Scheduled Tribes women are illiterate. These disparities are compounded by higher dropout rates in formal education resulting in disproportionately low representation in higher education. Not surprisingly, the cumulative effect has been that the proportion of Scheduled Tribes below the poverty line is substantially higher than the national average. The estimate of tribal poverty made by Planning Commission for the year 2010–11 shows that more than 51 percent rural and about 49 percent urban Scheduled Tribes were still living below the poverty line.

A majority of tribal land holdings (60 percent) are below 2 hectare and only 5 percent are above 10 hectares. However, the ownership of large holdings does not give a distinct advantage unless the land is of good quality. There are areas in which even large holdings beyond 5 hectares are not sufficient to meet the food necessity of the tribal families all-round the year. Some initiatives e.g. grain-golas, jhum cultivation, wadi project, Joint Forest Management (JFM), enhancing Livelihood and Health through Traditional Knowledge Management, Associating Individual Rural Volunteers (IRVs) in SHG Bank Linkage Programme have been taken in various tribal areas of the country.

The tribal population constituting around 8 percent of the population is mainly dependent on forests, livestock and agriculture. But the dwindling forest resources, shrinking water table and poor fuel and fodder supply have jeopardized their agriculture and livestock productivity. The small and marginal, fragmented and un-irrigated holdings capable of raising a mono crop and low productive livestock population do not provide adequate resources and incomes for their livelihood. Such factors, including their bigger family size, compel them to starve or migrate to nearby towns and many a time to distant localities for subsistence. Efforts are being made by the Government and Non-Government Organizations (NGO) to provide financial and technical assistance to the tribes through various schemes and development programmes in the country since 1947. These existing development schemes offer some relief to the tribes, but there are recurrent relapses to poverty due to various reasons. As a result, more than half of tribal population is still below poverty level and unable to join the mainstream.

Promotion of all round development of tribes inhabiting the length and breadth of our country has received priority attention of the government. There are numerous government policies for ensuring the welfare and well-being of tribes. The Governments at State as well as Central levels have made sustained efforts to provide opportunity to these communities for their economic development by eradicating poverty and health problems and developing communication for removal of isolation of their habitats. The Constitution of India seeks to secure for all its citizens, among other things, social and economic justice, equality of status and opportunity and assures the dignity of the individual. The Constitution further provides social, economic and political guarantees to the disadvantaged sections of people. Some provisions are specific to both Scheduled Castes and Scheduled Tribes, whereas some are specific to only Scheduled Tribes.

There are innumerable constraints responsible for lower pace of tribal development process than desired. Some of the major constraints are the destruction of forests, lack of awareness and protection of tribal rights and concessions. The forests are not only the source of livelihood for tribes but there exists an intricate relationship between tribes and forests in forest ecosystems. The depleting forest resources are threatening imminent food security for a good portion of the tribal population. There exists lack of awareness among tribal population about various developmental programmes launched by Government of India and States, resulting in their exploitation. The Tribes have been given numerous rights and concessions under various statutes of Central as well as State Governments but they remain deprived of the benefits arising out of such statutory provisions due to their ignorance and apathy of enforcing agencies.

The tribal situation in the country presents a varied picture. Some areas have high Tribal concentration while in other areas; the tribes form only a small portion of the total population. There are some tribal groups, which are still at the food gathering stage, some others practice shifting cultivation, yet other may be pursuing primitive forms of agriculture.

The Constitution of India provides for a comprehensive framework for the socio-economic development of Scheduled Tribes and for preventing their exploitation by other groups of society. A detailed and comprehensive review of the tribal problem was taken on the eve of the Fifth Five Year Plan and the Tribal sub-Plan strategy took note of the fact that an integrated approach to the tribal problems was necessary in terms of their geographic and demographic concentration.

Accordingly, the tribal areas in the country were classified under three broad categories:

- States and Union Territories having a majority scheduled tribe population.
- States and Union Territories having substantial tribal population but majority tribal population in particular administrative units, such as block and tehsils.

- States and Union Territories having dispersed tribal population.

In the light of the above approach, it was decided that tribal majority states like Arunachal Pradesh, Meghalaya, Mizoram, Nagaland and U.Ts. of Lakshadweep and Dadra and Nagar Haveli may not need a Tribal sub-Plan, as the entire plan of these States/Union Territories was primarily meant for the S.T. population constitutioning the majority. For the second category of states and Union Territories, Tribal sub-Plan approach was adopted after delineating areas of tribal concentration. A similar approach was also adopted in case of states and Union Territories having dispersed tribal population by paying special attention to pockets of tribal concentrations, keeping in view their tenor of dispersal. To look after the tribal population coming within the new tribal sub-Plan strategy in a coordinated manner, Integrated Tribal Development Projects (ITDP) were conceived during Fifth Five Year Plan and these have been continued since them. During the Sixth Plan, Modified Area Development Approach (MADA) was adopted to cover smaller areas of tribal concentration and during the Seventh Plan, the TSP strategy was extended further to cover smaller areas of tribal concentration and thus clusters of tribal concentration were identified. This will be discussed in further detail in the following chapters.

The Constitution of India incorporates several special provisions for the promotion of educational and economic interest of Scheduled Tribes and their protection from social injustice and from all forms of exploitation. These objectives are sought to be achieved through a strategy known as the Tribal Sub-Plan (TSP) strategy, which was adopted at the beginning of the Fifth Five Year Plan. The strategy seeks to ensure adequate flow of funds for tribal development form the State Plan allocations, schemes/programmes of

Central Ministries/Departments, financial and Developmental Institutions. The cornerstone of this strategy has been to ensure earmarking of funds for TSP by States/UTs in proportion to the ST population in those State/UTs. Besides the efforts of the States/UTs and the Central Ministries/ Departments to formulate and implement Tribal Sub-Plan for achieving socio-economic development of STs, the Ministry of Tribal Affairs is implementing several schemes and programmes for the benefits of STs.

There are now 194 ITDPs in the country, where the ST population is more than 50% of the total population of the blocks or groups of block. During the Sixth Plan, pockets outside ITDP areas, having a total population of 10,000 with at least 5,000 scheduled tribes were covered under the Tribal Sub-Plan under MADA. So far 252 MADA pockets have been identified in the country. In addition, 79 clusters with a total population of 5,000 of which 50 percent are schedule tribes have been identified.

In order to give more focused attention to the development of Scheduled Tribes, a separate Ministry, known as the Ministry of Tribal Affairs was constituted in October 1999. The new Ministry carved out of the Ministry of Social Justice and Empowerment, is the nodal Ministry for overall policy, planning and coordination of programmes and schemes for the development of Scheduled Tribes. The mandate of the Ministry includes social security and social insurance with respect to the Scheduled Tribes, tribal welfare planning, project formulation research and training, promotion and development of voluntary efforts on tribal welfare and certain matters relating to administration of the Scheduled Areas. In regard to sectoral programmes and development of these communities, the policy, planning, monitoring, evaluation and also their coordination is the responsibility of the concerned Central Ministries/Departments, State Governments and UT Administrations. Each Central Ministry/Department will be the nodal Ministry of Department concerning its sector. Ministry of Tribal Affairs supports and supplements the efforts of State Governments/U.T. Administrations and the various Central Ministries/Departments for the holistic development of these communities.

For the welfare and development of STs, an annual outlay of ₹ 4090 crore has been made in the annual plan for 2012–13. During 2012–13, ₹ 1200 crore has been provided by as Special Central Assistance (SCA) to Tribal Sub-Plan (TSP). The SCA to TSP is a 100 percent grant extended to states as additional funding to their TSP for family-oriented income-generating schemes, creation of incidental infrastructure, extending financial assistance to Self-Help Groups (SHGs), and community-based activities development of forest villages. The outlay for grants-in-aid under Article 275(1) during 2012–13 is ₹ 1317 crore.

The Haque Committee set up by the Panchayati Raj Ministry estimated in its May 2011 report that 275 million tribal women and men depend on Minor Forest Produce (MFP). The report detailed the rampant exploitation of MFP trade and strongly recommended that the government set up a commission to ensure a Minimum Support Price (MSP) for MFP on the lines of MSP for foodgrains. The estimated cost of procurement according to the committee was between ₹ 4000 and ₹ 5000 crore a year.

The Planning Commission in the 12th Five Year Plan brought down the cost to ₹ 2000 crore for the entire Plan period or just ₹ 400 crore per year. However contrary to this though some assistance has been provided to TSP and that too it is only 0.22 percent of GDP the same as last year, not even a small amount has been allocated for MSP for minor forest produce. Nor even a commission has been set up so far.

For economic empowerment of STs, financial support is extended through the National Scheduled Tribes Finance and Development Corporation (NSTFDC) in the form of loans and micro-credit at concessional rates of interest for income-generating activities. Market development of Tribal products and their retail marketing is done by the Tribal Co-operative Marketing Development Federation of India Limited (TRIFED) through its sales outlets. Till 31ˢᵗ October 2012, 32.37 lakh claims had been filed and 12.76 lakh titles distributed under the provisions of the 'The Scheduled Tribes and Other Traditional Forest Dwellers Act 2006'. Further 14,603 titles were ready for distribution. A total of 27.88 lakh claims have been disposed so far. This is applaudable but a very small dent to the glaring problem of land alienation and indebtedness.

For promoting education the government has also introduced many schemes for helping ST students. Under the post matric scholarship scheme, 100 percent financial assistance is provided to ST students whose family income is less than or equal to ₹ 2 lakh per annum to pursue post-matric level education including professional, graduate, and post-graduate courses in recognized institutions. The Top Class Education Scheme for STs provides financial assistance for quality education to 625 ST students per annum to pursue studies at degree and post degree level in any of the 125 identified institutions, family income not exceeding ₹ 2 Lakh as above. Financial assistance is also provided to 15 eligible ST students for pursuing higher studies abroad in specified fields at Master's and Ph.D. level under the National Overseas Scholarship Scheme. A scheme for strengthening of education among ST Girls in Low Literacy Districts is also being implemented to bridge the gap in literacy levels between the general female population and tribal women. But here again we find that the percentage allotted under these schemes are too meager and inadequate to meet the dire needs of the tribal population all India basis.

ETHNIC TRIBES AND THEIR PREDICAMENT IN ANDHRA PRADESH

Andhra Pradesh ranks tenth compared to all Indian States in the Human Development Index scores with a score of 0.416.

The National Council of Applied Economic Research district analysis in 2001 reveals that Khammam, Krishna, West Godavari, Chitoor and Medak are the five districts with the highest Human Development Index scores in ascending order in rural AP. The data show that the poor make up 16.3 percent of the total population in rural AP and expenditure on consumption is around 13.5 percent of the total consumption expenditure. The female literacy rate is 0.66 compared to male literacy rate in rural AP. The district wise variations for poverty ratio are high and low for the ratio of female/male literacy rate.

In Andhra Pradesh there are 32 lakh tribes, and 50 lakh nomads. Their habitat is spread along coastal and mountain strips and hilly regions from Srikakulam district to Khammam district and Godavari district, right up to north eastward to Adilabad region. Tribes of A.P. are classified into 2 groups- hilly tracts of Deccan Plateau and by Godavari and Krishna rivers. 33 tribes of Scheduled Tribes are found in 8 districts of A.P. Most pronounced are Khondas, Kolamis, Koyas, Valmikis, Bhagatas, Savaras, Jatayas and many more.

The lush green jungles of the Eastern Ghats, spread over nine districts of Andhra Pradesh and comprising 11,595 sq. miles of the State, are no longer a secure haven for nearly 33 tribal communities, including seven primitive groups, inhabiting these highlands. In the four decades since Independence, the tribes have steadily lost their hold on much of this area. While many have lost their sources of livelihood, others have sought refuge in deep **forests**. According to the 1991 census, the region's tribal-non-tribal ratio had dropped to 2:1 from the 1950 proportion of 6:1. And this demographic change has been largely brought about by official policies. Thanks to amendments made to the land transfer regulations in the tribal belt by the government, the non-tribes are holding almost 55 percent of tribal lands either benami or through clandestine means.

ETHNIC TRIBES AND THEIR PREDICAMENT IN GUJARAT

Dahod known as Dohad is a district bounded by Panchmahals in the west, Vadodara in the south, Jhabua district of MP in the east and Banswara district of Rajasthan in the north. Dahod covers an area of 3,646 Kms and has got seven talukas namely Dahod, Jalod, Dhanpur, Devgadh Baria, Garbada, Limkheda and Fatepura. The population of Dahod is 2,126,558 according to 2011 census and it is mainly dominated by tribes. These are marginalized indigenous tribal people comprising of different sub-groups such as Bhils, Damor, Choudry, Gamit, Rathwa, Vasava and Patelia. When we talk about ethnic group, it is basically the Bhil tribe. They are very much attached to their own culture and tradition. Not only this, they are talented in sculpture work and make beautiful statues of horses, elephants, tigers and deities out of clay. A forested landscape with a variety of flora and fauna offer motivation and inspire the local population in acts of creative intensity. Teracotta figurines, utensils and storage items grace Rathwa and Bhill dwelling area, while rituals give way to profession of wall paintings.

Here, we notice a large number of economically poor and socially excluded adivas is with extremely low health status of women, low education and a very high number of migrations.

Its natural resources like forest and water have been either with forest department or with the irrigation department barring access to these by the community. Due to the lack of any major river, water cannot be conserved easily in this area. Also because the area is on a slope, there is lot of soil erosion. This has resulted in disappearing forest cover.

The massive migration has led to loss of tribal traditional knowledge. In Dahod district there are several tribal villages where seasonal migration is very high. What is needed is that there should be more focus on development of water resource which would logically result in development of agriculture, horticulture, dairy and other ancillary activities related with agricultural development so that they could get sustainable income and could improve their socio-economic status.

When we look at tribes in general, they have not made any progress in any way. Almost 91 percent of tribal population lives below poverty line. When we talk about food security, tribes find hard to earn one square meal. Majority of the tribal population depend on agriculture but agriculture is affected by erratic rainfall. So migration has become a common phenomenon, in search of their basic necessity, food. They either move to other rural areas, urban areas and other distant places.

The main source of income is agriculture and animal husbandry. They possess the knowledge of manufacturing agricultural equipment and are also aware of repairing them. They also collect Gum, Ayurvedic Medicines (herbs) and Honey and try to generate income by selling it in the market. But the current trend of migration reveals that there is loss of traditional knowledge of herbs and other medicinal plants.

Regarding health and education, tribes in Dahod present a sorry spectacle. Malnutrition due to insufficient nutrient intake has made them more miserable. The greatest tragedy is that they are not aware of healthcare facilities. Children of the tribal families do not attend school, as there is widespread lack of awareness concerning the future benefits. Though ashram-shalas and primary schools are visible in talukas but the drop-out rate is very high. Children of the tribal families prefer to migrate with their parents for work to urban areas. The social consequences of migration are horrible and manifest themselves in the form of bonded labour, forced participation in flesh trade, high impact mortality and high level of absolute hunger.

At present some dedicated NGOs like Sadguru Foundation and Sahaj both are working very hard to provide benefit to the tribal population. There are at present 1,579 self-help groups who because of support of NGOs, have not only accumulated good savings but are actively leveraging their savings with institutional finance, mainly for productive purposes. SHG Federation Committee Members of five talukas (Dahod, Jalod, Garbada, Dhanpur and Limkheda) of Dahod district consists of 10,055 women workers. The district level and tehsil level SHG federations are actively planning to diversify and take up different livelihood programs. It is providing excellent opportunity for leadership development among tribal women. An unique development programme in Dhanpur is that Dhanpur Taluka Federation of women SHG groups has entrusted with the activity of mechanized agriculture. This federation has got 18 tractors free cost from John Deere India Pvt. Limited, Pune, an international tractor company under the programme of Tribal Development Department of Gujarat. The entire management is done by tribal women.

The horticulture programme which is popularly known as Wadi Programme has grown very fast in recent years in Dahod with the help of NGOs. At present, 25,000 farms have opted for this horticulture programme. In order to sustain and strengthen this programme, six taluka co-operatives have been formed by farmers. These co-operatives have accumulated worth ₹ 65 lakhs which are handy for various activities like nursery raising, mother beds, supply of seeds and other inputs. Floriculture has become highly profitable cultivation in Dahod where tribal women are helping their male counterparts. The earning from floriculture is between Rupees thirty thousand to Rupees one lakh.

Under bio-gas programme, women are trained as masons to construct bio-gas plant in villages. After training they are doing the jobs very well. This shows that tribal women have got both entrepreneurship and technical capability.

The tribes in Andhra Pradesh and Gujarat have been analyzed on the basis of three parameters namely, resource conditions relating to financial accessibility indebtedness and infrastructure, performance of agriculture, land alienation and forest produce and lastly, Human Development Indicators in relation to quality education and delivery of health services.

Majority of the tribal development policies and programmes are lopsided not taking into account what are the basic requirements of the concerned tribes. Hence, unless the root cause behind these poor indicators is addressed, there are little chances that the poverty, health and literacy will significantly improve in the long run.

THE GLARING DISPARITIES AND PROBLEMS OF TRIBES

The studies commissioned by the Government of India have revealed the causal chain that leads to this state of affairs and confirmed that the fundamental reason for tribal land alienation is the fragile, constantly shrinking economic base of the tribes. Their traditional skills in the gathering of forest produce lost significance with the introduction of state ownership of forests, so that from food-gatherers they were reduced to wage-earners or encroachers. Private property in land extinguished the erstwhile right of tribal communities to free access to land in consonance with their needs. Settled agriculture brought with it its inevitable linkages with credit, inputs and markets, rendering the tribal even more dependent and vulnerable.

As the tribes have an innate fear based on bitter past experience of banks, cooperative institutions and other government sources of credit; they prefer the predictability of the moneylender despite his usurious interest rates. In any case, most banks and cooperative institutions are unwilling to provide consumption loans, and moneylenders are the only sources of consumption credit. A combination of these factors leads to an extreme dependence on moneylenders on the part of the tribal, keeping him in perpetual debt and resulting in the mortgage and ultimate loss of his land. Though this phenomenon is common enough, another particularly tragic outcome of this indebtedness is the phenomenon of bondage, wherein people pledge their person and sometimes even that of their families against a loan. Repayments are computed in such terms that it is not unusual for bondage to persist until death, and to be passed on as a burdensome inheritance to subsequent generations. The practice of bonded labour is known by different names in different regions. In Andhra it is *Vetti*.

The empirical analysis also establishes the sad fact that government policy itself has, directly or indirectly, contributed to the phenomenon of tribal land alienation. It has been noted in several states that tribal land is being legally auctioned by co-operative credit societies and banks to recover dues. Auctioned land is purchased by non-tribes as well as rich tribes. Authorities responsible for regulating sale of tribal lands to non-tribes have been found to frequently collude with non-tribes to defraud the tribal landowners. The same collusion has deprived tribes of their rights to land in times of land settlement, or implementation of laws giving ownership rights to occupancy tenants.

Various studies commissioned by the Government of India with regard to other states, also establish that transfers of land from tribal landowners to non-tribes continued despite the various enactments, for a variety of reasons. Collectors or other agencies responsible for protecting the interests of tribes while regulating such transfers, in most cases did not apply their minds to issues of vital importance to the tribes. These include whether or not, the tribal had any other alternative livelihood, or sufficient land for viable cultivation even after sale, whether sufficient price was being paid, whether the sale was actually to enable repayment for usurious loans from a moneylenders etc. Legal transfers also took place by actions for recovery of dues and mortgages, by decrees of civil courts, misuse of provisions for settlement of occupancy tenants, settlement operations etc.

The persistent problem of indebtedness amongst the tribes is thus, one of the manifestations of their poverty. Despite the existence of legal/protective measures to curb the business of money-lending in tribal areas and provisions for debt-relief, their enforcement has been weak and ineffective. Also, the non-recognition of the tribal needs for their day-to-day consumption purposes by various credit extension programmes makes the otherwise vulnerable tribes fall as easy victims into debt-traps. Although the practice of bonded-labour stands abolished in the country through an Act of Parliament viz., the Bonded Labour System (Abolition) Act 1976, yet a total number of 2.52 lakh bonded labourers (including STs) were identified in March 1993 in 12 States i.e., Andhra Pradesh, Bihar, Karnataka, Madhya Pradesh, Orissa, Rajasthan, Tamil Nadu, Maharashtra, Uttar Pradesh, Kerala, Haryana and Gujarat. Immediate action is needed to review both laws and their implementation to restore alienated lands to tribes.

It is estimated that some 50 million persons have been displaced since 1950 on account of various development projects, of which more than 40 percent are tribes. These projects include large irrigation dams, hydroelectric projects, open cast and underground coal mines, super thermal power plants and mineral-based industrial units. In the name of development, tribes are displaced from their traditional habitats and livelihoods with little or no rehabilitation, and are rendered destitute, bewildered and pauperised by the development process. They are pushed into a vortex of increasing assetlessness, unemployment, debt bondage and hunger due to loss of access to traditional sources of livelihood viz., land, forests, rivers, pastures, cattle, etc. In these large development projects, tribes lose their land not only to the project authorities, but even to non-tribal outsiders who converge into these areas and corner both the land and the new economic opportunities in commerce and petty industry. Even wage employment to local tribes is rare. In Chotanagpur area, though the tribes constitute more than 50 percent of the total population, there are not more than 5 percent of them in the industrial working force. In some of the large firms like TISCO, Jamshedpur and Bharat Coking Coal Ltd., Dhanbad, the tribes employed are less than 5 percent. Development for the nation has meant displacement, pauperization, or, at its very best, peonage for the tribal.

The general question and debate going around in most academia circles is that the *'Money is spent, but who are the beneficiaries?'* and *'Is there any point in repeatedly allocating big sums of money exclusively for Dalits and Adivasis, without any idea of what is to be done with these?'* It is a relevant query to be directed at the Government's yearly budget, Union and states, which have been doing this for about two decades, in the name of social justice.

In 1989, the ideas were born of what is termed Special Component Plans for these deprived sections, under which each ministry or department was to set aside in its annual budget an amount proportionate to the population share of Scheduled Castes and Tribes (SC/ST) in the country. Yet, there is no plan even now as to how these funds are to be used.

In the Union budget presented this year, the allocations, called the Scheduled Caste Sub Plan and Tribal Sub Plan, registered a small increase from the previous year, with SCSP getting 0.4 percent more and TSP getting 0.3 percent more. These are still short of being proportionate to the population of SC/ST in the country. The other issue is the one mentioned, of the ends sought to be achieved by these allotment.

Just five ministries allocate 100 percent of funds for SC/ST dedicated programmes. Most ministries make a 20 percent allocation for SC/ST within various programmes, without designing any mechanisms to target SC/ST beneficiaries. For example, the seed infrastructure facility under the Ministry of Agriculture has set aside ₹ 79 crore to SCSP and TSP, while the National Food Security Mission (NFSM) has set aside ₹ 270 crore for it. NFSM is about raising of crop yields; there is no scheme for helping SC/ST. Even vague is the allocation under the National Vector-Borne Disease Control Programme of the health ministry. About ₹ 101 crore is set aside but there is no indication as to how this is to help SC or ST.

The Sarva Shiksha Abhiyan has set aside ₹ 4,793 crore for the SCSP and TSP. But there are no schemes specific to admission of SC or ST children or recruitment of SC/ST teachers. Again, ₹ 2,284 crore is set aside under the head of the Mid-Day Meal Scheme, though this is meant for all children. In the case of the rural development ministry, the approach has been straightforward. It has set aside funds only in the case of the Indira Awas Yojana and the Swarnajayanti Gram Swarojgar Yojana, where benefits can be extended directly to individuals from the SC/ST. A total of ₹ 7,492 crore has been allocated for SCSP and TSP from these two schemes. The flip side is that the ministry has refused to set aside funds for any other scheme, saying segregation of beneficiaries is not possible in, say, the National Rural Employment Guarantee Scheme or the Pradhan Mantri Gram SadakYojana. This is true of most schemes and, hence, calls for devising a method to spend the allocated funds. It is a grim situation that although allocations have been happening at the Centre and States, there is no mechanism to ensure that these funds actually reach the dalits and adivasis.

Central and State Schemes for Tribal Development

Promotion of all round development of tribal inhabiting the length and breadth of our country has received priority attention of the government. There are numerous government policies for ensuring the welfare and well-being of tribal. The Governments at State as well as Central levels have made sustained efforts to provide opportunity to these communities for their economic development by eradicating poverty and health problems and developing communication for removal of isolation of their habitats.

There are 67.8 million Scheduled Tribe people, constituting 8.08 percent of India's population. There are 698 Scheduled Tribes spread all over the country barring States and Union Territories like Chandigarh, Delhi, Haryana, Pondicherry and Punjab. Orissa has the largest number i.e. 68 of Scheduled Tribes. Article 366(25) refers to Scheduled Tribes as those communities who are scheduled in accordance with Article 342 of the Constitution. According to Article 342 of the Constitution, the Scheduled Tribes are the tribes or tribal communities or part of or groups within these tribes and tribal communities which have been declared as such by the President through a public notification. Scheduled Tribes are spread across the country mainly in forest and hilly regions. The President considers characteristics like the tribes' primitive traits, distinctive culture, shyness with the public at large, geographical isolation and social and economic backwardness before notifying them as a Scheduled Tribe. Seventy-five of the 698 Scheduled Tribes are identified as Primitive Tribal Groups considering they are more backward than Scheduled

Tribes. They continue to live in a preagricultural stage of economy and have very low literacy rates. Their populations are stagnant or even declining.

The tribal majority areas in the country are broadly divided into three categories, viz.: (i) predominantly tribal stated union territories, (ii) Scheduled area, and (iii) Non-Scheduled areas in the states. All the tribal-majority States and Union Territories are placed in a special category for availing funds. The development and administration of tribal areas is accepted as a special responsibility of the Central Government even though they are integral parts of the concerned states. Financial provisions for their development were considered in detail by the constituent assembly itself.

The schemes have been divided into two categories, viz.: (i) Central Sector Programmes which are fully financed by the Central Government, (ii) Centrally Sponsored Programmes which are partly financed by the Central Government, and rest of the expenditure meted out by the concerned State Government.

The utilisation of State funds is broadly classified under two categories-plan and non-plan. The plan technically covers all those items which are included in the State or the Central plan. The non-plan includes expenditure on general administration as also on the maintenance of development schemes.

The Special Central Assistance (SCA) for tribal sub-plans is allocated between different states on the basis of three criteria as under:

1. The tribal population of Sub-Plan area;
2. The geographical area of the Sub-Plan; and
3. The per capita gross output of the state.

The weightage for these three elements has been fixed in a certain proportion. While the first two criteria are simple, the quantum of assistance on the basis of the third criterion is determined with reference to the difference between the inverse of the State's per capita gross product and the inverse of the per capita gross national product. The financing agencies rendering their services in the tribal areas are Central Government, State Governments, institutions, viz., commercial banks, co-operative banks, NABARD and some voluntary organs.

The main causes of poverty among Tribal population are identified as illiteracy, unemployment, under employment and low productivity in agriculture. Since farmers in TSP area have land holding mostly on hill slopes, the fertility of land is very low. Further, droughts and soil erosion are now recurring features in the tribal areas. This has reduced employment opportunities for the tribal. For improving the economic status of tribal, special programmes were launched, during 1980's, mainly:

(a) The Asset Programme, and

(b) The Employment Programme.

The Asset Programme aims at the over-all integrated development of rural life through the removal of poverty and unemployment in rural areas. In this programme productive assets are directly given to the poor. It is believed that income generated from these productive assets would not only be sufficient to repay the bank loans but will help the assisted families to cross the 'poverty line'. This programme is popularly known as Integrated Rural Development Programme (IRDP).

The Employment Programme on the other hand aims at providing employment through public works during the adverse agricultural season. The employment programme asserts that poverty persists because of the lack of employment opportunities. The earlier employment schemes were ad hoc in nature but the employment programme launched from Oct.1 1980, popularly known as National Rural Employment

Programme (NREP) is considered as a permanent plan programme.

The travails of tribal development need to be understood properly. The programmes should be related to the specific needs of the tribal community. Also, tribal development programmes should be integrated with the on-going rural development programmes meant for poverty alleviation. A pragmatic and holistic approach to tribal development alone can produce good results.

The Constitution of India provides for a comprehensive framework for the socio-economic development of Scheduled Tribes and for preventing their exploitation by other groups of society. A detailed and comprehensive review of the tribal problem was taken on the eve of the Fifth Five Year Plan and the Tribal sub-Plan strategy took note of the fact that an integrated approach to the tribal problems was necessary in terms of their geographic and demographic concentration:

Accordingly, the tribal areas in the country were classified under three broad categories:

- States and Union Territories having a majority Scheduled Tribe population.
- States and Union Territories having substantial tribal population but majority tribal population in particular administrative units, such as block and tehsils.
- States and Union Territories having dispersed tribal population.

In the light of the above approach, it was decided that tribal majority States like Arunachal Pradesh, Meghalaya, Mizoram, Nagaland and U.Ts. of Lakshadweep and Dadra and Nagar Haveli may not need a Tribal sub-plan, as the entire plan of these States/Union Territories was primarily meant for the S.T. population constituting the majority. For the second category of States and Union Territories, tribal sub-Plan approach was adopted after delineating areas of tribal concentration. A similar approach was also adopted in case of States and Union Territories having dispersed tribal population by paying special attention to pockets of tribal concentrations, keeping in view their tenor of dispersal. To look after the tribal population coming within the new tribal sub-Plan strategy in a coordinated manner, Integrated Tribal Development Projects (ITDP) were conceived during Fifth Five Year Plan and these have been continued since them. During the Sixth Plan, Modified Area Development Approach (MADA) was adopted to cover smaller areas of tribal concentration and during the Seventh Plan, the Tribal Sub-Plan (TSP) strategy was extended further to cover smaller areas of tribal concentration and thus cluster of tribal concentration were identified.

The Constitution of India incorporates several special provisions for the promotion of educational and economic interest of Scheduled Tribes and their protection from social injustice and all forms of exploitation. These objectives are sought to be achieved as mentioned above through the strategy known as the Tribal Sub-Plan (TSP) strategy, which was adopted at the beginning of the Fifth Five Year Plan. The strategy seeks to ensure adequate flow of funds for tribal development form the State Plan allocations, schemes/programmes of Central Ministries/Departments, financial and Developmental Institutions. The cornerstone of this strategy has been to ensure earmarking of funds for TSP by States/UTs in proportion to the ST population in those State/UTs. Besides the efforts of the States/UTs and the Central Ministries/Departments to formulate and implement Tribal Sub-Plan for achieving socio-economic development of STs, the Ministry of Tribal Affairs is implementing several schemes and programmes for the benefits of STs.

In 1951, the government of India had started making efforts to raise the general standard of living of the weaker sections as well as tribal development in the form of National Extension Schemes (NES) with the objective to intensify the block level development activities. It was actually done to translate the spirit of the fundamental rights and Directive Principles of State Policy provided in Article 46: "the State shall promote with special care the educational and economic interests of the weaker sections of the people, and, in particular, of the Scheduled Castes and Scheduled Tribes, and shall protect them from social injustice and all forms of exploitation".

The NES was followed by the Community Development Project (CDP). In 1962, the block level programmes became found to be a blockade to the development of the weaker sections, and the Tribal Development Block (TDB) was introduced later. Since desired goals could not be realized through these programmes, the Tribal Integrated Development Project (ITDP) was started in 1972, and when it failed in practice another scheme, Tribal Sub-plan Scheme for Tribal Development (SSTD), was introduced in 1972 without defining the coverage area, and plan objectives. Integrated Tribal Development Projects (ITDP) and Integrated Area Development Programme (IADP) were started functioning under this in almost all States.

MAIN PROVISIONS FOR SCHEDULED TRIBES UNDER OUR CONSTITUTION

As present in the Fundamental Rights and Directive principles of state policy:

(a) Statutory recognition of tribal communities.
(b) Creation of scheduled areas for the thorough development of the tribal.
(c) Special representations in the parliament, in the legislative assemblies and local bodies.
(d) Special privileges in the form of reservation of a certain percentage of posts in government services and seats in educational institutions.

(e) Recognition of the right to use local language for administration and other purposes and to profess one's faith.

In addition to the above, three provisions of the constitution
deserve special mention:

1. According to the fifth schedule, Union Executive is given
   the power of giving direction to the States in matters
   relating to the administration of scheduled areas.
2. Article 275(1) of the constitution provides for grant-in-
   aid from the Union to the States for promoting the
   welfare of the Scheduled Tribes or for raising the level of
   administration of the Scheduled Areas.
3. The constitution also provides for the appointment of a
   commission for Scheduled Tribes for safeguarding their
   interests. The (Sivaraman committee) has recommended
   the "Sub-plan approach" with suitable adaptation for other
   backward areas for the better planning and development.

Thus the Constitution of India seeks to secure for all its
citizens, among other things, social and economic justice,
equality of status and opportunity and assures the dignity of
the individual. The Constitution further provides social,
economic and political guarantees to the disadvantaged
sections of people.

Before we analyse the various Central and State Schemes for
Tribal Development, let us briefly glance at the historical
importance given to Tribal development during our plan
periods.

DEVELOPMENT PROGRAMMES FOR
TRIBAL WELFARE

A number of employment oriented and developmental
programmes for tribal have been introduced by the
government of India. The major programmes are Integrated
Rural Development Programme (IRDP), Jawahar Rozgar
Yojana (JRY), Prime Minister's Rozgar Yojana (PMRY) and

Training for Self Employment for Rural Youth (TRYSEM). IRDP scheme is absolutely for rural people those belong to below poverty line and others are for both rural as well as urban youth. All these schemes are implemented in the state by the District Rural Development Agencies (DRDA's) in collaboration with Commercial and Cooperative Banks. PMRY was initiated in October 1993 to tackle the burning problem of educated unemployment. PMRY relates to setting up of self-employment ventures through industries and services. Any unemployed youth who is metric failed/passed or above or IT1 passed, is eligible for the benefits of the scheme subject to the condition that if he is between the age group of 18–35 years and his family income does not exceed ₹ 24,000 per annum. The youth should also be the permanent resident of the areas for at least three years and he should not be defaulter to any bank or financial institution. The scheme envisages 22.5 percent reservation for Scheduled Caste/ Scheduled Tribe and 27 percent for OBC. A maximum loan of ₹ 1 lakh per candidate is provided under this scheme, at an interest rate of 12.5 percent to 15.5 percent. The entrepreneur has to contribute 5 percent of project cost as margin money. No collateral security guarantee is asked on such loans. Period of repayment starts after a moratorium of six to eighteen months and range over 3 to 7 years. The government provides subsidy to the extent of 15 percent of the total loan disbursed with a ceiling of ₹ 7,500 per entrepreneur. In case of joint venture each partner may be provided a loan of ₹ 1 lakh subsidy. In such cases the interest is calculated for each partner separately at a rate of 15 percent of his share in the project cost limited to ₹ 7,500 for each partner.

The provision of compulsory training for entrepreneurship development is a salient feature of the scheme. Duration of this training is one month and trainees are provided stipend of ₹ 500 during the training period. With the objective of providing technical skills to rural youth to enable them to take up self-employment in the fields of agriculture and allied activities, industries, services and business activities, the scheme of TRYSEM was introduced in the year 1979 on Independence Day. The scheme works as a part of Integrated Rural Development Programme and aims at imparting training to about 2 lakhs rural youths every year from the 5,011 development blocks of the country and to lift them above the poverty line.

Under this scheme, those rural youth who are in the age group of 18 to 35 years with annual timely income from all sources are not exceeding ₹ 85,001 are eligible for selection. Preference is given to Scheduled Caste scheduled Tribe (50 percent) women (40 percent) and physically handicapped (3 percent). The selected beneficiaries are trained into the field of agriculture and allied activities, industry, service and business activities. The trainees are paid a monthly stipend or daily allowance during the training period. The training institution is provided honorarium along with ₹ 75 per trainee per month for purchase of raw materials. After completion of training, the beneficiaries are assisted in getting finance from the banks. A maximum of ₹ 35,000 can be sanctioned to each beneficiary as a composite loan. Trained youths are granted a subsidy by the government at the rate of l/3 of the cost of the project to set up self-employment venture. Beneficiaries are also provided marketing support for their finished products. The amount spent on this scheme is contributed by the Central and the State governments in 50:50 ratios. Since 1983 the scope of TRYSEM scheme has been enlarged. The main thrust of the development strategies during the recent past has been on the removal of poverty among tribal.

FIVE YEAR PLANS AND TRIBAL DEVELOPMENT

The planning commission laid down the objectives and strategies for tribal development from time to time. The following are the account of the tribal welfare programmes in India during the various plans.

The First Five Year Plan (1951–1956)

The First Five Year Plan outlined a positive policy for assisting the tribal as under:

- Assisting them to develop their natural resources and to evoke a productive economic life wherein they will enjoy the fruits of their own labour and will not be exploited by more organized economic forces from outside.
- It is not desirable to bring about changes in their religions and social life, except at the initiative of the tribal people themselves and with their willing consent.
- It is accepted that there are many features in tribal life which should not only be retained but also developed.
- The quality of their dialects as well as the rich content of their arts and crafts also needs to be appreciated and preserved.

In the First Five Year Plan, Community Development Projects for all round development of rural areas especially the weaker sections were started.

Second Five Year Plan (1956–1 961)

During this plan the Ministry of Home Affairs provided fund to the Ministry of Community Development to establish Special Multi-purpose Tribal Blocks (SMPT) in areas with prominent tribal population.

Third Five Year Plan (1961–1966)

Towards the end of the Second Plan, i.e., in 1959, SMPT Blocks were renamed as Tribal Development Blocks (TDB) and suggested it to be opened in all areas where over 60 percent of the population were tribal. In addition to the normal allotment of ₹ 12 lakhs to a community development block, a provision of ₹ 10 lakhs for 1st stage, and ₹ 5 lakhs for 2nd stage for TDB was also made.

Three Annual Plans (1966–1969)

During this period no special funds were provided for tribal development. However in 1969–70 a decision was taken to extend the total life of TDBs to 15 years by incorporating a new stage three. During the 3rd stage each TDB was given ₹ 10 lakhs.

Fourth Five Year Plan (1969–1974)

During the Fourth Five Year Plan, a series of programmes were conceived and addressed to specific target groups. The Small Farmers Development Agencies (SFDA) and Marginal Farmers Agricultural Labourers Development Agencies (MFAL) were the first two in the series. The Drought Prone Area Programme (DPAP) were initiated. Tribal Development Agencies (TDA's) were established and the level of investment in the new programme was much higher compared to TD Block. Six tribal development agencies were started during the Fourth Plan. Each Tribal Development Agency covered a group of TD Blocks. Tribal Development Agencies were expected to comprise elements of economic development, social services and prospective measures.

Fifth Five Year Plan (1974–1979)

Taking into account of the recommendations of the task force and other previous committees, during the Fifth Five Year Plan, an altogether new approach was adopted towards tribal development. This was termed as Tribal Sub-plan. It envisaged the total development of the tribal areas by financing through the Integrated Tribal Development Project (ITDP). The percentage wise investment for tribal development was high during the Fifth Five Year Plan with 3.01 percent of total plan outlay.

Sixth Five Year Plan (1980–1985)

The Sixth Plan continued the Sub-Plan approach of the Fifth Plan. This was to be supplemented by target beneficiary approach with the objective of narrowing the gap between the level of development of the tribal and other developed communities and bringing about a qualitative change in the life of a tribal community.

The broad objectives of the Sixth Plan were:

- A progressive reduction in the incidents of poverty and unemployment.
- Improving the quality of life through minimum needs programme.
- A reduction in inequalities of income and wealth.
- Infrastructure development for further exploitation of potential of the tribal region.

The States have to give due importance to the integration of programmes in the field and effective delegation of powers to the Project Authorities in ITDPs. The approach in the Sixth Plan for the development of backward areas in general was to rely, to a greater extent, on the development of agriculture, village and small-scale industries subsidiary occupations and related services and also the Minimum Need Programmes and Area Development Programmes. Improvement of economic status of the tribal should be the first concern and suitable programmes of horticulture, cattle development, poultry and piggery, etc. were carried out. Emphasis was placed more on family- oriented programmes than on infrastructure develop-ment unlike in the previous Plans.

Seventh Five Year Plan (1985–1990)

During the Seventh Plan, the Tribal Sub-Plan strategy comprised the following:

- Identification of the Development Blocks where tribal population is in majority and their constitution into

ITDPs with a view to an integrated and project-based approach for development.

- Marking of funds for the Tribal Sub-Plan and ensuring the flow of funds from the control of State plan, sectoral outlays and from financial institutions.
- Creation of appropriate administrative structures in tribal areas and adoption of appropriate personnel policies.

The programme of tribal development with ITDP pattern was continued in the Seventh Plan also without any basic or major changes in the approach Seventh Plan paid attention towards the rehabilitation of poor tribal and the removal of tribal women's backwardness.

Eighth Five Year Plan (1992–1997)

The strategy of Eighth Plan specifically aimed at improving the living environment of the tribal by giving them better social and civic amenities and facilities. The working group has recommended that the objective of the Seventh Plan would continue for the eighth plan period.

The objectives for the Eighth Plan are detailed below:

- Progressive reduction in poverty and creation of employment thereby providing reduction in income inequalities.
- Improving the quality of life through a minimum needs programme.
- Development and strengthening of infrastructure for further economic exploitation of the Tribal Sub-Plan area.
- Development of confidence of tribal along the desired lines through intensive educational efforts.

In the Eighth Five Year Plan, Tribal Sub-Plan (TSP) area, MADA (Modified Area Development Approach), Scattered Development Plans, and Primitive Tribe Development Plans for the tribal development approach have been stressed. Expansion of irrigation facilities and electrification of tribal settlements, expansion of irrigation wells, fertilizers, improvement of cattle breed and mining activities have also been given impetus.

In this plan, family oriented schemes have been also stressed to uplift the tribal families.

Table 1.1: Flows to Tribal Sub-Plan

Year	ST Population (%)	State Plan Outlay (₹ in crores)	Flow to Tribal Sub-Plan (TSP: ₹ in crores)	% of TSP Annual Plan
2008–09	34.2	1660.00	731.73	44.10
2009–10	34.2	2000.00	741.15	37.1
2010–11	34.2	2600.00	1017.50	39.1
2011–12	34.2	3210.00	1168.37	36.4

Source: Five Year Plans.

Ninth Five Year Plan (1997–2002)

Ninth Five Year Plan (1997–2002) has the strategy to achieve a seven percent growth rate for the economy. The main objectives of the Ninth Plan are the generation of adequate productive employment, eradication of poverty, empowerment of women and socially disadvantaged groups. It aims to ensure food and nutritional security for all, particularly the vulnerable sections of society.

The draft report of the working group on decentralized planning and Panchayati Raj for formulation of the Ninth Five Year Plan (1997–2002) noted that "large parts of the country and vast section of the population have been untouched by this progress. Effects will be made to ensure that the tribal economy is protected and supported against threats from the external markets. The ownerships/patent rights of the tribal people in respect of minor forest produces vis-a-vis the use of medicinal plants will be protected as per the provision of intellectual property Rights (IPR).

Tenth Five Year Plan (2002–2007)

This includes.

National Tribal Policy 2006

In 2004, the government of India unveiled Draft National Tribal Policy. It held a series of regional consultations. Indigenous/tribal people's organizations too held similar consultations and provided comments and suggestions. On 21 July 2006, the Government of India released its revised Draft National Tribal Policy. This time, indigenous organizations were given only 20 days to provide their comments. AITPN organized a National Consultation and key recommendations adopted at the National Consultation are given below. The participants of the National Consultation on the draft National Tribal Policy (A Policy for the Scheduled Tribes of India) from different parts of India, assembled in Guwahati, Assam on 6–7 August 2006 unanimously adopted the Declaration.

The Constitution through several Articles has provided for the socio-economic development and empowerment of Scheduled Tribes. But there was no national policy, which could have helped translate the constitutional provisions into a reality. Five principles were spelt out in 1952, known as Nehruvian Panchasheel, which had been guiding the administration of tribal affairs. These were:

- Tribal should be allowed to develop according to their own genius.
- Tribal' rights in land and forest should be respected.
- Tribal teams should be trained to undertake adminis-tration and development without too many outsiders being inducted.
- Tribal development should be undertaken without disturbing tribal social and cultural institutions.
- The index of tribal development should be the quality of their life and not the money spent.

The policy aimed to bring Scheduled Tribes into the mainstream of society through a multi-pronged approach for their all-round development without disturbing their distinct culture.

Realising that the Nehruvian Panchasheel was long on generalities and short on specifics, the Government of India formed a Ministry of Tribal Affairs for the first time in October 1999 to accelerate tribal development. The Ministry of Tribal Affairs came out with the draft National Policy on Tribal. Based on the feedback from tribal leaders, the concerned States, individuals, organisations in the public and the private sectors, and the NGOs, the Ministry finalised the policy.

The National Policy recognises that a majority of Scheduled Tribes continue to live below the poverty line, have poor literacy rates, suffer from malnutrition and disease and are vulnerable to displacement. It also acknowledges that Scheduled Tribes in general are repositories of indigenous knowledge and wisdom in certain aspects.

The National Policy aims at addressing each of these problems in a concrete way. It also lists out measures to be taken to preserve and promote tribal cultural heritage.

Formal Education

Formal education is the key to all-round human development. Despite several campaigns to promote formal education ever since Independence, the literacy rate among Scheduled Tribes is only 29.60 percent compared to 52.21 percent for the country as a whole (1991 Census). The female literacy rate is only 18.19 percent compared to the national female literacy rate of 39.29 percent. Alienation from the society, lack of adequate infrastructure like schools, hostels and teachers, abject poverty and apathy towards irrelevant curriculum have stood in the way of tribal getting formal education.

To achieve the objective of reaching the benefit of education to tribal, the National Policy ensures that:

- Tribal are included in the national programme of Sarva Shiksha Abhiyan run by the Ministry of Human Resource Development.
- Schools and hostels are opened in areas where no such facilities exist.
- At least one model residential school is located in each tribal concentration area.
- Education is linked with provision of supplementary nutrition.
- Special incentives like financial assistance, pocket allowance, free distribution of textbooks and school uniforms are provided.
- Teaching is imparted in tribal' mother tongue at least up to the primary level. Educated tribal youth are given employment as teachers, wherever possible. (This will obviate the need to employ teachers belonging to far-off places who find commuting is as difficult as staying in a village with no basic amenities.
- Pedagogy is made relevant so that tribal do not find it as alien.
- Curriculum and co-curriculum include aspects of skill up-gradation of tribal children.
- Curricula for skill up-gradation are to include aspects of tribal games and sports, archery, identification of plants of medicinal value, crafts art and culture, folk dance and folk songs, folk paintings, etc.
- Emphasis is laid on vocational/professional education. Polytechnics are set up for studies in subjects like forestry, horticulture, dairying, veterinary sciences and polytechnics.

Traditional Wisdom

Dwelling amidst hills, forests, coastal areas, deserts, tribal over the centuries have gained precious and vast experience in combating environmental hardships and leading sustainable livelihoods. Their wisdom is reflected in their water harvesting techniques, indigenously developed irrigation channels, construction of cane bridges in hills, adaptation to desert life, utilisation of forest species like herbs, shrubs for medicinal purposes, meteorological assessment, etc. Such invaluable knowledge of theirs needs to be properly documented and preserved lest it should get lost in the wake of modernisation and passage of time.

The National Policy seeks to:

- Preserve and promote such traditional knowledge and wisdom and document it.
- Establish a centre to train tribal youth in areas of traditional wisdom.
- Disseminate such through models and exhibits at appropriate places.
- Transfer such knowledge to non-tribal areas.

Health

Although tribal people live usually close to nature, a majority of them need health care on account of malnutrition, lack of safe drinking water, poor hygiene and environmental sanitation and above all poverty. Lack of awareness and apathy to utilise the available health services also affect their health status. In wake of the opening of tribal areas with highways, industrialization, and communication facilities, diseases have spread to tribal areas. Endemics like malaria, deficiency diseases, and venereal diseases including AIDS are not uncommon among tribal populations. However, lack of safe drinking water and malnutrition are well-recognised major health hazards. Tribal suffer from a deficiency of calcium, vitamin A, vitamin C, riboflavin and animal protein in their diets. Malnutrition and under-nutrition are common among Primitive Tribal Groups who largely depend upon food they either gather or raise by using simple methods. The poor nutritional status of tribal women directly influences their reproductive performance and their infants' survival, growth and development.

Tribal people, who are self- reliant and self-sufficient, have over the centuries developed their own medicine system based on herbs and other items collected from the nature and processed locally. They have also their own system of diagnosis and cure of diseases. They believe in taboos, spiritual powers and faith healing. There are wide variations among tribal in their health status and willingness to access and utilise health services, depending on their culture, level of contact with other cultures and degree of adaptability.

Against this background, the National Policy seeks to promote the modern health care system and also a synthesis of the Indian systems of medicine like Ayurveda and siddha with the tribal system.

The National Policy seeks to:

- Strengthen the allopath system of medicine in tribal areas with the extension of the three-tier system of village health workers, auxiliary nurse, mid-wife and primary health centres.
- Expand the number of hospitals in tune with tribal population.
- Validate identified tribal remedies (folk claims) used in different tribal areas.
- Encourage, document and patent tribal' traditional medicines.
- Promote cultivation of medicinal plants related value addition strategies through imparting training to youth.
- Encourage qualified doctors from tribal communities to serve tribal areas.
- Promote the formation of a strong force of tribal village health guides through regular training-cum-orientation courses.

- Formulate area-specific strategies to improve access to and utilisation of health services.
- Strengthen research into diseases affecting tribal and initiate action programmes.
- Eradicate endemic diseases on a war footing.

Displacement and Resettlement

Displacement of people from traditional habitations causes much trauma to the affected people. Compulsory acquisition of land for construction of dams and roads, quarrying and mining operations, location of industries and reservation of forests for National Parks and environmental reasons force tribal people to leave their traditional abodes and land—their chief means of livelihood. Nearly 85.39 lakh tribal had been displaced until 1990 on account of one mega project or the other, reservation of forests as National Parks, etc. Tribal constitute at least 55.16 percent of the total displaced people in the country. Cash payment does not really compensate the tribal for the difficulties they experience in their living style and ethos. Displacement of tribal from their land amounts to violation of the Fifth Schedule of the Constitution as it deprives them of control and ownership of natural resources and land essential for their way of life.

The National Policy for Tribal, therefore, stipulates that displacement of tribal people is kept to the minimum and undertaken only after possibilities of non-displacement and least displacement have been exhausted. When it becomes absolutely necessary to displace Scheduled Tribe people in the larger interest, the displaced should be provided a better standard of living.

The National Policy, therefore, mandates that the following guidelines be followed when tribal are resettled:

- When displacement becomes inevitable, each scheduled tribe family having land in the earlier settlement shall be given land against land. A minimum of two hectares of cultivable land is considered necessary and viable for a family (comprising man, his wife and unmarried children).

- Tribal families having fishing rights in their original habitat shall be granted fishing rights in the new reservoir or at any other alternative place

- Reservation benefits enjoyed at the original settlement shall be continued at the resettlement area.

- Additional financial assistance equivalent to nearly one and a half year's minimum agricultural wages for loss of customary rights and usufructory rights of forest produce shall be given.

- Tribal are to be resettled close to their natural habitat by treating all the people so displaced as one group to let them retain their ethnic, linguistic and socio-cultural identity and the network of kinship and mutual obligations.

- Free land is to be provided for social and religious congregations.

- If resettlement is possible only away from the district/taluka, then substantively higher benefits in monetary terms shall be given.

- When tribal families are resettled en masse, all basic minimum amenities shall be provided at the new sites. These include roads and passages, electricity, drainage and sanitation, safe drinking water, educational and health care facilities, fair price shops, a community hall and a panchayat office.

Forest Villages

Tribal's age-old symbiotic relationship with forests is well known. Recognising this fact, even the National Forest Policy committed itself to the close association of tribal with the protection, preservation and development of forests and envisaged their customary rights in forests. It is, however, a matter of serious concern that about 5000 forest villages do not have minimum basic living conditions and face a constant threat of eviction.

The National Policy suggests that any forceful displacement should be avoided. Human beings move on their own to places with better opportunities. The forest villages may be converted into revenue villages or forest villages may be developed on par with revenue villages to enable the forest villagers enjoy at least the minimum amenities and services that are available in revenue villages.

The National Policy, therefore, mandates that:

- Educational and medical facilities, electricity and communication, approach roads and such other basic amenities to be provided to forest villagers.
- Public Distribution System (PDS) and Grain Banks to be established to prevent food problems.
- Advanced agriculture and animal husbandry technologies to be introduced so that forest villagers raise their production, incomes and economic standards.
- Bank and other institutional loans be made available for entrepreneurs with viable projects of income generation.
- Tribal be given opportunities to partake in joint forest management and encouraged to form cooperatives and corporations for major forest related operations.
- Integrated area development programmes be taken up in and around forest areas.
- Tribal' rights in protection, regeneration and collection of minor forest produce (MFP) be recognised and institutional arrangements made for marketing such produce
- Efforts be made to eliminate exploitation by middlemen in cooperatives like Tribal Development Cooperative Corporations (TDCCs), Large Sized Multi-Purpose Societies (LAMPS) and Forest Development Cooperatives by introducing minimum support prices for non-agricultural produce on the lines of minimum support prices for agricultural produce.

Shifting Cultivation

In the evolution of human civilisation, shifting cultivation preceded agriculture as we know it today. In shifting cultivation, tribal do not use any mechanized tools or undertake even ploughing. A digging stick and a sickle are the usual tools. It is widely practised in whole of North-Eastern region besides the States of Andhra Pradesh, Orissa, Tamil Nadu and to some extent in Chhattisgarh and Jharkhand. Though the practice is hazardous to environment, it forms basis of life for tribal. Traditionally, shifting cultivation has been in vogue in hilly terrains where tribal have had the right on land either individually or on community basis. Because of poor yields, crops do not meet their food requirement for more than four months or so in a year.

The tribal involved in shifting cultivation do not seem to have any emotional attachment to the land as an asset or property needing care and attention as in non-tribal areas. In shifting cultivation lands, no attention is paid to the replenishment of soil fertility. Tribal merely believe in harvesting crops without putting in efforts or investments. Land is just left to nature to recoup on its own.

To handle the problem of shifting cultivation, the National Policy focuses on the following aspects:

- Land tenure system to be rationalised giving tribal right to land ownership so that they can invest their energy and resources in checking soil erosion and fertility—which have hitherto been neglected as land belonged to no one but was subject to exploitation by everyone.
- Agricultural scientists will be asked to focus on shifting cultivation and evolve suitable technologies to improve production.
- The shifting cultivators will be ensured sufficient food supply through the public distribution system and grain banks. Tribal will be encouraged to raise cash crops and horticultural plantations.

- Training and extension programmes will be organised to sensitise tribal about alternative economic strategies so that they can come out of shifting cultivation.

Land Alienation

Scheduled Tribes being simple folk are often exploited to forgo their foremost important resource-land-to non-tribal. Although States have protective laws to check the trend, yet dispossessed tribal are yet to get back their lands. Another form of land alienation takes place when States promote development projects like hydro-electric power stations and mining and industries. These developmental activities, which do not confer any benefit on tribal directly, render them landless.

The National Policy for Tribal seeks to tackle tribal land alienation by stipulating that:

- Tribal have access to village land records.
- Land records be displayed at the panchayat.
- Oral evidence be considered in the absence of records in the disposal of tribal' land disputes.
- States prohibit transfer of lands from tribal to non-tribal.
- Tribal and their representatives be associated with land surveys.
- Forest tribal villagers be assigned pattas for the land under their tillage since ages.
- States launching development projects take adequate care to keep tribal lands intact and when not possible, allot land even before a project takes off.

Intellectual Property Rights

Scheduled Tribes are known for their knowledge and wisdom of ethnic origin. There is, however, no legal and/or institutional framework to safeguard their Intellectual Property Rights.

The National Policy, therefore, aims at making legal and institutional arrangements to protect their Intellectual Property Rights and curtailing the rights of corporate and other agencies to access and exploit their resource base.

Tribal Languages

The languages spoken by tribal-tribal languages—are treated as unscheduled languages. In the wake of changing educational scenario, many of the tribal languages are facing the threat of extinction. The loss of language may adversely affect tribal culture, especially their folklore.

The National Policy aims at preserving and documenting tribal languages. Education in the mother tongue at the primary level needs be encouraged. Books and other publications in tribal languages will be promoted.

Primitive Tribal Groups (PTGs)

Primitive Tribal Groups (PTGs) are Scheduled Tribes known for their declining or stagnant population, low levels of literacy, pre-agricultural technology, primarily belonging to the hunting and gathering stage, and extreme backwardness. They were considered as a special category for support for the first time in 1979. There are 75 Primitive Tribal Groups spread over 15 States and Union Territories. The 25 lakh PTG population constitutes nearly 3.6 percent of the tribal population and 0.3 percent of the country's population. PTGs have not benefited from developmental activities. They face continuous threats of eviction from their homes and lands. They live with food insecurity and a host of diseases like sickle cell anaemia and malaria.

The National Policy envisages the following steps to tackle PTGs' problems:

- To boost PTGs' social image, their being stigmatized as *'primitive'* shall be halted.

- Efforts shall be made to bring them on par with other Scheduled Tribes in a definite time frame. Developmental efforts should be tribe-specific and suit the local environment.
- Effective preventive and curative health systems shall be introduced.
- PTGs' traditional methods of prevention and cure shall be examined and validated.
- To combat the low level of literacy among PTGs, area and need specific education coupled with skill up-gradation shall be given priority.
- Formal schooling shall be strengthened by taking advantage of 'Sarva Shiksha Abhiyan'. Trained tribal youth shall be inducted as teachers.
- Teaching shall be in tribal' mother tongue/dialect.
- Considering PTGs' poverty, school-going children shall be provided incentives.
- Emphasis shall be on laid on vocational education and training.
- PTGs shall enjoy the 'right to land'. Any form of land alienation shall be prevented and landless PTGs given priority in land assignment.
- Public Distribution System (PDS) shall be introduced to ensure regular food supply. Grain banks shall be established to ensure food availability during crises.
- PTGs' participation in managing forests shall be ensured to meet their economic needs and nourish their emotional attachment to forests.

Scheduled Tribes and Scheduled Areas

Although the Constitution is clear about the concept and strategy adopted for defining Scheduled Areas and tribal areas in terms of Fifth and Sixth Schedules under Articles as 244(1) and 244(2), there is some confusion among those concerned with implementing them.

The National Policy, therefore, envisages the following steps:

- The regulation making powers of State Governors to maintain good governance, peace and harmony in tribal areas will be further strengthened. It will be ensured that Tribal Advisory Councils meet regularly and focus on speedy developmental works and prohibition of land transfers. Money lending menace shall be curbed through implementation of money lending laws.
- Tribal Advisory Councils will be established in States which have Scheduled Areas and even in States where a substantial number of tribal people live although Scheduled Areas have not been declared.
- The Autonomous District/Regional Councils in North-Eastern States will be further strengthened. The Councils are elected bodies having powers of legislation and execution and administration of justice.

Administration

The existing administrative machinery in States and districts comprising Integrated Tribal Development Agencies (ITDA) and Integrated Tribal Development Projects (ITDP) have not been up in terms of the quality of performance and development indicators.

The National Policy seeks to revitalise the administration by proposing the following:

- Skill up-gradation-cum-orientation programmes shall be conducted for tribal administration officials.
- Infrastructure development shall be given priority to so that officials will function from their places of posting.
- Only officials who have adequate knowledge, experience and a sense of appreciation for tribal problems shall be posted for tribal administration.

- As the schemes meant for improving tribal' condition take time, a tenure that is commensurate with their implementation shall be fixed for officials.

Research

The National Policy acknowledges the importance of a good database to deal with Scheduled Tribe's affairs. Research on tribal' ethnic profile, spectrum of problems and prospects and developmental constraints and monitoring and evaluation of schemes and projects needs priority attention. The National Policy for Tribal proposes that the existing Tribal Research Institutes located in different States shall be further strengthened for carrying out purposeful research and evaluation studies and work towards the preservation of the rich tribal cultural heritage. It also envisages the establishment of a national-level research institution.

Participatory Approach

The National Policy recognises the importance of participatory approach to development. NGOs (Non-Governmental Organisations) and Voluntary Agencies (VAs) act as catalysts in reaching benefits of Government programmes and policies to the grass-root level and thus optimise the desired accomplishment. Such organisations have direct linkages with people and are conversant with their problems. NGOs can undertake and promote family and community based programmes and mobilise resources in tribal areas. Some well-established NGOs are eager to take part in the development of Scheduled Tribes in general and Primitive Tribal Groups in particular.

The National Policy, therefore, seeks to enlist and encourage NGOs in tribal development activities. They can play an important role in the opening of residential and non-residential schools, hostels, dispensaries, hospitals and vocational training centres, promotion of awareness programmes and capacity building.

Assimilation

To bring the tribal into country's mainstream, the National Policy envisages the following

- Identification of tribal groups with *'primitive traits'* shall be done away with on a priority basis.
- The 'distinct culture' of the tribes reflected in their folk art, folk literature, traditional crafts and ethos shall be preserved. Their oral traditions shall be documented and art should be promoted.
- Opportunities shall be provided for tribal to interact with outside cultures.
- Their geographical isolation shall be minimised through development of roads, transport and means of communication and provision of concessional travel facility.

Thus the major issues covered in the policy include:

- *Wrongful Alienation of Tribal Land or Tenurial Insecurity:* Under the draft policy, the issue of tenurial insecurity among tribal—the single most important cause of pauperisation among tribal despite laws to prevent wrongful alienation of land—will be addressed by amending state anti-alienation land laws, amending the Indian Registration Act, and the establishment of fast-track courts.
- *Tribal-Forest Interface:* Various steps are proposed to improve this natural resource base so that the socio-economic conditions of STs improve, including recognition of their age-old occupation rights, ownership over forest produce, conversion of forest villages into revenue villages, etc.
- *Displacement, Rehabilitation and Resettlement:* A legislative regime will be put in place that ensures the least displacement of tribal, exploration of all alternatives to displacement, and appropriate compensation, including land-for-land, giving the displaced market value for their

land, social impact assessments, etc. For industrial enterprises in scheduled areas, the community will receive suitable benefits.

- *Enhancement of the Human Development Index (HDI):* The government will take steps to improve education, sports and employment opportunities for STs by ensuring an annual increase of 3 percent in literacy growth rate, among both males and females, 100 percent enrolment of tribal children, and a reduction of dropout rates, especially among tribal girls, to achieve parity with others by the end of the 11th Five-Year Plan (2008–2013).
- *Livelihood Opportunities:* Livelihood opportunities will be enhanced though training, skills and design development, provision of market linkages and scientific inputs to enhance agriculture and horticulture production.
- *Migration:* Steps taken to reduce migration among tribal will include enhancing land productivity and providing guaranteed employment under the National Rural Employment Guarantee Act 2005.
- *Moneylending and Indebtedness:* Steps will be taken to improve the institutional flow of credit and provide consumption loans to STs who are easy prey to moneylenders.
- *Conservation and Development of Primitive Tribe Groups (PTGs):* Special and new initiatives will be taken for the conservation and development of PTGs (proposed to be renamed Particularly Vulnerable Tribal Groups that are the most backward among tribal communities) through the adoption of approaches that will result in heritage conservation as well as socio-economic development.
- *Gender Equity:* While ST women are, in many respects, better placed than their counterparts in the general population in areas like education, efforts will need to be made for the uplift of tribal women though special literacy programmes and the elimination of certain practices that result in the oppression of women.

- *Tribal Culture and Traditional Knowledge:* All efforts will be made to support and preserve tribal culture, traditional heritage, arts and crafts, dance and music, through documentation and dissemination, market linkages, cultural festivals and *meals* and encouragement and support of tribal artistes and folk art performers. Efforts will be made to preserve, document and promote traditional wisdom.
- *Scheduling and De-Scheduling of Tribes:* Steps will be taken to ensure that the benefits granted to ST communities are evenly spread among all ST communities, and, if so warranted, those populations that have caught up with the general population be de-scheduled. A time-bound programme will be initiated to identify the needs of nomadic tribes and their development.

Eleventh Five Year Plan (2007–2012)

Thus complete elimination of the abhorrent practice of manual scavenging needs to be accomplished by the middle of the 11th Five Year Plan. This needs to be done through effective measures of liberation and rehabilitation of scavengers such as sustainable employment and income generating activities. Efforts also need to be made on a continuing basis to identify and rehabilitate bonded labour and their children. There is a need to effectively implement the special component plan and the tribal sub-plan both at the Central and State level. Also, a comprehensive National Tribal Policy to ensure protection, all-round development, welfare and empowerment of the tribal and tribal areas with special emphasis on rehabilitation and resettlement of project affected people needs to be announced and effectively implemented. Expeditious adoption and implementation of the National Tribal Policy in the 12th Plan is an urgent imperative.

CATEGORISATION FOR IMPLEMENTATION OF SCHEMES FOR TRIBAL DEVELOPMENT

Integrated Tribal Development Projects/ Agencies (ITDPs/ITDAs)

The ITDPs are generally contiguous areas of the size of a Tehsil or Block or more in which the ST population is 50 percent or more of the total. On account of demographic reasons, however ITDPs in Assam, Karnataka, Tamil Nadu, and West Bengal may be smaller or not contiguous. Andhra Pradesh and Orissa have opted for an Agency model under the Registration of Societies Act and the ITDPs there are known as ITD Agencies (ITDAs). So far 194 ITDPs/ITDAs have been delineated in the country in the states of Andhra Pradesh, Assam, Bihar, Gujarat, Himachal Pradesh, Karnataka, Kerala, Madhya Pradesh, Maharashtra, Manipur, Orissa, Rajasthan, Sikkim, Tamil Nadu, Tripura, Uttar Pradesh, West Bengal and Union Territories of Andaman and Nicobar Island and Daman and Diu. In Jammu and Kashmir though no ITDP has been delineated yet the areas having ST Population in the State are treated as covered under the TSP strategy. In eight states having scheduled areas the ITDPs/ITDAs are generally co terminus with TSP areas. The ITDPs/ITDAs are headed by Project Officer though they may be designated Project Administrators or Project Directors.

Modified Area Development Approach (MADA) Pockets

These are identified pockets of concentration of ST population containing 50 percent or more ST population within a total population of minimum of 10,000. The total number of MADAs identified so far in the various TSP States is 259. Generally, MADA pockets do not have separate administrative structures to implement development programmes. The line Departments of the State Govt. are expected to implement development programmes in MADA pockets under the overall control of the District authorities.

Clusters

These are identified pockets of tribal concentration containing 50 percent or more ST population within a total population of about 5,000 or more. As in the case of MADA pockets, there are no separate administrative structures for Clusters. So far 82 Clusters have been identified in various T.S.P. states.

Primitive Tribal Groups (PTGs)

Primitive tribal groups are tribal communities among the STs who live in near isolation in inaccessible habitats. They are characterized by a low rate of growth of population, pre-agricultural level of technology and extremely low levels of literacy. So far 75 PTGs have been identified.

The Ministry of Tribal Affairs sanctioned proposals of State Governments and NGOs covering about 62 PTGs during this year. The proposals covering mainly the activities relating to food, security, promotion of primary education and extending basic minimum health services to the primitive tribes were approved and funds released to the State Governments and NGOs. The annual allocation made under the scheme since its inception in 1998–99 saw an increase in the amount released. From ₹ 663 lakhs released in 1999–2000, it has increased to more than ₹ 3000 lakhs at present.

VARIOUS ACTS AND SCHEMES OF CENTRAL AND STATE GOVERNMENTS

Forest (Conservation) Act 1980

After the enactment of Forest (Conservation) Act, 1980 State Governments faced problems in taking up non-forestry developmental activities relating to infrastructure for improving socio-economic conditions of people living in the villages located in the forest areas. Consequent to the intervention of this Ministry, steps like stopping of illegal eviction of genuine tribal people living in the forests, allowing diversion of forest lands for providing the basic and essential developmental facilities to the tribal/forest villages, etc. have been achieved. This programme was launched during the 10ᵗʰ Plan as a onetime measure with for Integrated development of 2690 forest villages originally identified with about 2.5 lakh tribal families with a view to:

- To raise the Human Development Index (HDI) of the inhabitants of the Forest Villages
- Provide basic facilities and services like food, safe drinking water, health care, primary education, approach roads, other infrastructural facilities, etc.

During the 10ᵗʰ Five Year Plan, ₹ 450 crore was allocated to the Ministry of Tribal Affairs for the development of forest villages under Special Central Assistance to Tribal Sub Plan (SCA to TSP).

Presently there are 2,474 forest villages/habitations (reduced from the original 2,690) spread over 12 States (reduced from the original 13 States). As per the latest information available in the Ministry of Environment and Forests on forest villages/ habitations based on reports received from States, details are as under:

Under the programme, infrastructure work relating to basic services and facilities viz. approach roads, healthcare, primary education, minor irrigation, rainwater harvesting, drinking water, sanitation, community halls, etc. and activities related to livelihood are taken up for implementation.

The implementing Agencies are Forest Development Agency (FDA)—forest division level Joint Forest Management Committees (JFMCs)—village level, composed of all willing adult members of the village. The funding is done under the programme of 'Special Central Assistance' to the Tribal Sub-plan Fund flows from Ministry of Tribal Affairs to Department of Tribal Welfare/Tribal Development of the States and then to the implementing agencies.

Year-wise allocation of the funds as seen under various Plans shows that amount has been coming down year after year. In spite of concerted efforts allocation has not increased to such an extent so as to make a dent in the lives of tribal population in India.

The Protection of Civil Rights Act, 1955

An Act to prescribe punishment for the preaching and practice of—"Untouchability" for the enforcement of any disability arising there from for matters connected therewith.

The Scheduled Castes and the Scheduled Tribes (Prevention of Atrocities) Act, 1989

An Act to prevent the commission of offences of atrocities against the members of the Scheduled Castes and the Scheduled Tribes, to provide for Special Courts for the trial of such offences and for the relief and rehabilitation of the victims of such offences and for matters connected therewith or incidental there to.

The Provisions of the Panchayats (Extension to the Scheduled Areas) Act, 1996

This is an Act to provide for the extension of the provisions of Part IX of the Constitution relating to the Panchayats to the Scheduled Areas. Village level democracy became a real prospect for India in 1992 with the 73rd amendment to the Constitution, which mandated that resources, responsibility and decision making be passed on from central government to the lowest unit of the governance, the Gram Sabha or the Village Assembly. A three tier structure of local self-government was envisaged under this amendment.

Since the laws do not automatically cover the scheduled areas, the PESA Act was enacted on 24 December 1996 to enable

Tribal Self Rule in these areas. The Act extended the provisions of Panchayats to the tribal areas of nine states that have Fifth Schedule Areas. Most of the North Eastern States under Sixth Schedule Areas (where autonomous councils exist) are not covered by PESA, as these states have their own Autonomous Councils for governance.

The Constitution (Eighty-ninth Amendment) Act, 2003

The amendment provided for:

- There shall be a Commission for the Scheduled Tribes to be known as the National Commission for the Scheduled Tribes.
- It shall be the duty of the Commission:
  - (a) To investigate and monitor all matters relating to the safeguards provided for the Scheduled Tribes under this Constitution or under any other law for the time being in force or under any order of the Government and to evaluate the working of such safeguards;
  - (b) To inquire into specific complaints with respect to the deprivation of rights and safeguards of the Scheduled Tribes;
  - (c) To participate and advise on the planning process of socio-economic development of the Scheduled Tribes and to evaluate the progress of their development under the Union and any State;
  - (d) To present to the President, annually and at such other times as the Commission may deem fit, reports upon the working of those safeguards;
  - (e) To make in such reports recommendations as to the measures that should be taken by the Union or any State for the effective implementation of those safeguards and other measures for the protection, welfare and socio-economic development of the Scheduled Tribes; and

(f) To discharge such other functions in relation to the protection, welfare and development and advancement of the Scheduled Tribes as the President may, subject to the provisions of any law made by Parliament, by rule specify.

Forest Rights Act, 2006

An Act to recognize and vest the forest rights and occupation in forest land in forest dwelling Scheduled Tribes and other traditional forest dwellers who have been residing in such forests for generations but whose rights could not be recorded; to provide a framework for recording the forest rights so vested and the nature of evidence required for such recognition and vesting in respect of forest land.

This Act may be called as Scheduled Tribes and Other Traditional Forest Dwellers (Recognition of Forest Rights) Act, 2006.

This aims to compensate the "historical injustice" done to forest dwelling tribes and provide the adivasis rights to forest resources. The bill for the first time recognises that tribal have rights over forests. The proposed forest rights include: the right to hold and live in the forest land; community rights over forest such as 'nistar'; right of ownership access to use and dispose of minor forest produce; rights over disputed lands; rights for conversion of pattas or leases or grants on forest land into titles; rights of conversion of forest villages into revenue villages; right to manage any community forest resource; and any other traditional right enjoyed by the forest-dwelling STs. In concrete terms, the bill proposes pattas to forest lands occupied before 1980 but subject to a ceiling of 2.5 hectares per family. No tribal person is to be evicted from forest land until the process of determining rights is completed. The bill proposes wide-ranging powers for the gram sabha that include determining the nature and extent of forest rights, regulating access to forest resources, and punishing those who violate the provisions. Although the bill is a step in the right direction, it addresses tribal land issues in isolation from the related legislations on wildlife protection and forest conservation. Another weakness of the bill concerns the issue of displacement by development projects; the bill should clearly delineate the role of the gram sabha vis-à-vis development-induced displacement. The rights proposed to be conferred with regard to the lands occupied before 1980 are essentially compensatory in nature. Because the bill tries to compensate the loss which tribal had to suffer without looking at the processes that have resulted inland dispossession; nor does it refer to the failure of the state in restoring the alienated land and in providing adequate rehabilitation for the displaced. Because loss of land to non-tribal is among the major factors driving tribal to "encroach" on the forest land the cut-off date of 1980 and the ceiling on the extent of land proposed to be regularised would drastically reduce the scope of the bill. It also excludes from its purview a large number of non-ST forest dwellers. Although the proposed legislation promises a great deal, the scepticism remains given the track record of the state in enforcing the earlier laws and the constitutional provisions.

Grants under Article 275(1) of the Constitution of India

Article 275(1) of the Constitution of India guarantees grants from the Consolidated Fund of India each year for promoting the welfare of Scheduled Tribes and in pursuance of this Constitutional obligation, the Ministry of Tribal Affairs provides funds through the Central Sector Scheme "Grants under Article 275(1) of the Constitution". The objective of the scheme is the promotion of welfare of Scheduled Tribes and raising the level of administration of Scheduled Areas.

The scheme covers all the 21 Tribal Sub-Plan and 4 other tribal majority States of the country. Some of the guidelines for release of grants under this scheme are as follows:

- The grants are to be used essentially for creation and up-gradation of critical infrastructure required bringing the tribal areas with the rest of the country. The basic purpose is to create opportunities conducive to income and employment generation. Due emphasis has been given to infrastructure in sectors critical to enhancement of Human Development Indices such as in health, education, income generation.
- Peoples' participation is the central thread around which the entire fabric of tribal development is to be woven. The approach towards tribal development should, therefore, ensure the participation of tribal population while planning and implementing the schemes out of the grants.
- The concerns/issues effecting women should occupy central position in preparation of the projects/schemes, including the involvement of women right from planning to the implementation stage. The projects should be so planned that substantial benefits, at least 30 percent in proportion, are targeted for women.
- Each State, Region, ITDA, MADA and Cluster is required a specific plan, based on the felt local needs such as low literacy, poor health services, critical gaps in sectors like irrigation, roads, bridges, electricity, technical/ vocational institutes, forests, sports promotion, etc. Efforts are therefore, to be made to identify thrust areas for each ITDA, MADA and Cluster and on that basis for the region or the State, as a whole.

The grants are provided to the States on the basis of ST population percentage in the State.

The Ministry of Tribal Affairs, which used to release the funds without identifying the projects in earlier year, has now decided to release funds to the State Governments against specific infrastructure development and welfare projects from the year 2000–01.

As has been mentioned earlier, from the year 2000–01, the releases are made against specific developmental works/ projects identified by the State Governments. One of the major constraints is that the State Governments often do not release the funds in time to the implementing agencies.

For the first time State Governments were asked to submit specific Schemes for infrastructure development. A Minister level meeting was held with the State Governments and Schemes were approved prepared by the State Governments for improvement of infrastructure in the Scheduled Areas. At the Conference following were emphasized:

- Timely implementation of the Scheme.
- Timely submission of utilization certificates, quarterly report, etc.
- Undertaking only infrastructure building Schemes under Article 275(1) but not individual beneficiary Schemes.
- Exercising strict vigilance on NGOs working in their state through District Collectors.

Thus the Ministry provides Grant-in-Aid to TSP and tribal majority States under Article 275 (1) of the constitution to meet the cost of such projects for tribal development as may be undertaken by the State Government for raising the level of administration of Scheduled Areas therein to the level of the rest of the state.

Special Central Assistance to Tribal Sub-Plan (SCA to TSP)

The Ministry of Tribal Affairs extends special central assistance to the TSP States and Union Territories and also to North Eastern States of Assam, Manipur and Tripura as an additional grant to these states/UTs. These grants are basically meant for family oriented income generating Scheme in various TSP areas to meet the gaps, which have not otherwise been taken care of by the State Plan.

Vocational Training Centers in Tribal Areas

The scheme aims at upgrading the skills of the tribal youths in various traditional/modern vocations depending upon their educational qualification, present economic trends and the market potential, which would enable them to gain suitable employment or enable them to become self-employed. The scheme provides 100 percent grant, and is implemented through State Governments, UT Administration and NGOs. The scheme prescribes fixed financial norms. No construction cost is provided.

The proposals by NGOs are required to be routed through State Government and the recommendation of the "State Committee for Supporting Voluntary Efforts" constituted under the chairmanship of Principal Secretary/Secretary, Tribal Welfare/Development Department of the State/UT are mandatory. The recommendation of State Committee is valid for that financial year in which it is made.

Some Components of the Scheme include:

- The scheme will be implemented for the benefit of the Scheduled Tribes as well as PTGs and can be taken up anywhere in the country but priority will be given to remote tribal areas, areas inhabited by particularly vulnerable tribes and areas affected by extremist activities.
- Under the scheme, the training for trades including modern trades having employment potential in the region should be provided.
- As far as possible, minimum 33 percent seats will be reserved for tribal girl candidates.

Strengthening Education among Scheduled Tribe Girls in Low Literacy Districts

It is a gender scheme of the Ministry. The scheme aims to bridge the gap in literacy levels between the general female population and tribal women, through facilitating 100 percent enrolment of tribal girls in the identified Districts or Blocks, more particularly in Naxal affected areas and in areas inhabited by Primitive Tribal Groups (PTGs), and reducing drop-outs at the elementary level by creating the required ambience for education. The scheme recognizes the fact that improvement of the literacy rate of tribal girls is essential to enable them to participate effectively in and benefit from, socio-economic development.

The scheme covers 54 identified districts in 12 States and 1 Union Territory where the ST population is 25 percent or more, and ST female literacy rate is below 35 percent or its fractions, as per 2001 census. In addition, any other tribal block in a district, other than aforesaid 54 identified districts, which has scheduled tribal populations 25 percent or above, and tribal female literacy rate below 35 percent or its fractions, as per 2001 census, are also covered. The scheme also covers PTG areas and gives priority to areas affected by naxalites. The scheme is implemented by Non-Governmental Organizations (NGOs) and autonomous societies of the State Governments/Union Territory.

The scheme primarily envisages the running and maintenance of hostels linked with schools running under Sarva Shiksha Abhiyan or other schemes of Education Department. Where such schooling facilities are not available, the scheme has provision for establishing a complete educational complex with residential and schooling facility. The scheme has provision for tuitions, incentives and periodical awards to encourage the ST girls. The scheme does not provide and construction cost. The scheme prescribes fixed financial

norms. The scheme also envisages the establishment of
District Education Support Agency (DESA), which would be
a nongovernment organization or a federation of non-
governmental organizations, for varied functions like ensuring
100 percent enrolment, reducing drops outs, arrangement of
preventive health education, monitoring the performance of
NGOs, etc. The proposals by NGOs are required to be routed
through State Government and the recommendation of the
"State Committee for Supporting Voluntary Efforts" constituted
under the chairmanship of Principal Secretary/Secretary,
Tribal Welfare/Development department of the State/UT are
mandatory. The recommendation of State Committee is valid
for that financial year in which it is made.

The Scheme for construction of Girls Hostels for STs is a
useful instrument for spreading education among tribal girls
whose literacy is only 18.91 percent as per 1991 census. Under
the Scheme funds are provided to all the TSP States and
Union Territories having tribal population for construction of
hostels on sharing basis (50:50) to States and 100 percent to
UTs.

Like the Scheme for Girls Hostel, under this Scheme funds
are provided to states on sharing basis (50:50) and
100 percent to UTs for construction of Boys Hostel for STs.

For Ashram Schools in Tribal Sub-plan areas, the Ministry
under this Scheme provides funds to all the States and UTs
having tribal population for establishment of residential
schools for STs in an environment conducive to learning near
their habitations on sharing basis (50:50) to States and
100 percent to UTs.

Grant-in-Aid to Voluntary Organizations working for the Welfare of Scheduled Tribes

The prime objective of the scheme is to enhance the reach of
welfare schemes of Government and fill the gaps in service

deficient tribal areas, in the sectors such as education, health, drinking water, agro-horticultural productivity, social security net, etc. through the efforts of Voluntary Organizations (VOs)/Non-Governmental Organizations (NGOs), and to provide an environment for socio-economic upliftment and overall development of the Scheduled Tribes (STs). Any other innovative activity having direct impact on the socio-economic development or livelihood generation of STs may also be considered through voluntary efforts.

Under this scheme 90 percent grant is provided by the ministry and 10 percent cost is required to be borne by the non-governmental organizations from their own resources, except in Scheduled Areas where the Government bears 100 percent cost. The scheme provides a list of categories of projects viz. residential school, non-residential schools, 10 or more bedded hospitals, mobile dispensaries, computer training centres, etc., which could be covered under the scheme, and also prescribes fixed financial norms. The scheme does not provide any construction cost.

The Proposals by NGOs are required to be routed through State Government and the recommendation of the "State Committee for Supporting Voluntary Efforts" constituted under the chairmanship of principal Secretary/Secretary, Tribal Welfare/Development Department of the State/UT are mandatory. The recommendation of State Committee is valid for that financial year in which it is made.

Scheme of Development of Primitive Tribal Groups (PTGs)

Based on pre-agricultural level of technology, low level of literacy, declining or stagnant populations, 75 tribal communities in 17 States and 1 Union Territory of Andaman and Nicobar Island, have been identified and categorized as Primitive Tribal Groups (PTGs). Considering the vulnerability of these groups, a Central Sector Scheme was introduced in the year 1998–99 for the all-round development of PTGs.

The scheme is very flexible, and covers housing, infrastructure development, education, health, land distribution/development, agriculture development, cattle development, social security, insurance, etc. During 2007–08, comprehensive long term "Conservation-Cum-Development (CCD) Plans" for PTGs has been formulated for Eleventh Plan period through baseline surveys conducted by respective State Governments/ Union territory. These Plans envisage a synergy between efforts of State Governments and non-governmental organizations.

Based on pre-agricultural level of technology, low level of literacy, declining or stagnant populations, 75 tribal communities in 17 States and 1 Union Territory of Andaman and Nicobar Island, have been identified and categorized as Primitive Tribal Groups (PTGs). Considering the vulnerability of these groups, a Central Sector Scheme was introduced in the year 1998–99 for the all round development of PTGs. The scheme is very flexible, and covers housing, infrastructure development, education, health, land distribution/ development, agriculture development, cattle development, social security, insurance, etc. During 2007–08, comprehensive long term "Conservation-cum-Development (CCD) Plans" for PTGs has been formulated for Eleventh Plan period through baseline surveys conducted by respective State Governments/Union territory. These Plans envisage a synergy between efforts of State Governments and non-governmental organizations

Post-Matric Scholarship for STs Book Bank Scheme and Overseas Scholarships

The post-metric scholarship Scheme provides financial assistance to all ST students for pursuance of post-metric studies in recognized institutions within India. The Scheme provides for 100 percent assistance from the Ministry to State Governments and UT Administrations implementing the Scheme, over and above their respective committed liabilities.

The Ministry also gives financial assistance for setting up Book- Banks in institutions running professional courses like Medicine, Engineering, Law, Agriculture, Veterinary, Chartered Accountancy, Business Management, and Bio-Sciences. Annually, Ministry provides financial assistance to 9 meritorious ST students for Post-graduate, Doctoral and Post-Doctoral studies in foreign universities/institutions of repute.

Under the Scheme "Research and Training" the Ministry provides financial assistance under three components:

1. Grants to Tribal Research Institutes on 50:50 sharing basis; for conducting Research and Evaluation Studies, Seminars, Workshops etc.
2. Award of Research Fellowship to Tribal Students on 100 percent basis registered in Indian Universities.
3. Supporting projects of All-India or Inter-State nature on 100 percent basis to NGOs/Universities, etc. for conducting research on tribal matters, Travel Grants and for Publication of Books on tribal.

Up-gradation of Merit of ST Students and Scheme for Coaching

The up gradation of merit Scheme is for arranging coaching classes in reputed colleges for developing competence among ST students for their better performance in competitive examinations conducted by various universities institutes for admission to Medical and Engineering courses while the Scheme for coaching is for conducting Pre-Examination Coaching for tribal students for various examinations conducted by UPSC, SSC, Banking Services Recruitment Boards, etc. The scheme supports free coaching to scheduled tribe students for various competitive examinations, viz. Civil Services/State Civil Services/Other Exams conducted by UPSE like CDS, NDA, etc./professional courses like Medical,

Engineering, Business Administration/Banking/Staff selection Commission/Railway Recruitment Boards/Insurance Companies, etc. The financial norms of the scheme have been revised during 2007–08. The scheme covers coaching fees, monthly stipend @ ₹ 1000/- per ST student per month and boarding/lodging charges for outstation students @ ₹ 2000/- per ST student per month for the period of coaching.

Grants-in-Aid to State Tribal Development Co-operative Corporations and Others

This is a Central Sector Scheme, with 100 percent grant, available to the state Tribal Development Cooperative Corporation (STDCCs) and other similar corporations of State engaged in collection and trading of Minor Forest Produce (MFP) through tribal Grants under the Scheme are provided to strengthen the Share Capital of Corporations, construction of Warehouses, establishment of processing industries of MFPs, etc. to ensure high profitability of the corporation so as to enable them to pay remunerative prices for MFPs to the tribal.

Scheme of Marketing Development of Tribal Products/Produce

The Tribal Cooperative Marketing Development Federation of India Limited (TRIFED) was established in August 1987 by the then Ministry of Welfare, Government of India, under the *Multi State Cooperative Societies Act 1984* (which has now been replaced by the *Multi-State Cooperative Societies Act, 2002*).

TRIFED was established with the basic mandate of bringing about the socio-economic development of tribal of the country by institutionalizing the trade of Minor Forest Produce (MFP) and Surplus Agriculture Produce (SAP) collected/cultivated by them—because tribal are heavily dependent on these natural products for their livelihood. But in many cases they did not use to get remunerative prices due to middle-men and unscrupulous traders exploiting the naiveté of tribal.

TRIFED was expected to help tribal by ensuring purchase of their products and that too by paying them remunerative prices. Further TRIFED was required to provide marketing support to State Tribal Development Cooperative Corporations, State Forest Development Corporations and other State level Agencies engaged in procurement of such products from tribal. Since inception, TRIFED focused its activities mainly on procurement of Minor Forest Produce (MFP) and Agriculture Produce (AP) with the idea of providing remunerative prices to the tribal and also to help member societies in disposing their stocks procured from tribal.

TRIFED was expected to perform the MFP operations as a welfare activity and not as a commercial activity. Thus TRIFED was expected to trade in MFP irrespective of the commercial prudence of purchasing goods at cheaper rates and resorting to purchase and sale only to maximize profit. As a consequence TRIFED suffered cumulative loss of ₹ 92.62 crore till 31.3.2003, resulting in the erosion of the equity share capital provided by the Central Government.

Price Support to TRIFEDs

The Ministry provides Grants-in-aid to its corporation, TRIFED to set off losses on account of fluctuations in prices of MFPs being marketed by it for ensuring remunerative prices to tribal engaged in collection of MFPs either directly or through STDCCs and other such Cooperative Societies. From 1990–91 to 2006–07, the Central Government had extended a total amount of ₹ 51.40 crore under the *'Price Support Scheme.'*

Investment in Share Capital to TRIFED

The Ministry is the largest shareholder of TRIFED with over 99 percent contribution in its Share Capital. Under this Scheme, the Ministry provides funds to TRIFED as its contribution in the Share Capital. After a thorough review and careful consideration of the past performance, in the year 2003 TRIFED reoriented its activities. Under its new strategy, TRIFED ceased from bulk procurement of MFP and AP. Instead it started concentrating on marketing development activities for tribal products. TRIFED has thus become a *"Service Provider"* to its member federations and a *"Marketing Developer"* for the tribal produce and products. TRIFED has been marketing tribal products through its own shops called *'TRIBES India'* and through the outlets of State Emporia on consignment basis. This is a new scheme introduced during the year 2007–08 to replace the existing scheme *'Price Support to TRIFED'.* As per the approved Road Map, the Central Government would extend a total amount of ₹ 69.59 crore as grants under the scheme to TRIFED during the 11th Plan period. The details of the requirements, activity-wise, are as under:

Table 1.2: Activity-Wise Financial Requirements of TRIFED

Activity-wise financial requirements of TRIFED during 11th Plan

	Activity	2007–08	2008–09	2009–10	2010–11	2011–12	Total for 5 years
Fund Requirement from Ministry							
A	Retail Marketing Development Activity	550	623	392	−10	−243	1312
B	MFP Marketing Development Activity	761	710	500	380	414	2765
C	Vocational Training, Skill Up-gradation and Capacity Building of ST Artisans and MFP Gatherers	371	403	438	488	530	2230
D	Research and Development/IPR Activity	187	146	119	99	101	652
	Funds required for A+B+C+D	1869	1882	1449	957	802	6959

Village Grain Bank Scheme

This Scheme provides Grants for establishment of Village Grain Banks to prevent deaths of STs specially children in remote and backward tribal villages facing or likely to face starvation and also to improve nutritional standards. The Scheme provides funds for building storage facility, procurement of Weights and Measures and for the purchase of initial stock of one quintal of food grain of local variety for each family. A Committee under Chairmanship of village Headman runs the Grain Bank thus established.

Central Rural Sanitation Programme

The Central Rural Sanitation Programme (CRSP) was launched in 1986 with the objective of improving the quality of life of rural people and to provide privacy and dignity to the women. The programme provided 100 percent subsidy for construction of sanitary latrines for Scheduled Castes, Scheduled Tribes and landless labourers and subsidy as per the prevailing rates in the States for the general public. The programme was supply-driven, highly subsidized and gave emphasis for a single construction model.

The CRSP was restructured in 1999 and was replaced by the Total Sanitation Campaign (TSC). The restructured scheme, i.e. TSC moves away from the principle of State-wise allocation primarily based on poverty criterion to a "demand-driven approach". It also gives emphasis on school sanitation and hygiene education for changing the behavior of the people from younger age itself. This programme is being implemented in 451 districts of the country.

Other Welfare Schemes for Rural Scheduled Tribes

Under the National Old Age Pension Scheme, 2.4 million STs were covered during the Ninth Plan accounting for

7.4 percent of the total beneficiaries. Similarly, while 1 lakh ST families were benefited under the National Family Benefit Scheme accounting for 10.2 percent, 4 lakh ST women were benefited under the National Maternity Benefit Scheme (NMBS) accounting for 7.4 percent of the total beneficiaries during the Ninth Plan (NMBS now stands transferred to the Department of Family Welfare with effect from 2001–2002).

LEGAL AND POLICY FRAMEWORK FOR TRIBAL IN ANDHRA PRADESH

The government, both at Centre and State, has not only formulated a number of policies to safeguard the interests of the tribes but also has initiated a number of development schemes for the welfare and upliftment of the tribal communities. These have been discussed in details in the earlier chapter. They are broadly categorized into the following and discussed in the subsequent sections:

Constitutional Safeguards

A number of constitutional provisions are already in place to safeguard the interests of the tribal in the country. Some of the important ones are indicated below:

- *Administration:* Under Clause (1) of Article 244, the Fifth Schedule applies to the administration and control of the Scheduled Areas and STs in a state.
- *Tribal Development:* Article 275(1) provides for Grants-in-Aid of the revenues of a state to enable it to meet the cost of development schemes for the welfare of STs in that state.
- *Promotion of Education:* Article 15(4) along with subsequent amendments empowers the state to make any special provision for the advancement of any socially and educationally backward classes including STs and also

enables the state to reserve seats for them in educational institutions.

- *Political Safeguards:* Article 330 and 332 provides for reservation of representation of SCs and STs in the Lok Sabha (Parliament) and Vidhan Sabhas (State Legislative Assemblies).
- *Employment:* Article 16(4) empowers the state to make, "any provision for the reservation of appointments or posts in favour of any backward class of citizens (including STs) if not represented adequately in the services under the state".
- *Reservations in Educational and Employment Opportunities:* The Constitution of India provides for reserving certain percentage of seats in all educational institutions and public employment in proportion to the tribal population. Residential or "Ashram Schools" are being run in the ITDA areas to provide primary and secondary education for the STs. According to Article 17: Civil Rights: "Untouchability" has been abolished and its practice in any form is forbidden. Enforcement of any disability arising out of "Untouchability" shall be an offence punishable in accordance with law.

Policy Regulations

The following laws, rules and regulations and policies pertaining to tribal and tribal tracts have special relevance to the project under assessment:

- *The Agency Tracts Interest and Land Transfer Act, 1917* restricts transfer of land in the Agency (tribal) tracts. It regulates debt and interest on the borrowings by the hill tribes and transfer of their immovable property. It was enacted primarily to safeguard the interest of the hill tribes in the area over which it extended and to protect them from exploitation by non-tribal and moneylenders. It

permitted transfer of land only among tribal and lay down
that the interest accrued over the debts borrowed by the
tribal shall not exceed the principal amount.

- *The Andhra Pradesh Scheduled Arecas Land Transfer
  Regulation, 1959* extends the provisions of the above Act.
- *The Andhra Pradesh (Andhra Scheduled Areas) Estate
  (Abolition and Conversion into Ryotwari) Act 1948, The
  Andhra Pradesh Mahals (Abolition and Cconversion into
  Ryotwari) Regulation, 1969, and The Andhra Pradesh
  Mutta (Abolition and Conversion into Ryotwari)* Regulation, 1969: These are landmark enactments and promulgations that facilitated state ownership of private estates
  and lands in the Scheduled Areas and paved the way for
  settlement of land tenure. Prior to the seenactments and
  promulgations, lands in the Scheduled Areas were under
  private ownership in the form of estates. Mahals were
  private estates in certain parts of the present Khammam
  District. Estates' and Mahals' owners leased parts of their
  lands to tenants for cultivation. In the Scheduled Areas of
  Vishakhapatnam and East Godavari districts, the then
  rulers granted "Mokassas" and "Mutta rights" to certain
  individuals in recognition of the service rendered by them
  like assisting in collection of land revenue, maintaining
  law and order, etc. Since these were basically grants, the
  tribal did not have absolute rights over these properties.
  Through abolition of Estates and Mahals, the state paved
  the way for settlement of rights of all the tribal tenants
  who tilled these lands. The forested areas of these Estates
  were taken over and reserved as State Forests. Further,
  through abolition of Mutta rights and their conversion
  into Ryotwari Pattas, the Mokassas and the Mutta rights
  were settled in favour of the tribal who tilled these lands.
  Thus, the enactments and promulgations paved the way
  for settlement of land rights to the tribal.

- National Forest Policy 1988: The GOI, through a Resolution dated 7th December 1988, has revised its Forest Policy. The strategies relevant for Tribal welfare and development in this policy states: "Having regard to the symbiotic relationship between the tribal people and forests, a primary task of all agencies responsible for forest management, including the forest development cor-porations should be to associate the tribal people closely in the protection, regeneration and development of forests as well as to provide gainful employment to people living in and around the forest".

Indira Kranthi Patham (IKP) in Tribal Sub Plan Areas

In order to give greater focus and achieve convergence between the *Indira Kranti Patham* and the Integrated Tribal Development Agencies (ITDAs) in the project districts, under the overall framework, the government has developed a tribal development strategy with exclusive implementation arrangements. The following implementation arrangements are ordered in the TSP areas. In the TSP areas, the Project Officer, ITDA, has the responsibility of implementing the Project. A separate Tribal Project Management Unit (TPMU) is being set up to work under the administrative control of Project Officer, ITDA. The TPMU's mandate is social mobilization and empowerment of tribal communities in the TSP areas. The TPMU shall be provided with necessary support staff and functional specialists by the SERP. The TPMU's day-to-day functioning shall be the responsibility of Additional Project Director who works under the Project Officer, ITDA, and under technical control of Project Director, *Indira Kranthi Patham*. At the state level, there shall be a State Tribal Management Unit (STMU) as part of State Project Management Unit of SERP for effective implement-ation of Tribal Development Plan. The STMU shall function under close guidance and coordination of Commissioner, Tribal Welfare.

IFAD (International Fund for Agricultural Development)

Government of Andhra Pradesh has started IFAD-assisted programme for the comprehensive development of tribal in the interior agency areas of the state. The first phase of the IFAD programme for the coastal districts like Srikakulam, Vizianagaram, Vishakhapatnam and East Godavari was started in 1991 and was completed in 1999, with a total expenditure of ₹ 165 crores. The second phase of the IFAD programme for the tribal areas of Adilabad, Warangal, Khammam, West Godavari and Srisailam was started in 1995 and continued up to 2003. The programme was being implemented at a cost of ₹ 183 crores. Under the IFAD programme, apart from taking up schemes like irrigation, horticulture, land development, health and education; a lot of emphasis is being given for beneficiary participation.

Adivasi Mahila Sashaktikaran Yojana

Upliftment of tribal women has been a prime focus of the NSTFDC. It is felt that tribal women can contribute significantly to the process of economic development of the STs. With this object in view, NSTFDC introduced an exclusive concessional scheme for the economic development of eligible ST women titled "*Adivai Mahila Sashaktikaran Yojana*".

Due to the efforts put in by TPMUs, 40,842 Self-Help Groups (SHGs) have been mobilized in tribal area with about 5.22 lakh ST women as members. So far, 2995 Village Organisations have been formed and they have federated into 77 *Mandal Samakhyas* in tribal areas. So far 18,129 Self-Help Groups have been provided with an amount of ₹ 68.38 crores under Community Investment Fund for taking up micro-projects for gainful employment, thereby, benefiting 1,97,546 ST women.

For the first time in India and in A.P., a land mark decision was taken by the government to implement and monitor all the economic support schemes through Women Self-Help Groups in coordination with *Indira Kranthi Patham*. The groups not only ground the assets but also monitor the scheme and recovery of the amount sanctioned. The SHGs will prepare a micro-credit plan and submit to *Mandal Samakhya* and it will be submitted to Project Officer/District Tribal Welfare Officer for sanctions. The releases will be made directly to *Mandal Samakhya* and thereon to Village Organizations. This will simplify the procedure of grounding the schemes. They are empowered to decide their economic-enhancement activities, including land purchase schemes.

AP Tribal Power Company Limited

The State Government established the AP Tribal Power Company Ltd. (AP TRIPCO) under the Companies Act 1956 (July 2002) with a view to explore the feasibility of harnessing the hydro-power available in the tribal areas and improve the conditions of living in those areas by establishing mini hydro power projects (1–3 MW) in Scheduled Areas by utilizing the natural streams and waterfalls. These mini hydal power projects are to be established in partnership with the local tribal women organizations. The entire profits from such projects will accrue to the local tribal and to be used for developing the local tribal areas.

Janashri Bhima Yojana

The Government of India has introduced a new scheme called "*Janashri Bhima Yojana*" during 2004–05. It is a group insurance scheme to provide life insurance protection to the rural and urban poor persons below poverty and marginally

above poverty line, such as workers engaged inforest products
and leaf collectors in forest. Persons between the age of 18
years and 60 years are eligible under this scheme. Sum assured
is ₹ 20,000. The annual premium payable for securing the
assurance is ₹ 200 out of which ₹ 100/- has to be contributed
by the nodal agency/member of the group/State Government
and the remaining amount of ₹ 100 will be subsidized from
Social Security Fund of Central Government. During 2004–
05, the Government of India released an amount of ₹ 60 lakh
for providing insurance coverage to 12,000 families of PTGs
for five years starting from 2004–05 under the *Janashri
Bhima Yojana* Scheme of LIC of India. This grant is towards
beneficiary contribution, and the subsidy part of amount will
be obtained by LIC of India from Social Security Scheme of
GOI. During 2005–06, Government of India released an
amount of ₹ 120 lakh to cover (24,000) ST families under this
scheme.

Janshala

Janshala was launched in this state in 1999. The programme
covers 28 mandals (blocks) in three districts—East Godavari,
West Godavari and Krishna, and 136 slums in four mandals
of Hyderabad City. It is being implemented through a state-
level society which also implements the District Primary
Education Programme (DPEP) and *Sarva Shiksha Abhiyan*
(SSA). In convergence with *Janshala*, the ITDA established
alternative schools in habitations where there were no schools.
These schools are known as *Girijana Vidya Vikas Kendras*
(GVVKs). Usually, GVVKs only had class I and II, after
which children either went to a nearby primary or middle
school, or were sent to residential schools (*Ashramshalas*) run
by the Tribal Welfare Department. However, it was found
that many GVVK children dropped out after class II due to
the distance of the nearest primary school and also due to

reluctance of some parents to send their children tohostels. To address this problem, ITDA and *Janshala* have expanded some of the GVVKs up to class IV.

Jawahar Gram Samrudhi Yojana (JGSY)

This scheme launched in 1999 aims to enable the village community to strengthen the village infrastructure through creation of durable assets as per the local needs. The works taken up provide gainful employment to the rural poor. The Gram Sabha while according approval to conform to the felt needs of schemes given to SC/ST families living below poverty line and physically handicapped persons gives preference to works in the area inhabited by the SC/STs in selection of the works. Further, 22.5 percent of the State Budget is marked exclusively for the benefit of SCs/STs.

Employment Assurance Scheme (EAS)

This scheme seeks to provide additional wage employment opportunities in the form of manual work to the rural poor living below the poverty line. In the process, the effort is to create durable community assets. Minimum wages are paid under the scheme. While providing employment, preference is given to SC/ST and parents of child labour withdrawn from hazardous occupation, and who are below the poverty line.

Swarnjayanti Gram Swarojgar Yojana (SGSY)

Under this scheme, assistance is provided to the poor families living below the poverty line in rural areas for taking up self-employment activities, either individually or in groups called the Self-Help Groups. SGSY is a credit-cum-subsidy pro-gramme. Subsidy is given so as to make it easy for the poor to start their own self-employment activities. An individual is given loan up to ₹ 50,000 and SHGs up to 3 lakh without any collateral security. Subsidy is given at the rate of 30 percent of the project cost with a limit of ₹ 10,000 for SC/ST.

Sectorial Programs

In addition to the above special programs focused on tribal there are a number of other development schemes which are being implemented under different sectors including agriculture, animal husbandry, horticulture, fisheries, health and education. In tribal areas, majority of beneficiaries under these programs are from tribal groups.

Coffee Project

A project on coffee plantation in an area of 60,000 acres has been taken up in the 10th Five Year Plan in the agency area of ITDA, Paderu with financial assistance from the Government of India, Coffee Board and NSTFDC. The total outlay of the project for 7 years is ₹ 144 crores out of which 50 percent is beneficiary contribution in the form of labour. Of the remaining 50 percent, the Government of India assistance is ₹ 36 crores (25 percent), State Government's share is ₹ 12 crores (8.33 percent) and NSTFDC's share is ₹ 24 crores (16.67 percent).

GUJARAT GOVERNMENT INITIATIVES FOR TRIBAL IN DAHOD DISTRICT

The Tribal Development Department of the Government of Gujarat has brought out several policies to enable the tribal of Gujarat in upgrading their skills so that they receive sustainable employment and thus increase their earnings. The government policies include various kinds of programmes, implemented through institutions and NGOs having expertise in their respective fields. These programmes vary in duration and cost. With a view to understand the process of implementation of government policies in Gujarat's tribal region and emerging issues, we need to study the government policies initiated by the Government of Gujarat in detail. The present study deals with various government policies that have been implemented for the tribal in Dahod for their upliftment.

The Constitution of India has advocated the policy of affirmative action and positive non-discrimination in order to ensure better quality of life for the tribal population. Special protection has also been provided to Scheduled Areas that are largely populated by Scheduled Tribal. Specially empowered Project Administrators implemented the ITDP (Integrated Tribal Development Projects) in the 1970s in order to improve the quality of life of tribal population. The Project Administrators have considerable powers over activities of other agencies working in the same field. They also monitor the work of other departments. Recognizing the constitutional rights of the tribal, the concept of Tribal Area Sub Plan (TASP) was also introduced to back the tribal population with financial provisions. The Tribal Development Department in each Indian State is entrusted with the budgetary and planning powers for Tribal Area Sub Plan funds.

The Government of Gujarat has set about to evolve a development example for tribal communities that focus on social justice and equity. The State's approach is people-centred, participatory and decentralised. The State Government has tried to make strategies favourable to the tribal people at all levels of planning, policy making, and imple mentation, leading empowerment to the tribal. The development strategies of Gujarat Government ensure that the tribal population's interests are safeguarded and the strategies assist in bringing ownership of the resources traditionally inherited by the tribal. While ideating the tribal development schemes, programmes, and plans, the Government's focus has not been on merely the maintenance of the continuation level of living for survival of the tribal. The focus has in fact been on assuring dignified living and working conditions for the tribal populations across the State.

Vanbandhu Kalyan Yojana (Hon. Chief Minister's Ten Point Programme)

The Government of Gujarat announced the 'Chief Minister's Ten Point Programme for the Development of Tribal Areas' (Vanbandhu Kalyan Yojana) in the Assembly on February 27, 2007. The bold and unprecedented initiative seeks to enable the tribal regions to get along into mainstream development by bridging the gap between the Integrated Tribal Development Projects (ITDP) blocks and other parts of Gujarat. Under the Ten Point Programme, the Government of Gujarat allocated a package of ₹ 15,000 crore for a period of five years, to make social and civil infrastructure development and permanently remove persistent poverty in ITDP areas. Vanbandhu Kalyan Yojana is a quality oriented programme, aimed to improve the quality of civil infrastructure and social infrastructure in ITDP areas and thus build a positive environment by creating quality employments for the tribal families. Vanbandhu Kalyan Yojana's strategies include harnessing of private initiative, training and modern facilities, technology and infrastructure to lead Dahod's tribal into the new age of information technology, global linkages, and value addition.

Vanbandhu Kalyan Yojana includes the following ten features:

1. Quality and sustainable employment for 5 lakh tribal families
2. Emphasis on quality education and higher education
3. Accelerated economic development of tribal areas
4. Health for all
5. Housing for all
6. Safe drinking water to all
7. Irrigation
8. All weather roads
9. Universal availability of electricity
10. Urban development.

Vanbandhu Kalyan Yojana started up from the year 2007 and since then, there has been a lot of progress for the tribal of Dahod. The progress under Vanbandhu Kalyan Yojana includes programmes like Project Sunshine, Integrated Dairy Development Project, Jeevika Project 1, 2 and 3 and Skill Development Training, which have benefited several bene-ficiaries and increase their basic income. Female tribal are receiving an increased income of ₹ 4000/- per month through the sale of milk from cows and buffaloes under IDDP. Many heifers (improved breed) have been produced under the cattle development programme. Science stream-based higher secondary schools have been started to increase the literacy among tribal students. A Nursing school has been started in Dahod. The students of primary schools in most of the tribal talukas are been given 200 ml. of flavoured milk on daily basis under the Doodh Sanjeevani Yojana. Due to this scheme, which was started in 2007, the attendance in the primary schools has improved and the health of tribal students has also improved. Several BPL families have been allotted houses under Sardar Awas Yojana, Indira Awas Yojana, and other such schemes. Health check- up of tribal has been conducted under the Health Check-Up Programme. Individual taps, mini pipelines, individual water connection and other measures have been taken to ensure safe drinking water in tribal areas. Check dams have been constructed, ponds have been constructed and other significant measures have been taken to provide better irrigation facilities in tribal areas. Many electric connections have been provided under Universal Electrification Programme. Poor households have been given electricity connections free of cost. Tribal areas have been provided with all-weather roads.

Key Components of the Vanbandhu Kalyan Yojana:
- Gender framework for the ten point programme.
- Result oriented interventions.

- Involvement of local people in planning and monitoring.
- Focus on individual family and the ITDP areas.
- Involvement of every implementing department in the programme.

Integrated Tribal Development Projects

The Integrated Tribal Development Projects (ITDP) schemes have been implemented through specifically empowered officials addressed as the Project Administrators. The Project Administrators have varied powers over activities of other authorities working in the field. Each Project Administrator on an average handles a population of five lakh people along with development funds of over ₹ 800 million currently. Each Project Administrator is supported by 5–6 subject experts. The tribal region in Gujarat consists of 43 tribal talukas, 15 pockets and 4 clusters. The entire tribal region is covered under the 12 Integrated Tribal Development Projects. All the tribal zones in the State are characterized by hilly terrain, uncertain rainfall, and rocky soil and hence, those areas are among the most backward region in the State. Minerals, agricultural land, and forests are the main resources in the tribal zones, specifically in Dahod. Unfortunately, the human resources available in Dahod are undeveloped and unskilled, thus leading to poor growth of the tribal region. The task of developing Dahod is hence a big challenge before the administration.

Tribal Area Sub-Plan Implementation to Improve the Socio-Economic Condition of the Tribal in Dahod

The Tribal Sub-Plan is an area development plan. Earlier, scheduled tribal areas had special development projects formulated every year, such as Integrated Tribal Development Projects, Tribal Sub Plans, etc. The plan objectives were modified from the year 1986, in order to cover family oriented programmes along with beneficiary oriented pro-grammes. These programmes now began to be implemented also for the tribal residing outside the scheduled tribal areas and were incorporated in the Tribal Sub Plan. Therefore, the new provision made on the development schemes incorporates not just the tribal in the scheduled areas but also the tribal outside the scheduled areas. The Gujarat State Government has been implementing the Tribal Area Sub Plan as a part of its commitment to implement Constitution of India's enshrined Directive Principle of State Policy. The present strategy for tribal area's development was initiated with the commencement of the Fifth Five Year Plan, early in the year 1975–76.

The Tribal Sub-Plan

The State Government been geared up to undertake activities to bring about overall development of the tribal in Gujarat. Efforts have been made to create a New Gujarat Pattern parallel to Maharashtra Pattern of Tribal Sub Plan. Under the Chairmanship of the Guardian Ministers of the District in Tribal Areas, the 'District Adivasi Vikas Mandal' has been constituted to monitor, review, and evaluate all Tribal Sub Plan schemes. Taluka Panchayat President and District MPs/ MLAs selected from the tribal areas are the members of the 'District Adivasi Vikas Mandal'. Its members also include two lady tribal leaders of the district, two experts in educational field, and two members working for tribal welfare at district level. An expenditure of ₹ 351.69 crore has been provided as a reserved fund for the year 2011–12 for special Tribal Sub Plan. The Tribal Development Department of Gujarat is entrusted with the planning and budgetary powers for the state's TASP funds.

Tribal Sub-Plan assistance is offered to tribal families in Dahod through Integrated Rural Development Programme

(IRDP) and other variety of programmes. The programmes enable the tribal families to cross the poverty line with the help governmental assistance such as subsidy, loan, etc. An exclusive programme, known as 'Gujarat Pattern of Financial Allocation' was launched in order to facilitate participatory and decentralized plans in tribal areas in Gujarat. This program was launched in the year 1998. The Gujarat Pattern funds are specifically intended for bridging over the missing links in interventions and aims at creation of local infra-structure and economic development. 10 percent of the funds are earmarked under this initiative to support major inter-district projects.

Agricultural Development in Dahod through Tribal Area Sub-Plan (TASP)

The tribal area of Dahod, though having greater forest cover, is characterized by less urbanization, limited access to irrigation and sparse population in comparison to other parts of the state. These major factors lead to far lower agricultural productivity per hectare in comparison to other non-tribal regions. Thus TASP seeks to improvise the agricultural sector in tribal areas like Dahod. The essential features of the Tribal Area Sub Plan includes recognition that there can be no uniform solution to the variety of problems faced by the tribal and therefore accept their uniqueness and formulate programmes, schemes, and policies to suit each individual situation; developing appropriate frame for development through Sub-Plan exercise, securing as much quantification from State and Central Plan funds as required, to ensure full utilization, accountability, and non-divertability; according topmost priority to protective measures for eliminating the exploitation of tribal people; restructuring the institutional and administrative set up to suit the needs and aspirations of tribal and supplementing efforts of the State and Central Government through Special Central Assistance (SCA).

The following are the major long-term objectives formed under TASP:

- To sustain agriculture in the tribal areas.
- To support the farmers who are below poverty line.
- To increase the coverage under quality seeds/planting materials.
- To narrow the gaps between the level of development of the tribal in Dahod and the people residing in other parts of the State.
- To increase productivity of agricultural crops.
- Extension functionaries with use of latest technology.
- Technical guidance through agricultural scientists.
- To increase income from agriculture.
- To improve the quality of living of the tribal farmers.

The tribal of Dahod depend upon forests for their subsistence, for most part of the year. The forests of Dahod provide not only food, shelter, healthy climate and nourishment for the tribal, but also help them improve various day-to-day needs. Under the National Bamboo Mission, a project on Bamboo Development was approved in Gujarat state. Under the Bamboo Development scheme, ₹ 4154.28 lakhs were approved for implementation from 2007–08 to 2011–12. Against the release of ₹ 1275.90 lakhs till 2011–12, ₹ 1254.90 has been spent till today. The Bamboo Development project also has a scheme for training, under which the tribal youth are taught skills to develop and make traditional bamboo articles, home décor, furniture and other fancy items. Various market linkages are also modernised so that the value addition may fetch the tribal youth more economic benefit. Several community development works such as schools, construction of roads, drinking water facilities, community wells, etc. have been developed under the Development of Forest Settlement Scheme. These community development schemes help in enhancing the income and livelihood opportunities of the tribal people residing in Dahod. The schemes include providing assistance for house construction, irrigation facilities, land improvement and offering agricultural kits.

The Government of Gujarat has undertaken suitable methods to ensure active participation of the tribal of Dahod in protection and development of forests, by participating in Joint Forest Management (JFM). The Government has given the responsibility of development and protection of forest to the local tribal under the formation of village level Forest Protection Committee. FDAs have been constituted in Gujarat State for planning and implementing various forest development activities in tribal pockets of the state. Gujarat State Forest Development Agency—a state level federation of the Forest Development Agencies—has been formed for coordination, macro-level planning, implementation and convergence of various schemes run by Gujarat Government for the upliftment of the tribal of Dahod. Various other forest development activities have been undertaken by the Gujarat Government in the forest areas for tribal under the Tribal Welfare, SMC (Tribal) and Development of Communication Schemes. Under these schemes, ₹ 2496.66 lakhs has been spent against the total provision of ₹ 2498.78 lakhs.

'Dasmula' (Ten medicinal plants)—has been developed as a project for restoration and development of the important medicinal plants. This project is under implementation and is being assisted by a financial assistant in South Gujarat. An expenditure of ₹ 39.58 lakhs has been made till March'12 against the total approved and released amount of ₹ 40.57 lakhs. Another special project of 'Canopy Plantation' has been undertaken, under which, locally available important medicinal plants are raised in the forest which can later provide employment for the local tribal.

Swarnim Krushi Mahotsav

Swarnim Krushi Mahotsav is an enlightened agriculture—extension initiative by the State Government to herald a revolution in agriculture sector. The project strategizes to improve the yield immensely by opening up bright avenues of progress and prosperity. The Krushi Mahotsav has been an exhaustive effort in agricultural extension organized by Government of Gujarat between the months of May and June, just before the onset of monsoon. The primary aim of this project is to increase agricultural income by promoting a scientific approach to farming. The project was conceived in such a manner that the farmers in tribal areas could receive immediate benefits and they can begin preparations for the next kharif season. Under the programme, the farmers have adopted innovations and modern technologies, learnt sustenance of agriculture and nurturing natural resources.

Krushi Rath, under the Swarnim Krushi Mahotsav, covers all 18000 villages, spreads awareness among farmers, provides know-how about how to select appropriate crop, proper insights about animal husbandry and latest technologies. Gujarat has simulated Krushi Mahotsav to find solutions to the various problems faced by farmers. Massive projects have been undertaken by the State under this programme, such as water-conservation drives by constructing Bori-Bandhs, Farm-ponds, check-dams and terrace-ponds. Under Krushi Rath, a team of horticulture, agriculture, animal husbandry and cooperation department's team members along with agricultural scientists travel with the Kisan Rath unit to every village. Organic farming is also encouraged under the Swarnim Krushi Mahotsav programme. The Mahotsav has created a forum for the convergence of all major stakeholders. It has also facilitated doorstep availability of critical agricultural requirements such as seeds, fertilizers, pesticides and credit for the farmers.

VARIOUS SCHEMES IMPLEMENTED BY THE TRIBAL DEVELOPMENT DEPARTMENT OF GUJARAT ARE AS UNDER

Health, Housing and Other Schemes

Free medical assistance, Balwadi Scheme, financial assistance for individual housing, housing for PTG, Halpati Housing Scheme, assistances for free legal aid, Kunwarbai nu Mameru Scheme, Nucleus Budget, Saat Phera Samuh Lagna Scheme (Group Marriage Scheme), financial assistance victims of Exploitation and Abuse and social awareness camps are part of the health, housing and other schemes brought out by the State Government.

Balwadi Scheme

The Balwadi scheme has been started in Dahod for the tribal children of the age of three to five years, so that they can learn cleanliness; etiquettes like how to stand up and talk; prayers; and also learn about the good virtues and basic morals. The tribal children also become accustomed to school life. Under the Balwadi scheme, tribal children between the age of three and five years are given free education. The women escorting the children receive ₹ 600 per month, along with ₹ 100 as transport allowance and ₹ 600 for miscellaneous expenses annually. The women managing the Balwadi are given a salary of ₹ 1200 to ₹ 1500, depending on their qualifications. The Balwadi scheme is implemented by NGOs and assistance is subject to annual provisions.

Halpati Housing Scheme

Gujarat has implemented several rural housing schemes for BPL families, SC families, ST families, tribal and other primitive groups. The main schemes include the Sardar Patel Awaas Yojana, the Dr. Ambedkar Awaas Yojana, Adin Jati and

Halpati Housing Scheme. All the above mentioned schemes share a common feature—the unit cost of ₹ 40,000 or above is either subsidised by the State Government fully or has part beneficiary contribution. In Dahod, the Gujarat government provides ₹ 11000 per annum in addition to supplement the unit cost of the Halpati Housing Scheme and no income limit has been prescribed for the primitive ST group. Financial assistance of ₹ 54,500 is provided per house to provide housings for members of Halpati Caste in Dahod.

Sardar Patel Awas Yojana

Sardar Patel Awas Yojana materially the slogan "free plot, free house". The State Government provide Free plots scheme for landless agricultural labourers and village artisans living Below Poverty Line in rural areas of Gujarat is under implementation since 1972. A scheme to pay assistance for construction of houses on such allotted plot came into in 1976. Price of a house under the scheme was ₹ 20,000 in ordinary areas and ₹ 22,000 in hilly and inaccessible are a formally. Now price of the one unit house was raised to ₹ 43000 since 2001. Dahod people also get benefit of this scheme.

Kunwarbai nu Mameru Scheme

Under the Kunwarbai nu Mameru Yojana, the Gujarat Government provides financial assistance of ₹ 5,000 to ₹ 10,000 to the poor tribal brides. Parents of Scheduled Tribes' brides in Dahod with an annual income up to ₹ 27,000 in rural area and ₹ 36,000 in urban area can avail this scheme.

Scheme of Grant-in-Aid to Voluntary Organizations

The major objective of the scheme of grant-in-aid to voluntary organizations is to improve the reach of welfare schemes of the Gujarat Government and fill the gaps in service deficient tribal areas, in the sectors such as agro-horticultural productivity, drinking water, social security, education, health, etc. to provide an environment for socioeconomic upliftment and overall development of the tribal in Dahod. Majority of the welfare schemes of the Gujarat Government are carried out through the efforts of voluntary organizations. All other innovative activities having direct impact on the socio-economic development or generation of the tribal in Dahod are also being considered through voluntary efforts. The scheme of grant-in-aid to voluntary organizations began on 1st April 2008.

Manav Garima Yojana

Under the Manav Garima Yojana, the Government provides financial assistance for the tribal in Dahod, who are desirous to start cottage industry for self-employment without obtaining bank loans. This scheme is implemented through Gujarat Scheduled Caste Development Corporation, Gandhinagar. The income limit under this scheme is ₹ 20,000 for rural areas and ₹ 25,000 for urban areas. Further, financial assistance of ₹ 4,000 is provided for equipment assistance.

Drought Prone Area Programme (DPAP)

The basic objectives of the Drought Prone Area Programme is to minimise the adverse effects of drought on productivity of land, water and human resources and production of crops and livestock with drought proofing techniques, ultimately leading to drought proofing of the affected areas. The DPAP scheme also aims to promote overall economic development and improve the socio-economic conditions of the vulnerable groups inhabiting the programme areas. Dahod district is also getting help under this scheme from the Government of Gujarat. The programme was first launched during 1973–74 by the Government of India to address special problems of drought prone areas.

Beti Bachavo Abhiyan (Save the Girl Child)

Beti Bachavo Abhiyan, also known as 'Save the Girl Child' campaign, is a public movement for spreading awareness to the society that no discrimination is made on gender basis. Jyotigram, a free bus journey for the girl students, the Kishori-Shakti Yojana, an upgrading of primary education, and various other steps have been taken to improve the condition of girl students.

Mid-Day Meal Programme/Bal Pravesh

Mid-Day Meals in schools has a long history in India. The Mid-Day Meal Programme was introduced in 1925 for the underprivileged children in Chennai then known as Madras Municipal Corporation. It took another 55 years for the three states—Gujarat, Kerala and Tamil Nadu to join the Mid-Day Meal Programme with their own resources for primary schools. Soon, the programme was also implemented to be provided to children in Tribal Areas of Madhya Pradesh and Orissa. Because of this programme, the enrolment rate has substantially increased in primary schools and the dropout ratio has also substantially decreased. The objectives of the Mid-Day Meal Programme include providing nutritional support to children of primary stage in drought affected areas during summer vacation; improving the nutritional status of children in from standards 1 to 5 in Government, Local Body and Government aided schools, and EGS and AIE centres; encouraging poor children, belonging to disadvantaged sections, to attend school more regularly and help them concentrate on classroom activities; protecting children from classroom hunger; increasing school enrolment and attendance; improving socialisation among children belonging to all castes; addressing the issue of malnutrition among children; and social empowerment of women by creating employment. The Government of Gujarat ensures 100 percent literacy in rural areas by encouraging Bal Pravesh (Child Admissions as it is a prime factor to combat poverty.

Nirogi Bal (Healthy Child)

The Gujarat Government emphasizes on Nirogi Bal scheme as health is a primary concern for children who attend the classroom. Literacy to Health with Nirogi Bal guarantees universal reach and delivery of quality health services. This scheme was announced for safe health with impact to social development of Gujarat in 2008–09 with mass movement. One of the major goals of this scheme is to ensure life skills education and elementary education for all children.

Chiranjeevi Yojana (Hospital Facilities for Maternity)

The Chiranjeevi Yojana implemented by the Government of Gujarat is aimed to encourage the BPL families to improve access to delivery in hospital. The scheme was launched as a one year pilot project in December 2005 in five backward districts Banaskantha, Dahod, Kutch, Panchmahals, and Sabarkantha and covered all BPL families financial assistance is provided for protection to the BPL families, covering their out-of-pocket costs incurred on travel to reach the healthcare facility centre. Assistance of ₹ 200/- for transportation expenses with ₹ 50/- for the attendant is provided. Approximately, 1,63,609 women have availed the benefit of this scheme.

Scholarship Schemes

A provision of ₹ 884.00 crore has been proposed for 2012–13 for Tribal Development Department for Welfare of Scheduled Tribes against, the provision of ₹ 700.05 crore for 2011–12. This provision mainly includes free uniform in primary schools, increase in the rates of scholarships, assistance for bicycle, starting residential schools for talented students, Government hostels, ashram shalas, Pre-SSC Scheme, scholarship for Students of Class 1–4, post-metric scholarship scheme, special state scholarship scheme for working ST girls, fellowship scheme for ST students of MPhil and PhD courses, along with other schemes.

Stipends

Various different kinds of stipends are provided to SC students for IAS, IPS Courses and Allied Services, for the tribal trainees who are in Training cum Production Centres (TCPC), pre-examination centre and shorthand, typing classes with the stipend to the trainees. There are other stipends for Technical and Commercial Courses for the SC students. Assistance for food bill for S.T. students of Medical and Engineering colleges, assistance for educational kits for medical, engineering and technical diploma students is also provided.

Other Assistance for Education

Varied other kinds of assistance such as VidyaSadhna Scheme, assistance for uniforms to students of Class 1–7, economic assistance to ST students studying in reputed private schools, book-bank scheme for ST students and assistance for private tuitions for ST students of Class 12 is also provided.

Prizes

The Government awards prizes to state-level ST high rank holders in Class 10 and 12 board exams, district-level ST high rank holders in Class 10 and 12 board exams and to first rank holders in degree courses.

Hostels and Educational Institutions

A fully functional school in the tribal area is required to have 420 residential students, out of which 50 percent must consist of girls. The accommodation must be of dormitory type, with each dormitory not having over 8 beds and they must be equipped with individual cupboards for students, beds with mattresses, and facilities of light and fan. Each dormitory is provisioned to have external main switches so that the power supply can be easily switched off by maintenance staff when they are not being used.

One can consider construction of four small hostels, with each one housing approximately 105 students. The flooring material needs to be maintenance free and durable. There must be separate dormitories for girls and boys. Provisions for dry hostels for students of class 8–12, financial assistance to NGOs to build grant-in-aid hostel for ST students, assistance for extra coaching classes in grant-in-aid hostel, assistances for development and maintenance of Government hostels for S.T. boys and girls, assistance for dry hostels for college students, working women's hostel for S.T. women, financial assistance to build premises for Govt. Hostels, assistance to grant-in-aid hostels, Adarsh Nivasi Shalas (Model Residential Schools) and Ashram Shalas are also there. There needs to be a medium size common room where at least 25 percent of students can have access in general at any time. Facilities for indoor games such as carom and chess, a TV, a notice board, and a small library needs to be there in the common room. Each hostel is required to have a small store to keep extra bed sheets, towels, mattresses, and other items. Each hostel must have at least two entries and exits, so that at least one of them can be used during emergencies. There must be a common washing room with facilities for drying clothes. The place should be protected from direct sun light and must be easily accessible to the students. The dormitories must always be protected from direct sun light. Maximum use of solar power must be made for lighting and water heating in bathrooms. Each hostel must have an apartment for the warden and the warden must be provided with a separate entry. The warden's apartment should have a bed room cum living room, a cupboard, toilet cum bath room, and internet facility.

Teachers' Quarters

Based on successful results of a previous financial assistance scheme, a special scheme of allocating special quarters for teachers in the tribal areas was introduced for the first time in the Eleventh Five Year Plan. Under this new scheme, 10-blocks unit has been proposed to be constructed in the tribal areas where teachers find difficulty in finding housing facilities. An expense of ₹ 667.25 lakhs has been provided for 85 units in the Tribal Area Sub Plan programme in 2011–12 and the disbursement of the same has been incurred through fund allotment to SarvaSikshaAbhiyan (SSA), Gandhinagar.

Computerised Projects

Computerised Projects have been designed as one of the major aims of elementary education initiatives in order to improve the quality of education imparted through Municipal or Panchayat Schools (government schools). The Computerised Projects are aimed to cover both computer education as well as computer-aided learning.

THE TRIBAL SELF-GOVERNANCE INITIATIVES IN INDIA

There are three major components of Self-Governance. These components include the planning phase, the negotiations process, and actual implementation. To whatever extent a Tribe chooses to enter into Self-Governance, completion of each of these components is essential to successful implementation.

Planning

One of the primary objectives of Self-Governance is to provide the maximum flexibility to Tribal governments to design programs, activities and services to address Tribal priorities and respond to local concerns. When programs intended to serve Indian people have been managed by the Bureau of Indian Affairs (BIA) and Indian Health Service (IHS) in the past, or managed by Tribes under PL 93–638 grants and/or contracts, most of the decision making and funding priorities were made by the Federal bureaucracy. Tribal or local concerns often did not fit into the funding and program parameters established under BIA and IHS policies and regulations. Most of the BIA and IHS guidelines, policies and regulations are prepared for national application and are not tailored to specific Tribes, Reservations, or local conditions.

Self-Governance is designed to allow Tribes to plan and implement BIA and IHS programs, activities, and services that best meet their needs. In effect, along with existing Tribal responsibilities, Tribal governments become the primary policy makers for the programs, services and activities on their Reservations, including the allocation of fiscal resources. Under Self-Governance, Tribes become responsible for BIA and IHS programs, services, functions, and activities assumed by the choice of the Tribes.

Legislative Requirements

As outlined in both the permanent Self Governance law (P.L. 103–413) and the Self-Governance demonstration legislation (Title III, P.L. 100–472, as amended), a qualified Tribal applicant shall:

- Successfully complete the planning phase including legal and budgetary research; and internal tribal government planning and organizational preparation;
- Request participation in the Self-Governance by resolution or other action by the Tribal governing body; and
- Demonstrate financial stability and financial management capability for the previous three years by having no material audit exceptions in the required annual audit.

Initial Contacts

Tribes which meet the legislative requirements, depending on which programs they wish to compact, should send a tribal resolution and cover letter to either the Department of the Interior Office of Self-Governance or to the Indian Health Service Office of the Tribal Self-Governance.

Additionally, interested Tribes may request additional information from the Self-Governance Communication and Education Office of the Department of the Interior. This Office was formed to share information regarding the purpose, process, and benefits of Self-Governance. The administrator for the Communication and Education Project has been distributing materials and information, providing educational workshops, coordinating national conferences and other forums discussion concerning critical Self-Governance issues.

As the demand for Tribal-specific technical assistance and interest in Self- Governance has greatly increased, it is helpful to contact other participating Self-Governance Tribes, Tribal leaders, and Self-Governance Coordinators. Information such as specific Self-Governance job descriptions, sample Tribal budget ordinances, internal personnel policies and procedures, other administrative and fiscal processes, and Tribal laws can be obtained and reviewed for application and adaptation to each Tribe's unique governmental and administrative structure.

Internal Reorganization

The planning basis for internal Tribal reorganization should be determined by the particular needs of the individual Tribal government and should take into consideration the requirements included in the law, provisions contained in the Tribe's Constitution, Tribal Laws, Tribal policies and procedures, the Self-Governance Compact and Annual Agreement, and the federal audit requirements as reflected in OMB Circular A-87. How an Indian Tribe reorganizes its government for participation in Tribal Self-Governance is solely an internal Tribal matter for each individual Tribe to decide.

The "new partnership" and reaffirmation of the "government-to-government" relationship under Self-Governance enhances the authority, responsibility, and opportunity to function as an independent Tribal government. Under a typical 638 contract, a Tribe's obligation was principally to the Contracting Officer at the Area or Agency level who reported to the multiple layers of the BIA and IHS bureaucracies. Tribes and Tribal program managers often had to respond to the 638 contract/grant "Scopes of Work" rather than to the elected Tribal Council or needs of their people.

Under a Self-Governance Compact, the participating Tribe, the Department of the Interior and/or the Indian Health Service identifies "Designated Officials" as the individuals responsible for resolving issues, problems, or for any matter arising under this new relationship. Generally, the Tribes have identified the Tribal Chairman as their "Designated Official" and the Department of the Interior and the Indian Health Service has identified either an Area Director or the Director of either of the Office(s) of Self-Governance as the Federal "Designated Official".

Because of this "new partnership" role, internal Tribal government reorganization takes on additional importance. Tribal reorganization may be as simple as identification of the Tribal Designated Official, or may be a major restructuring of how the Tribal government conducts its business and activities. Reorganization may be at the policy, legislative, administrative, or program levels. For example, some Self-Governance Tribes have undertaken major reorganizations of Tribal governmental structure and have amended their Tribal Constitutions. This reorganization effort has also included the enactment of several new Tribal laws designed to address specific areas of concern and, at the same time, to prevent unnecessary intrusion into internal Tribal affairs by outside forces. For other Self-Governance Tribes, most of the reorganization has occurred within existing federal programs and Departments. Increased program responsibilities have required the development of new processes and procedures to handle the new responsibilities. Many Self-Governance Tribes, found their existing institutional structures, Constitutions, and Ordinances adequate to address the responsibilities of Self-Governance and to serve the needs of Tribal members.

Many Tribes also found the need to develop or expand:

- budget procedures;
- internal monitoring procedures;
- performance and evaluation procedures; and,
- Internal compliance systems.

Major considerations in approaching Tribal reorganization are: identifying methods for timely decision-making; communicating policy decisions from the Tribal Council to Tribal programs and to Tribal members; and, developing cost-efficient program operations. Effectiveness of organizational structure will in part determine how well Tribes can respond to problems and issues as they arise. Cost efficiency of program operations dictate how much it costs to provide programs and services. Combined, effectiveness and cost efficiency will affect the opportunities the Tribe will have to redesign programs, reallocate funding, and most importantly, improve the delivery of services to people.

As with any organization, a hierarchy of decision-making authority must be established. Reasons for delegation of authority must be established by Tribal Councils and understood by all levels of Tribal government. Generally, the closer decision-making is to the actual implementation of decisions, the more efficient the government operates. Tribal Councils retain policy and legislative authority while administrators make administrative decisions, managers make management decisions, and program line staff makes program decisions. The respective roles and responsibilities need to be defined and understood. Government operations, including Tribal government, require the delegation of authority and responsibility. The concept of delegation of authority and responsibility to Program Managers is essential for effective and efficient government operations.

Tribal Budget Process

With a few limitations contained in P.L. 103–413, Title III of P.L. 100–472, as amended, and the Compacts of Self-Governance, Self-Governance Tribes are free to design and allocate funds based on Tribal needs and priorities. Self-Governance Tribes may also need to establish or expand their own internal budgeting process. This may depend on the extent of their existing budgeting process for Tribal funds or "hard money" budgets.

A few important limitations exist for how a Self-Governance Tribe decides to design its programs and allocate its funds. Those limitations are:

- No more than 30 percent of funding for BIA trust programs may be reallocated within any year without an explanation of how the trust responsibility will be met, (trust programs are limited to physical resources and financial management).
- Funds specifically appropriated or that are "earmarked" for specific activities by the Congress may only be used for those statutory purposes.
- Funds awarded to a Tribe from BIA or IHS statutory designated competitive grants and incorporated into Annual Funding Agreements must be allocated for the purposes of the grants: except grant funds may be combined with other funds provided the objectives are

accomplished—for example Indian Child Welfare funds may be combined with other social services funds to create stability for an overall comprehensive program that deals with matters involving child welfare, alcohol, drug abuse and family counseling; and

- Construction funds must be spent on construction activities, but operating dollars may be spent for construction.

Based on the annual Self-Governance negotiations, a Self-Governance Tribe receives a block of funds based on what funds the Tribe would be eligible to receive at all levels, including the dollars from the BIA Central, Area and Agency Offices and IHS Headquarters, Area and Service Unit associated with the programs, services, functions and activities assumed by the Tribe. Essentially, each Self-Governance Tribe is responsible for internally allocating these funds, subject to the limitations identified above. Under Self-Governance, it becomes a practical matter for the Tribe to have a formal or defined budgeting process established. The budgeting process should be responsive to the needs of the Tribe, Tribal members, and Tribal programs.

Some Self-Governance Tribes have enacted Budget Ordinances which set forth formal mechanisms for handling the Tribal budget process. These Ordinances can serve as Tribal "anti-deficiency" laws enabling Tribal programs to operate within the established budgets approved by Tribal Councils. The procedures established by these Ordinances help prepare the Tribes for assuming their responsibilities under Self-Governance. For example, prior to Self-Governance, the BIA and IHS would establish program budgets. Now, Tribes are solely responsible for internally allocating or appropriating the funding for each program through internal budgeting procedures. All of the budget procedures and decisions require better information, programmatic and community involvement, and formal adoption by the Tribal Councils.

In general, Tribal managers and program staff prepare operational plans, justifications and corresponding budgets for the next fiscal or calendar year. Depending on the Tribal budget procedures these programs/budgets are presented to the Tribal Council and/or the responsible Tribal authority. The Council then allocates funds according to its priorities and availability of funds. It is very important that these program plans include evaluation tools so the Tribal Government and Tribal management can periodically assess program progress.

Self-Governance planning requires a complete review of existing operations, establishment of internal policies and procedures, communication and education, efficient and effective use of management resources, determination of Tribal priorities, and the identification of short and long-term goals. The intensity of the planning process will vary for each Tribe. For Tribes just entering Self-Governance, typically this process will range anywhere from six months to two years. Self-Governance planning does not end with negotiations and implementation. Planning activities for Self Governance is an ongoing effort. It is only hoped that preferential treatment approach towards the tribal population will be a milestone in their path of development.

Socio-Economic Profile of Tribal in Andhra Pradesh and Gujarat

SOCIO-ECONOMIC PROFILE OF TRIBAL DISTRICTS OF ANDHRA PRADESH

Andhra Pradesh is home to 35 communities officially designated as Scheduled Tribes (STs). They numbered at 50, 24, 104 in the 2011 Census. Out of the 35 STs, recently two communities, namely, Nakkala/Kurvikaran, Dhulia/Paiko/Putiya (in the districts of Vishakhapatnam and Vizianagaram) have been de-notified in the state. Twelve tribes, namely, Bodo Gadaba, Gutob Gadaba, Bondo Porja, Khond Porja, Parangi porja, Chenchu, Dongaria Khonds, Kuttiya Khonds, Kolam, Kondareddis, Konda Savaras and Thoti have been recognized as Primitive Tribal Groups (PTGs). Except Konda Reddis and Thoti, the population statistics of other PTGs are not available separately as these are notified as sub groups/sections of main communities. The Population of Konda Reddis is 132569 as per the 2011 Census and that of Thoti tribe was 2,074 as per 2001 census. No data was available about the tribe in 2011 census since authorities had lumped the tribe along with other scheduled tribes.

The STs of Andhra Pradesh constitute 5.68 percent of India's tribal population. Although the state's STs comprise only 6.99 percent of the state's population, they account for the largest tribal concentration in Southern India. The ST's in the state are living in the districts of Srikakulam, Vizianagaram, Vishakhapatnam, East Godavari, West Godavari, Warangal, Khammam, Adilabad and Kurnool. The 35 reported ST communities are mainly concentrated in nine districts declared as Scheduled Areas by special government order in 1950. Sixty percent of the STs live in forest areas in the

Eastern Ghats, on the banks of the river Godavari. Two-thirds of the ST population in the State of Andhra Pradesh live in these areas. This constitutes 11% of the total geographical area of the state. Among the 23 districts of Andhra Pradesh and Telangana, Khammam has the highest ST population (25.18%).

This is followed by Adilabad (18.09%), Vishakhapatnam (14.42%), Warangal (14.10%) and Nalgonda (11.30%). This

Table 2.1: District-Wise Population of Scheduled Tribes of Andhra Pradesh (2011 Census)

Sl. No.	District	Total Population	ST Total	ST Male	ST Female	% of STs to Total Population
1.	Srikakulam	2703114	166118	81382	84736	6.15
2.	Vizianagaram	2344474	235556	114687	120869	10.05
3.	Vishakhapatnam	4290589	618500	302905	315595	14.42
4.	East Godavari	5285824	297044	144548	152496	5.62
5.	West Godavari	3994410	133997	65439	68558	3.35
6.	Krishna	4517398	132464	66734	65730	2.93
7.	Guntur	4887813	247089	125105	121984	5.06
8.	Prakasam	3397448	151145	76677	74468	4.45
9.	SPSR Nellore	2963557	285997	145168	140829	9.65
10.	Kurnool	4053463	82831	42052	40779	2.04
11.	Anantapur	4081148	154127	78573	75554	3.78
12.	YSR Kadapa	2882469	75886	38571	37315	2.63
13.	Chittoor	4174064	159165	79756	79409	3.81
Telangana						
14.	Ranga Reddy	52,96,741	2,18,757	1,12,768	1,05,989	4.13
15.	Hyderabad	39,43,323	48,937	25,556	23,381	1.24
16.	Nizamabad	25,51,335	1,92,941	95,679	97,262	7.56
17.	Medak	30,33,288	1,68,985	86,574	82,411	5.57
18.	Mahabubnagar	40,53,028	3,64,269	1,87,035	1,77,234	8.99
19.	Nalgonda	34,88,809	3,94,279	2,03,876	1,90,403	11.30
20.	Warangal	35,12,576	5,30,656	2,68,976	2,61,680	14.10
21.	Khammam	26,07,066	6,56,577	3,26,225	3,30,352	25.18
22.	Karimnagar	37,76,269	1,06,745	53,495	53,250	2.83
23.	Adilabad	27,41,239	4,95,794	2,47,472	2,48,322	18.09
Telangana		**3,50,03,674**	**31,77,940**	**16,07,656**	**15,70,284**	**9.08**
Andhra Pradesh		**84,665,533**	**5,918,073**	**2969362**	**2948711**	**6.99**

Source: Census 2011.

zone forms the traditional habitat of 31 tribal communities in Scheduled Areas (sprawling 30,030 sq. km.) and the rest outside. The other three tribal groups, i.e., Lambada, Yerukala and Yanadi mostly live outside the Scheduled Areas. Out of the 33 STs, Sugalis are numerically the largest ST with a population of 2,077,947 constituting 41.4 percent of the state's ST population. They are followed by Koya 568,019 (11.3 percent), Yanadis 462,167 (9.2 percent), Yerukulas 437,459 (8.7 percent) and Gonds 252,038 (5 percent). These five ST communities account for 76 percent of the total ST population in the state. Of the total ST population, 92.5 percent live in the rural areas. Among the major STs, Gonds have the highest (97.6 percent) rural population, followed by Koya (95.5 percent), Sugalis (93.7 percent), Yanadis (86.4 percent) and Yerukulas (77.5 percent).

Economic Status

In the state, agriculture labour among STs is 10.3 percent with 115.31 lakh land holdings. However in percentages STs have only 7.5 percent of holdings. Among total employees, STs represent only 4.9 percent. Whereas for Male work participation is 55.7 percent for female it is only 52 percent.

There has been a rise in the ST main workers from 7.38 percent of the total main workers at 2001 Census to 9.46 percent of the total main workers at 2011 Census. This, in turn, has resulted in corresponding decrease in the marginal workers from 20.7 percent in 2001 to 16.4 percent in 2011. Out of total workers, agricultural labourers constitute 49.3 percent, which is significantly higher when compared to 36.9 percent recorded for ST population at the national level. Cultivators account for 34.3 percent and 13.5 percent has been returned as other workers. Remaining 3 percent have been workers in household industry. At the individual caste level, among major STs, Yenadis have the maximum 76.2 percent agricultural labourers.

Table 2.2: District-Wise Rural and Urban Scheduled
Tribes Population and their Percentage (2011 Census)

Sl. No.	District	Rural	Urban	Total	% of ST Rural Population to Total ST Population	% of ST Urban Population to Total ST Population
1.	Srikakulam	160438	5680	166118	96.58	3.42
2.	Vizianagaram	226130	9426	235556	96.00	4.00
3.	Vishakhapatnam	579968	38532	61850	93.77	6.23
4.	East Godavari	282547	14497	297044	93.20	6.80
5.	West Godavari	124584	9413	133997	91.37	8.63
6.	Krishna	93915	38549	132464	70.90	29.10
7.	Guntur	190905	56184	247089	77.26	22.74
8.	Prakasam	124386	26759	151145	82.30	17.70
9.	SPSR Nellore	240972	45025	285997	84.26	15.74
10.	Kurnool	64735	18096	82831	78.15	21.85
11.	Anantapur	126362	27765	154127	81.99	18.01
12.	YSR Kadapa	58181	17705	75886	76.67	23.33
13.	Chittoor	128753	30412	159165	80.89	19.11
14.	Adilabad	463089	32705	495794	93.40	6.59
15.	Nizamabad	185297	7644	192942	96.03	4.12
16.	Karimnagar	92353	14392	106745	86.52	13.48
17.	Medak	156801	12184	168985	92.78	7.21
18.	Hyderabad	–	48937	48937	0	100.00
19.	Ranga Reddy	133890	84867	218757	61.20	38.79
20	Mahbubnagar	345359	18910	364269	94.81	5.19
21.	Nalgonda	366300	27979	394279	92.90	7.10
22.	Warangal	486034	44622	530656	91.59	8.41
23.	Khammam	709904	55661	765565	92.73	7.27
	Andhra Pradesh	**5340903**	**685944**	**6026847**	**88.61**	**11.38**

Source: Census 2011.

Table 2.3: District-Wise Scheduled Tribe Workers According to Activity Status in Andhra Pradesh as per 2001 and 2011 Census

Sl. No.	District	2011					2001				
		Cultivators	Agriculture Labourers	Manufacturing Households	Total Main Workers	Total Marginal Workers	Cultivators	Agriculture Labourers	Manufacturing Households	Total Main Workers	Total Marginal Workers
1.	Srikakulam	6988	42330	589	56489	34265	14775	32804	1005	55207	24309
2.	Vizianagaram	12949	73463	1878	98009	35553	31302	51291	3046	96317	27862
3.	Vishakhapatnam	138637	80635	5037	248972	110925	178376	53396	3676	250838	57007
4.	East Godavari	22183	55092	754	89071	32410	31057	31633	1951	73544	26505
5.	West Godavari	6901	295948	1114	362613	58307	9272	24742	893	42366	10310
6.	Krishna	1854	36857	1142	57209	11198	3115	28733	1981	46993	9186
7.	Guntur	8410	85938	1268	120613	18056	10304	65558	2384	97699	19472
8.	Prakasam	2841	43914	1052	66876	15656	3984	28432	2444	49702	13179
9.	Nellore	2201	91913	2041	122842	35979	3737	77175	2629	106581	28453
10.	Kurnool	3480	18274	4091	35819	4948	4456	10912	5590	29003	5752
11.	Anantapur	11286	30403	2386	60121	17360	16452	22827	3585	52300	14387
12.	YSR Kadapa	1977	18015	1993	31485	7359	2392	11293	3257	23384	7372
13.	Chittoor	25701	207917	63644	320389	3140	6869	34200	1504	53136	15425
14.	Ranga Reddy	21510	23860	2005	80793	18479	24846	15169	1470	57794	13103
15.	Hyderabad	196	285	329	13574	4621	71	45	449	10227	1075
16.	Nizamabad	37045	35041	3280	82653	16713	42282	19938	2976	71642	15794
17.	Medak	28731	31850	1134	70634	14530	26663	22456	1512	57135	12491
18.	Mahabubnagar	67720	67372	2906	166482	24005	56521	37668	3859	115418	32611
19.	Nalgonda	51889	102372	2130	180454	31565	63038	62016	3361	148560	36735
20.	Warangal	111405	107945	1944	245877	42506	118878	62863	3425	204497	51087
21.	Khammam	98071	224041	2348	358922	75054	120521	142984	3967	298625	79551
22.	Karimnagar	14165	23197	1552	47211	9357	16171	13358	2018	38547	10293
23.	Adilabad	109026	75898	4542	211230	56364	95071	48721	4344	166487	47675
	Andhra Pradesh	**785166**	**1772213**	**109159**	**3128338**	**678350**	**880153**	**898214**	**61326**	**2146002**	**559634**

Source: Census 2011.

Table 2.4: District-Wise Number of Operational Holdings and Area Operated by Scheduled Tribes (2005-06)
(Area in Hectares)

Sl. No.	District	Marginal (upto 1.0 Hect)		Small (1.0–2.0 Hect)		Semi Medium (2.0–4.0 Hect)		Medium (4.0–10.0 Hect)		Large (upto 10.0 and above)		Total	
		No.	Area	No.	Area	No.	Area	No.	Area	No.	Area	No.	Area
1.	Srikakulam	22376	9444	5297	7153	1576	3998	253	1394	13	174	29515	22163
2.	Vizianagaram	25221	11161	7626	10594	3101	8246	881	4891	59	807	36888	35699
3.	Vishakhapatnam	44319	21277	23719	34062	19059	53027	8506	48408	717	10002	96320	166677
4.	East Godavari	16793	8209	10167	14654	8798	23993	4115	23370	393	5676	40266	75902
5.	West Godavari	13797	5991	3919	5546	2461	6549	776	4333	51	769	21004	23188
6.	Krishna	11895	4831	2418	3304	900	2422	226	1217	12	161	15451	11935
7.	Guntur	12991	6223	4379	5945	1842	4596	421	2289	11	137	19644	19190
8.	Prakasam	8876	3970	3086	4398	1447	3501	240	1321	7	88	13656	13278
9.	Nellore	18077	6958	2364	3138	573	1354	54	283	5	65	21073	11797
10.	Kurnool	5574	3270	3640	5106	2032	5405	596	3247	30	364	11872	17392
11.	Anantapur	10475	6022	9827	14349	6379	15131	946	5238	76	1128	27703	41869
12.	YSR Kadapa	5825	2744	2032	2900	770	1898	91	496	3	36	8721	8075
13.	Chittoor	13400	6021	3591	5013	1107	2734	95	499	5	60	18198	14327
14.	Ranga Reddy	13255	7146	7336	10228	3862	9891	916	4981	73	1134	25442	33380
15.	Hyderabad	–	–	–	–	–	–	–	–	–	–	–	–
16.	Nizamabad	24845	12836	10059	13563	2431	5959	271	1448	26	570	37632	34376
17.	Medak	17002	8405	7909	11050	3092	7987	723	3992	68	959	28794	32392
18.	Mahabubnagar	32921	17469	20014	28307	10419	27148	2485	13638	179	2345	66018	88907
19.	Nalgonda	44473	21948	19285	26891	8819	23166	2242	12224	124	1886	74943	86114
20.	Warangal	53993	25753	20657	28772	8903	23829	2707	15035	287	4667	86547	98056
21.	Khammam	69191	34261	32633	46095	21850	57743	7483	40326	438	5948	131595	184373
22.	Karimnagar	13904	6303	4392	6094	1508	3957	294	1591	15	213	20113	18159
23.	Adilabad	33187	17653	27403	39329	26144	67290	8133	43502	479	6833	95346	174607
	Andhra Pradesh	**512390**	**247894**	**231753**	**326492**	**137073**	**359826**	**42454**	**233725**	**3071**	**44020**	**926741**	**1211956**

Source: Census 2011.

Work Participation Rate (WPR)

The Work Participation Rate (WPR) is the percentage of workers to the total population. The WPR of the ST population is 54.2 percent according to the 2011 Census, which is almost equal to 53.9 percent recorded in 2001. The WPR among males is 58.7 percent and females are 54.4 percent; more than half of the males/females have been returned workers among ST at 2011 Census. At the individual caste level, by and large, a consistent pattern is noted in the WPR. The highest WPR of 56.5 percent is reported for Yanadis and lowest among Yerukulas (50.5 percent). The Yerukulas have also recorded the lowest female WPR of 45.2 percent (Office of the Registrar General, India 2011).

Out of the total number of workers, "agricultural labourers" constitute 58.3 percent, which is significantly higher when compared to 39.3 percent recorded for ST population at the national level. "Cultivators" accounting for 34.3 percent and 13.5 percent, have been returned as "other workers". The remaining 3 percent have been workers in "household industry". At the individual caste level among the major STs, the Yanadis have the maximum 76.2 percent of "agricultural labourers" (Office of the Registrar General, India 2011).

Livelihoods of the Tribe

A Report in 2000 stated that 45% of Rural ST population and 35.6% in urban areas is below poverty line. According to NSS 66th round estimates, in India Monthly per capita expenditure of Tribes in rural areas is ₹ 873 and in urban areas is ₹ 1794. In Andhra Pradesh monthly per capita expenditure of ST in rural areas is ₹ 999 and in urban areas as ₹ 2114. Less population is able to use schemes of government for their opportunities. Population survival is based on their traditional occupations like making of toys, baskets, mats, cosmetics and collection of leaves, honey, shifting, agriculture, etc.

The economy and livelihood practices of the tribes are closely associated with the ecological factors and habitats which they inhabit. Among the plain tribes, the Yerukulas are the traditional basket makers and swine herders. They are known as the ex-criminal tribe of Andhra Pradesh. They live mostly in multi-caste villages, maintaining symbiotic relations with the non-tribal. The Yanadis' habitats are mostly found on the banks of rivers, lakes, tanks and canals. Their main livelihood is fishing. Besides this they also catch the field rats exclusively for their own consumption purpose. The settlements of the Lambadas are found in separate hamlets, locally termed as *Tandas*. Most of their habitats are located nearer to hillocks or in the places with green pastures where they could rear cattle. Earlier, the Lambadas were known to be nomads, but in modern times, they are becoming sedentary cultivators, and rearing of cattle has become their secondary occupation. They are mostly distributed in the Telangana Region and sparsely in Rayalaseema and the coastal areas. The Yerukulas are found throughout the state whereas the Yanadis are mostly concentrated in Nellore District and sparsely distributed in Coastal Andhra Region.

Fig. 2.1   *Fig. 2.2*   *Fig. 2.3*

Fig. 2.4   *Fig. 2.5*

Figs. 2.1–2.5: Cattle Rearing

ECONOMIC AND SOCIAL INCLUSION

Housing and Potable Water

Most of the tribal live in thatched houses and very few have 'pucca' houses with drinking water and sanitation facilities. The cooking is very traditional mostly through burning of fire woods collected from the forest. Water is procured mostly from wells situated far and in the outskirts of the villages where women have to walk to draw water from the wells for consumption. Some villages may have water hand pumps nearby but these again are few and scattered.

Fig. 2.6   *Fig. 2.7*   *Fig. 2.8*

Fig. 2.9   *Fig. 2.10*   *Fig. 2.11*

Figs. 2.6–2.11: Thatched Houses, Mostly Wells for Drawing Water, Mud Flooring, etc.

Literacy

It is widely accepted that there is a positive co-relation between literacy and Social inclusion. Extending the system of primary education into tribal areas and reserving places for tribal children in middle and high schools and higher education institutions are central to government policy, but efforts to improve a tribe's educational status have had mixed results. Recruitment of qualified teachers and determination of the appropriate language of instruction also remain troublesome. Commission after commission on the "language question" has called for instruction, at least at the primary level, in the students' native tongue. In some regions, tribal children entering school must begin by learning the official regional language, often one completely unrelated to their tribal tongue. The experiences of the Gonds of Andhra Pradesh provide an example. Primary schooling began there in the 1940s and 1950s. The government selected a group of Gonds who had managed to become semiliterate in Telugu and taught them the basics of written script. These individuals became teachers who taught in Gondi, and their efforts enjoyed a measure of success until the 1970s, when state policy demanded instruction in Telugu. The switch in the language of instruction both made the Gond teachers superfluous because they could not teach in Telugu and also presented the government with the problem of finding reasonably qualified teachers willing to teach in outlying tribal schools. From the table below we can see that drop-out rates in Andhra Pradesh for both ST boys and girls in all classes is highest compared to other States.

Table 2.5: Drop-out Rates among SC and ST Boys and Girls (2006)
(percentage)

Categories	AP	Karnataka	Maharashtra	Orissa	Rajasthan
Dropout SC Boys I–V	44.09	6.12	17.02	44.99	53.07
Dropout SC Girls I–V	44.12	14.03	18.21	42.36	36.29
Dropout SC Boys VI–VIII	63.41	27.19	30.03	63.73	69.65
Dropout SC Girls VI–VIII	68.87	51.61	38.22	67.17	80.07
Dropout ST Boys I–V	63.29	4.88	34.42	59.58	52.19
Dropout ST Girls I–V	68.47	4.96	42.82	63.19	38.31
Dropout ST Boys VI–VIII	76.80	53.81	59.12	76.49	70.42
Dropout ST Girls VI–VIII	82.49	56.80	65.14	76.56	79.63

Source: Select Education Statistics (2006), Government of India, Delhi.

Table 2.6: District-Wise and Sex-Wise Literates and Literacy Rates of Scheduled Tribes of Andhra Pradesh (2011 Census)

Sl. No.	District	Total			Literates			Literacy Rate		
		Persons	Male	Female	Persons	Male	Female	Persons	Male	Female
1.	Adilabad	495794	247472	248322	219922	130838	89084	44.36	52.87	35.87
2.	Nizamabad	192941	95679	97262	75837	47085	28752	39.31	49.21	29.56
3.	Karimnagar	106745	53495	53250	48910	28820	20090	45.82	53.87	37.73
4.	Medak	168985	86574	82411	63122	40976	22146	37.35	47.33	26.87
5.	Hyderabad	48937	25556	23381	29300	16659	12641	59.87	65.19	54.07
6.	Ranga Reddy	218757	112768	105989	104083	62588	41495	47.58	55.50	39.15
7.	Mahbubnagar	364269	187035	177234	129019	83464	45555	35.42	44.62	25.70
8.	Nalgonda	394279	203876	190403	164003	104938	59065	41.60	51.47	31.02
9.	Warangal	530656	268976	261680	226954	136361	90593	42.77	50.70	34.62
10.	Khammam	765565	378532	387033	351467	200493	150974	45.91	52.97	39.01
11.	Srikakulam	166118	81382	84736	78835	45731	33104	47.46	56.19	39.07
12.	Vizianagaram	235556	114687	120869	96700	55631	41069	41.05	48.51	33.98
13.	Vishakhapatnam	618500	302905	315595	241582	146129	95453	39.06	48.24	30.25
14.	East Godavari	213195	104422	108773	101638	54850	46788	47.67	52.53	43.01
15.	West Godavari	109072	53367	55705	54968	28726	26242	50.40	53.83	47.11
16.	Krishna	132464	66734	65730	62162	35510	26652	46.93	53.21	40.55
17.	Guntur	247089	125105	121984	99018	59459	39559	40.07	47.53	32.43
18.	Prakasam	151145	76677	74468	60915	35111	25804	40.30	45.79	34.65
19.	SPS Nellore	285997	145168	140829	106411	58051	48360	37.21	39.99	34.34
20.	YSR Kadapa	75886	38571	37315	31642	18875	12767	41.70	48.94	34.21
21.	Kurnool	82831	42052	40779	39272	23552	15720	47.41	56.01	38.55
22.	Anantapur	154127	78573	75554	74192	44757	29435	48.14	56.96	38.96
23.	Chittoor	159165	79756	79409	72775	40982	31793	45.72	51.38	40.04
	Andhra Pradesh	**5918073**	**2969362**	**2948711**	**2532727**	**1499586**	**1033141**	**42.80**	**50.50**	**35.04**

Source: Census 2011.

The commitment of tribes to acquiring a formal education for their children varies considerably. Gonds and Pardhans, two groups in the central hill region, are such cases. The Gonds are cultivators, and they frequently are reluctant to send their children to school, needing them, they say, to work in the fields. The Pardhans were traditionally bards and ritual specialists, and they have taken to education with enthusiasm. The effectiveness of educational policy likewise varies by region. In some parts of the northeast tribes schooling has helped tribal people to secure political and economic benefits. The education system there has provided a corps of highly trained tribal members in the professions and high-ranking administrative posts.

It is evident from the above table that the illiteracy rate is still at a high as 57.20 percent. In rural areas the illiteracy rate of ST's is even higher. It is around 70 percent. Many tribal schools are plagued by high dropout rates. Children attend for the first three to four years of primary school and gain a smattering of knowledge, only to lapse into illiteracy later. Few who enter continue up to the tenth grade; of those who do, few manage to finish high school. Therefore, very few are eligible to attend institutions of higher education, where the high rate of attrition continues. In Andhra Pradesh literacy rate is 67.2 percent. But, the literacy of schedule Tribe in the state is abysmally low at 42.80 percent.

For the improvement of literacy the Andhra Pradesh Government has started Hostels for boys and girls, residential schools, vocational training centers etc. National Policy of Education (1986 and revised Policy in 1992) suggested the following programmes for education of tribal people.

1. Opening primary schools in Tribal Areas.
2. Need to develop curricula of their language.
3. Promoting schedule tribal youth to work as teachers.
4. Ashram schools, Residential schools should be established in large scale in Tribal areas.
5. Incentives to encourage their life style through education.

Literacy and level of education are two basic indicators of the level of development achieved by a group/society. Literacy results in more awareness besides contributing to the overall improvement of health, hygiene and other social conditions. According to 2011 Census, the percentage of literate persons (those who can read and write with understanding), aged 7 years and above, among ST population of Andhra Pradesh is 49.2 percent, which is lower than 67.02 percent reported for state population as a whole. The literacy data show that the ST population of the state has made significant improvement in literacy during the decade 2001–2011. The literacy rate, which was 37 percent in 2001, has increased by 12.2 percentage points in 2011. But in comparison to other states/UTs, the position of ST population of Andhra Pradesh is not satisfactory. It is just above Madhya Pradesh and Jammu and Kashmir (50.6 percent) and Bihar (51.1 percent), which are bottom two states in literacy rate for ST population among all states/UTs. At the district level, the highest literacy rate has been recorded in Hyderabad (55.4 percent) and the lowest in Mahbubnagar (25.8 percent). Among the major STs, Yerukulas have reported the highest literacy rate (45.4 percent), followed by Koyas (41.8 percent), Gonds (36.4 percent), Yanadis (35.3 percent) and Sugalis (34.3 percent). Female literacy rate of 26.1 percent among the ST population is a matter of concern as almost a fourth of ST females are illiterate in the state.

Marital Status

Marital status is one of the important determinants of fertility and growth of a population. The 2011 Census data on marital status show that 45.77 percent persons among the STs of Andhra Pradesh are "never married". The "currently married" constitute 48.60 percent; while 5.04 percent are "widowed" and only 0.58 percent is "divorced and separated". Majority of the girls and boys among STs in Andhra Pradesh are getting married after attaining the legal age of marriage. However, marriages of ST girls below 18 years (1.91 percent) are lower than that recorded among ST population at the national level (1.98 percent). Similarly, the incidence of marriage among boys below 21 years at 2.75 percent is also lower than 3.20 percent aggregated for ST population at the national level. The mean number of children ever born per ever married ST woman of all ages as well as 45-49 years age group are 1.44 and 3.05 respectively, which are lower than corresponding figures of 2.87 and 3.68 for the ST population at the national level (Office of the Registrar General, India 2011).

Religion

The 2011 Census data show that Hindus constitute 49,84,478 (98.9 percent) of ST population of Andhra Pradesh, followed by 35,983 Christians (0.7 percent) and 4,643 Muslims (0.1 percent) (Office of the Registrar General, India 2011).

TRIBAL GROUPS PROFILE IN VISHAKHAPATNAM DISTRICT

According to the 2011 census Vishakhapatnam district has a population of 4,288,113. This gives it a ranking of 44th in India (out of a total of 640) and 5th in its state. The district has a population density of 384 inhabitants per square kilometre (990/sq mi). Its population growth rate over the decade 2001-2011 was 11.89%. Vishakhapatnam has a sex ratio of 1003 females for every 1000 males, and a literacy rate of 67.7%.

Vishakhapatnam district is home to 16 tribal groups of which 7 are notified as Primitive Tribal Groups. This district is home to around 14% of the tribal population in the state. An ethnographic profile of the tribal living in the district is given below.

Bagata

Bagata is one of the numerically preponderant and ethnically significant tribes of Andhra Pradesh and distributed predominantly in the Scheduled areas of Vishakhapatnam district. Majority of the former Muttadars and traditional village headmen in the tribal areas of Vishakhapatnam district belong to this tribe. They occupy highest rung in the local social hierarchical ladder. It is a Telugu speaking community with a population of 1,31,047 as per 2011 census constituting 2.21 percent to the total tribal population of the state. Literates constitute 40.80% among Bagatas. The percentage of female literacy is low with 26.76% when compared to male literacy rate, which is 54.72% among Bagatas.

The socially approved modes of acquiring mates include marriage by negotiation, marriage by capture, marriage by mutual love and elopement and marriage by service. Out of these, marriage by negotiation is widely practised. The custom of paying bride price to the bride's parents is in vogue in this community. Monogamy is common form of marriage while polygamy is rarely practised. Levirate (marriage of brother's widow) and sororate (marriage of wife's sister) are in vogue. Widow re-marriage is permitted. Divorce is socially accepted. Nuclear families are predominant over joint families among Bagatas. They are patriarchal, patrilineal and patrilocal. In the absence of son, daughter inherits the property of father.

Agriculture is the main stay of their livelihood while agriculture labour and collection of Non Timber Forest Produce (NTFP) are subsidiary occupations.

Bagatas worship plethora of gods and goddesses such as Sanku Devatha (village deity), Jakara Devata (goddess of rain and crops), Bali Devatha (goddess of group of villages or Muttas), Durga, Nandi devatha, etc., and attribute all the events in their daily life to the kindness or wrath of the deities. They celebrate the festivals along with other local tribal communities. Some festivals are celebrated before consuming produce like Korra Kotha Panduga, Kandi Kotha Panduga, Sama Kotha Panduga, Mamidi Kotha Panduga, etc.

There are traditional councils at village level and they are headed by a representative called as Peddamanishi. Most of the internal disputes are settled by these traditional councils and penalty will be imposed on the culprits.

Gadaba

Gadabas are predominantly found in tribal areas of Srikakulam, Vizianagaram and Vishakhapatnam districts. Their population according to 2011 census reports is 37798. Gadabas speak their own dialect. The total literacy rate among Gadabas is 36.63. The Gadaba tribe is divided into different sub divisions viz, Bodo or Gutob, Katheri, Kolloyi, etc., Each sub division which is endogamous (in marriage) is divided into various exogamous (inter marriage) clans. The modes of acquiring mates among Gadabas are marriage by negotiation, by mutual love and elopement, by capture and by service. Family is nuclear. Widow re-marriage and divorce are permitted.

At present Gadabas are cultivators and agricultural labourers. Those who inhabit the hilly areas practice shifting cultivation and they cultivate Ragi, Red gram, Niger in their Podu lands. They collect Non-Timber Forest Produce for household consumption and sale.

They worship Sankudevudu, Peddadevudu, Modakondamma, Jakaridevatha, Ippapolamma, etc. and they celebrate festivals like, Eetelapanduga, Ashadapanduga (Korrakotha), Kothamasa and Maridamma Panduga. In addition to the above festivals, they worship the spirits of their ancestors.

Gadabas have their own traditional council headed by a traditional village headman known as Naiko. His office is hereditary. He is assisted by Challan (messenger) and a Barika

(Village servant). In the areas of religious activities, Desari or Pujari officiate all the religious ceremonies. Gadabas are recognized as Primitive Tribal Group in A.P.

Goudu

The Goudus are a pastoral tribe in the agency tracts of Andhra Pradesh and they are recognized as Scheduled Tribe in the agency area of Srikakulam, Vizianagaram and Vishakhapatnam districts. They inhabit predominantly the hill tracts of Araku valley, Paderu, Munchingput areas of Vishakhapatnam district. According to 2011 census their population is 6997. The total literacy rate among Goudu is 26.14.

The Goudu tribe is divided into twelve endogamous sub-divisions which are further divided into exogamous clans. Goudus living in Vishakhapatnam, Vizianagaram and Srikakulam speak Adivasi Oriya. They practice shifting cultivation and also settled cultivation in the valley lands. The main occupation of Goudus of interior villages is cattle rearing.

The popular ways of acquiring mates are through negotiation, capture, love and elopement and service. Levirate (marriage of brother's widow) type of marriage is also in vogue. The Goudus have their traditional community council known as Kula Panchayath which maintains their customary laws, settles disputes and imposes fine on the offenders.

Kammara

Kammaras are a Scheduled Tribe inhabiting the Scheduled areas and adjoining areas in Srikakulam, Vizianagaram, Vishakhapatnam, East Godavari and West Godavari districts. They are also called Konda Kammaras and Ojas. Their population as per 2011 census is 48912. The total literacy rate among Kammara is 39.68.

Even though traditional occupation of Kammaras of scheduled areas is black smithy and carpentry, most of them gave up their traditional occupation and resorting to podu or shifting cultivation and settled cultivation.

Kammara tribe is divided into a number of totemic clans, which regulate marital relations among the Kammaras. The surnames of the Kammaras are identical with surnames of other tribal groups in Vishakhapatnam district. Marriage by mutual love and elopement, marriage by capture, marriage by service and marriage by negotiation is socially approved forms of acquiring mates. Both levirate and sororate are in vogue.

Kammaras worship Nisahani devatha, Sankudevata, Jakiri devatha and Gangalamma. They perform festivals like Chaitrapurab, Gangalamma Panduga and new fruit crop eating ceremonies such as Mamidikotha, Kandikotha, chikkudotha, and Korra, Samakotha. They perform Dimsa folk dance along with other tribal groups.

They have traditional tribal council of their own, which regulates the social life of Kammaras and to settle the disputes. Kammaras have been living in symbiosis with other tribes of the area. They manufacture agricultural implements and supply them to other tribal of the village and receive in kind for their services.

Konda Dora

The Konda Doras are found chiefly in the scheduled areas of Srikakulam, Vizianagaram, Vishakhapatnam and East and West Godavari districts of Andhra Pradesh. Their population according to 2011 census is 210509 and the total literacy rate among Konda Dora is 35.09.

They call themselves as Kubinga or Kondargia in their own dialect, which is called Kubia. Konda Doras living in Vishakhapatnam speak Adivasi Oriya and Telugu. Konda

Dora tribe is divided into a number of clans. Levirate type of marriage is customarily practised in this community. Polygyny (a man having more than one wife) is also in vogue. Marriage by capture, marriage by elopement, marriage by negotiation and marriage by service are traditionally accepted ways of acquiring mates. Divorce is socially permitted.

They are basically shifting cultivators. But they are adopting settled cultivation. They collect and sell Non-timber forest produce. They worship Boda devata, Sanku devata, Nisani devata and Jakara devata and offer sacrifices. They celebrate Chaitra Panduga, Balli Panduga, Korra and Samakotha, Chikkudu Kotha and pusapandoi (ceremonial eating of adda nuts). The most important festival is Kada Pandoi (seed charming festival) and this festival is followed by hunting festival. They perform the famous community dance called Dimsa and on marriage occasions. In the traditional panchayat headed by the headman, Guruvakadu the cases such as divorce, minor civil and social disputes are dealt and the decision of the headman is final.

Konda Kapu

Konda Kapus are synonymous with Konda Doras. Some of the Bagatas are also styling themselves as Konda Kapus whenever they interact with non-tribal population. The population of this tribe as per census 2011 was 10054.

Khonds

Khonds are chiefly residing in the densely wooded hill slopes in the scheduled areas of Srikakulam, Vizianagaram and Vishakhapatnam districts of Andhra Pradesh. They are also known as Samantha, Kodu, Jatapu, Jatapu, Dora, Kodi, Kodhu, Kondu and Kuinga. These terms are used for Khonds in different areas of Srikakulam, Vizianagaram and Vishakhapatnam districts. The Khonds call themselves in their own dialect as Kuinga or Kui Dora. Their population according to 2011 census is 45291 and the total literacy rate among Khond is 17.81. The Khonds are divided into the following sub-tribes:

1. Dongria Khond
2. Desya Khond
3. Kuttiya Khond
4. Tikiria Khond
5. Yeneti Khond.

Each sub tribe of Khond tribe is divided into a number of clans. Each clan has a distinct name and matrimonial alliances are permitted basing on clans names. Monogamy is the rule. Polygyny is rare. Both levirate and junior sororate are in existence. Marriages by exchange, mutual love and elopement and by service are socially approved ways of acquiring mates. They have their own dialect called Kui or Kuvi. The Khonds living in Araku and other bordering areas are multilingual. The Khonds have a tribal council usually consisting of four or five members headed by a man called Havanta, whose office is hereditary. The members of the council are selected. The main functions of the council are settlement of disputes on marriage, land and other property.

The Khonds mainly subsist on cultivation. They are experts in Podu cultivation (shifting cultivation). They grow millets like ragi, sama and korra and oil seeds like niger, castor and pulses like red gram in podu fields. They are adept in hunting and fishing also. They are well versed in the preparation of handicrafts like basket, mat weaving, oil extraction, etc.

They celebrate festivals called Hira parbu (seed charming) Maha parbu (new mango fruit eating), Kumda parbu (consuming maize and pumpkin products), etc. Khonds perform a folk dance called Mayura (peacock dance) which is an imitation of movements of peacock on every festive and marriage occasions.

Kotia

Kotia tribe is chiefly found in the tribal areas of Vishakhapatnam district of A.P., and joining to Orissa and their population as per 2011 census is 45,291. The total literacy rate among Kotia is 40.95. Kotia tribe is divided into the following sub divisions or sub groups:

1. Bodo Kotia
2. Sano Kotia
3. Putia Poika
4. Dhulia.

In Vishakhapatnam agency, Bodo Kotias are also called Doras and claiming equal status with Bagata, a tribe with higher social status. Bodo Kotia people do not accept cooked food from Sano Kotia people as they are considered inferior in social status. Similarly Sano Kotia people also do not accept food from those of Putia Poika. Kotia tribe is divided into various totemic clans and each clan is further divided into different surnames. Some of the clan names are Matya (Fish), Naga (Snake), Geedh (Eagle), Gorapitta (a kind of bird), etc. All the sub divisions of Kotia community speak corrupt form of Oriya.

Four types of acquiring mates are in vogue in this community. They are Bodobiba (marriage by negotiation), Udaliyajibar (marriage by mutual love and elopement), Dangdigikbar (marriage by capture) and Gorjuvai (marriage by service). Both levirate and sororate are socially accepted. Divorce is permitted. Widow or widower re-marriages are permissible. Traditional mechanism of social control among Kotias is called Nayaklok and it is headed by a traditional leader called Nayak. The messenger is called Barika. They settle disputes like theft, divorce, land disputes, quarrels, etc.

The principal deities worshipped by Kotias are Pedda demudu Sanku demudu, Nandi purab, Ashada Jathara, Gairam

Panduga, Pedda demudu panduga, Bheema demudu panduga and first new crop eating festivals like Korra-samakotha, Metta dhanyam kotha, Mamidi kotha etc. Kotias are agriculturists and raise food crops like ragi, jowar, maize and paddy and vegetables like cabbage, brinjal, tomato, potato, etc. Kotias also raise vegetables like beans, chillies, ladies finger, ginger, etc., in the back yards of their houses. They collect Non-timber forest produce items like adda leaves, tamarind sheekai, broom sticks, mohwa flower, etc., and sell to GCC.

Kulia

Kulia is numerically very small tribe inhabiting the tribal areas of Vishakhaptnam district. Their settlements are confined to the wooded tracts of Araku, Paderu, Pedabayalu and Munchingput mandals of Vishakhapatnam district. They are also called Mulias. Their population according to 2011 census is 385 and their total literacy rate is 41.44.

Kulias are divided into a number of exogamous patrilineal clans. The institution of Nestam (bond friendship), which is also called Goth band bar, is in vogue. Kulias observe clan exogamy. Though marriage by negotiation is the most common form of marriage, marriage by capture and marriage by elopement are also in practice. Polygyny is also in vogue. Both levirate and surrogate are permitted. They speak Oriya among themselves, but are equally proficient in Telugu. They celebrate Korra-samakotha, Mettadhanyamkotha, Chikkudu-kotha and Mamidi kotha festivals. Their traditional occupations are agriculture, selling bangles, beeds and trinkets. They also collect minor forest produce and sell in the weekly shandies.

Mali

Malis are predominantly found in tribal areas of Vishakha-patnam, Vizianagaram and Srikakulam districts. Their population according to 2011 census is 5,244 and their

literacy rate is 26.48. The Mali tribe is divided into two endogamous sub-groups, which are further divided into seven sub-groups as follows:
I. Bodo Mali II. Sano Mali

1. Khandya Mali, 2. Pannari Mali, 3. Pondra Mali, 4. Sorukava Mali, 5. Thagoor Mali, 6. Donguradiya Mali, 7. Kosalya Mali.

The Bodo Malis are considered superior sect and both men and women of this group wear sacred thread, whereas in the other sub-division, only men wear sacred thread. The traditional dormitories known as Kuppus were once popular in this community. Marriage by negotiation, marriage by mutual love and elopement, marriage by service are different ways of acquiring mates. They speak corrupt form of Oriya. Their traditional occupation was growing flower plants and making garlands. But now they are settled agriculturists. They grow vegetables and sell in the weekly markets. They have Kulapanchayat which deals with cases relating to social and economic disputes.

Manne Dora

Manne Doras inhabit the tribal areas of Vishakhapatnam, Srikakulam and East Godavari districts of Andhra Pradesh. Their population according to 2011 Census is 13,636 and their literacy rate is 38.72. The social organization of Manne Doras is based on exogamous, patrilineal descent group called Kulam in Paderu areas, Bamso in Araku and Kilagada areas and gotram in other areas. Though Kulam is exogamous, all the clans do not stand in marriageable relationship. Some of the Clans are considered to be brother clans. Nestam or Goth band bar, the traditional bond friendship is in vogue among Manne Doras.

Though marriages by capture, by service and by elopement are also socially accepted modes of acquiring mates, marriage by negotiation is the most common mode of acquiring mate. Levirate and surrorate are in practice. They mostly speak Telugu. But those who are living along the border areas of Orissa speak Oriya also.

They worship Jakara devatha, Ganga devudu, Sanku devatha etc., and main festivals they celebrate are Nishani festival, Jakara festival, Nandi devudu festival, Bodo devatha festival and Ganga devudu festival. Besides these, they perform all Kotha festivals. Manne Doras have their own traditional council called Kula Panchayat which consists of headman (Kula pedda) and a few members.

Mukha Dora

Mukha Doras are found in the tribal areas of Vishakhapatnam, Srikakulam and East Godavari districts. They are also known as Nooka Dora, Racha Reddy, Muka Raja and Sabarlu. Their population according to 2011 census is 42,357 and the total literacy rate among Mukha Dora is 28.02. Mukha Dora is divided into several exogamous clans such as Korra, Gammela, Kakara, Sugra, Kinchoyi, etc. The name of the clan is prefixed to their names. The elders of Mukha Dora community wear sacred thread and Tulasi beads. Marriage by capture, marriage by service, marriage by elopement and marriage by negotia-tion are the socially accepted ways of acquiring mates. Polygamous marriages are common. Levirate and sorrorate are permitted. Their mother tongue is Telugu but they also speak Adivasi Oriya. Mukha Doras abstain from eating of beef and pork. They worship Bodo devata, Jakara devata, Sanku devata, Nishani devata and Ganga devata. The most significant festival of Mukha Doras is Chaitra festival. They celebrate festivals in the honour of their deities.

Most of the Mukha Doras have settled on agriculture and they supplement their economy by the collection and sale of minor forest produce. They claim social status just below the

Bagatas in the social hierarchy of tribal areas of Vishakhapatnam district.

Porja

Porjas are found predominantly in the tribal areas of Vishakhapatnam district of Andhra Pradesh. Their population as per 2011 census is 36,145 among whom males are 17,741 and females are 18,761. The total literacy rate among Porja is 26.55. They are recognized as Primitive Tribal Group. They have their own dialect. In addition to their own dialect, they speak Telugu as well as Adivasi Oriya. Porja tribe is divided into following endogamous sub-divisions or sub-groups:

- Parangi Porja
- Jhodia Porja
- Gadaba Porja
- Banang Porja
- Pangu Porja
- Kolloi Porja
- Didoi Porja.

Each endogamous sub-group is further divided into the following totemic clans which are popularly known as 'bowsu' in local parlance. Clan names are pre-fixed to the individual names. The woman gets the clan name of the husband after marriage. The Porja family is generally nuclear. These people are patrilineal, patriarchal and patrilocal. Cross-cousin marriages are permissible among them. They marry after attaining adulthood.

Monogamy is prevalent. Polygyny is rare. Divorce is permissible among them. Widow re-marriages are socially accepted. Marriage by negotiation, marriage by elopement, marriage by capture and marriage by service are socially accepted ways of acquiring mates, but negotiation is held as the most prestigious and is common. As soon as the marriage is over, the son separates himself from the family of origin and sets up his family of procreation.

Porjas worship Bododevatha, Sankudevatha or Nishani-devatha, Jakara devatha, Nandi devatha etc., in addition to the spirits of their ancestors, on every festive occasion, the ancestor worship is paramount in Porja religious life and they offer sacred food and fowls are sacrified to the spirits of ancestors. They celebrate festivals like Giliab Parbu (hunting festival), Poduja (sowing festival), Gotnakiya (ploughing festival), Amflishuva (new mango eating festival), Bandaponpuras, Nandi Purab, Volpoda, Bali devatha panduga, etc.

Porjas perform a folk dance called Jhodianat or Nandinat at the time of Nandi devatha festival. It is also known as Jillinat because the songs which are sung during this dance performance are full of expressions of love and romance. Jilli in Porja dialect means love and romance. The entire movements of dance resemble the movements of Dimsa dance but swift movements which are found in Dimsa are not found in Jhodia nat.

There is a headman for each group in a village and a leader called Naidu for each village the offices of which are hereditary and these office bearers bear the responsibility of maintaining social order within the community. The inter-village disputes and disputes among the community people are settled by their traditional village council.

Most of the Porjas who are living in the interior places are largely subsisting on podu cultivation and collection of minor forest produce. They practice podu cultivation on hill slopes and use primitive implements like hoe cum digging stick, hand axe and sickle. They also practice plough cultivation on flat fields and irrigated terraces. The landless sections of them work as agricultural labourers. The dead are either cremated or buried, according to convenience. The pollution caused by death is observed for ten days and ancestor worship is observed.

Reddi Dora

The Mukha Doras of Vishakhapatnam district are known as Reddi Doras. Their number according to 2011 census reports is 930. The total literacy rate among Reddi Dora is 17.32. The Mukha Doras, who are also known as Nooka Doras, are mostly found in Vishakhapatnam and Srikakulam districts. They are endogamous and have exogamous clans, which serve as regulatory forces in their matrimonial alliances. They speak Telugu. They are mainly agriculturists and podu cultivators. They supplement their economy by the collection and sale of minor forest produce.

Rona

They are also known as Rena and Rana, which mean battle. They are found living in the agency areas of Vishakhapatnam and Vizianagaram districts of Andhra Pradesh. According to 2011 census, their population is 1012 and the literacy rate is 25.88. Their mother tongue is Oriya. Cross-cousin marriages are common and levirate and surrogate are allowed in the community. Elopement and negotiation are the modes of acquiring spouses. Bride price is paid in kind. Remarriage is allowed for widow and divorcee. Nuclear families are common. They follow the rule of patrilineal decent and patrilocal residence. Divorce is permissible.

Main occupation of Rona is settled agriculture. They work as wage labourers. Their traditional community council is headed by a Naidu. They worship village gods like Peddadevudu, Nandidevudu, Gangadevudu, Jatradevudu ancestral spirits. They celebrate the festivals of Itukala

Panduga, Korra Kotha, and Jodla Panduga besides Hindu festivals like Sivarathri, Ugadi and Diwali.

Valmiki

Valmikis living in the Agency tracts of Andhra Pradesh are only notified as Scheduled Tribes. They are found in the agency areas of Vishakhapatnam and East Godavari districts. They claim that they are descendants of the famous sage Valmiki, the author of Ramayana. According to 2011 Census, their population is 71,883. The total literacy rate among Valmiki is 58.22. The Valmiki tribe is divided into various gotrams in order to regulate the marriage institution in Vishakhapatnam tribal area. Marriage by mutual consent, marriage by elopement, is the methods of acquiring mates. Widow re-marriages and divorce are permissible. Valmikis are agriculturists and forest labourers. Some of them became traders and petty moneylenders. They sell the earthen pots also in the shandies. They practice podu cultivation on the slopes of hills.

TRIBAL GROUPS SITUATED IN WARANGAL DISTRICT

According to the 2011 census Warangal district has a population of 3,522,644. This gives it a ranking of 82nd in India (out of a total of 640). The district has a population density of 274 inhabitants per square kilometre (710/sq. mi). Its population growth rate over the decade 2001-2011 was 8.52%. Warangal has a literacy rate of 66.16%.

Koya

The Koyas are mainly inhabited in the hilly areas of West Godavari, East Godavari, Khammam and Warangal districts and are sparsely found in Adilabad and Karimnagar districts.

The Koya population as per 2011 Census is 1,04,348 in Andhra Pradesh and the total literacy rate is 41.85. The Godavari and Sabari rivers which are flowing through their area of habitation exercise profound influence on Koyas economic, social and cultural life. Koyas popularly call themselves as Dorala Sattam (Lords group) and Putta Dora (original lords). Koyas call themselves Koitur in their dialect. Though strongly influenced by neighbouring Telugu speaking people, they retained a typical cultural trait of Koya culture.

Koyas living in Adilabad, Karimnagar, Warangal and some parts of East Godavari have forgotten their own Koya (Basha) dialect and adopted Telugu as their mother tongue. The rest of the Koyas found in Khammam district (Bhadrachalam division), Polavaram area of West Godavari district speak Koya. It is also called Chettu Basha (Tree language) or Gali basha (Air language) in Telugu language as it is spoken by people living under the trees and forests.

The Koya tribe is divided into several functional, endogamous groups who are in turn divided into several exogamous phratries. Nuclear and monogamous families are predominantly found. Marriage among Koyas takes place after attainment of puberty and cross cousin marriages are encouraged. Levirate is socially accepted. The following four types of acquiring spouses are in vogue among Koyas:

1. Marriage by negotiation,
2. Marriage by love and elopement,
3. Marriage by capture
4. Marriage by service.

Marriage by negotiation is the most preferred mode of acquiring mates in modern times among Koyas. Monogamy is the general practice among Koyas though polygamy is socially approved. Descent is through male line only. Koya woman is industrious and she is an economic asset to the family. The woman attends to all agriculture operations except ploughing besides domestic work. Divorce is oral and conventional but not legal and it may be initiated from either side. The Kulapanchayath plays an important role in administering the divorce. Widow re-marriage known as Maru Manuvu is allowed among Koyas, though the remarried widow is not allowed to wear Puste (marriage badge), she is given equal status with other married women in all social and religious functions.

The Koyas are mainly settled cultivators. They grow Jowar, Ragi, Bajra and other millets. Most of the Koyas living in midst of forest collect tubers and roots such as Tella Chenna Gadda, Kirismatilu and edible green leaves such as Clencheli, Doggali, Gumuru Thotakura, Boddukura and prepare curries for their domestic consumption. Their lands are very fertile due to periodical floods of Godavari in the Koya habitat. Lord Bhima, Korra Rajulu, Mamili and Poturaju are the important deities to Koyas. Their main festivals are Vijji Pandum (seeds charming festival) and Kondala Kolupu (festival to appease Hill deities). Koyas have a number of religious functionaries who attend to different aspects of their religious life.

Most important fair celebrated by Koyas is the Sammakka Saralamma Jatra once in two years on full moon day of the Magha Masam (January or February) at Medaram village in Mulug taluk of Warangal district. It is said to be the largest tribal religious festival in Asia. In modern times, lakhs of non-tribal particularly from backward classes also attend to this fair with much devotion and traditional gaiety. The traditional village panchayat of Koyas (Kula Panchayat) consists of Poyi (headman), Pinapedda (who assists headman in conducting enquiries) and Vyapari (messenger). Disputes like divorce, inter-caste marriages etc., are dealt by this panchayath. It also takes active part in the marriage ceremonies and conducting of fairs and festivals.

Koyas perform a robust colourful dance called (Permakokata) Bison horn dance during festive and marriage ceremonies. The men put on Bison Horns on head and wear colourful dress. They carry a big cylindrical drum to their neck and beat it rhythmically. The women form into circles by holding each other's hands over their shoulders and perform splendid dance while singing.

APPALLING SOCIO-ECONOMIC STATUS IN VISHAKHAPATNAM AND WARANGAL DISTRICTS

As can be seen, the socio economic status of the tribal in both the districts is appalling. Their literacy rate is significantly lower than that of the state's literacy rate. One interesting aspect in their marital tradition is that many of the tribes permit levirate and surrogate marriages which are not commonplace in the mainstream Indian society. Many of the tribal groups continue to cultivate their crops inefficiently due to lack of awareness and continued negligence shown by successive governments in development aspects relating to tribal. Podu or shifting cultivation is still in vogue among many tribal groups. The government should be proactive in improving their economic condition. They have been the most neglected segment of the Indian society and the economic development which has seen its light in the country has not been able to bestow its benefits upon the tribal.

SOCIO-ECONOMIC PROFILE OF DAHOD DISTRICT IN GUJARAT

Gujarat State ranks fifth in India when total Scheduled Tribe's population is taken into consideration. Concentration of Scheduled Tribe's population in Madhya Pradesh, Maharashtra, Orissa and Bihar is much higher when compared to Gujarat.

Table 2.7: District-Wise Population of Scheduled Tribes of Gujarat (2011 census)

Sl. No	District	Total Population	ST Total	ST Male	ST Female	% of STs to Total Population
1.	Kachchh	24228	4731	2447	2284	19.53
2.	Banas Kantha	284155	66958	34327	32631	23.56
3.	Patan	13303	1902	976	926	14.30
4.	Mahesana	9392	1427	769	658	15.19
5.	Sabar Kantha	542156	108471	55835	52636	20.01
6.	Gandhinagar	18204	2180	1176	1004	11.98
7.	Ahmadabad	89138	12989	6797	6192	14.57
8.	Surendranagar	21453	3925	2044	1881	18.30
9.	Rajkot	24017	4401	2292	2109	18.32
10.	Jamnagar	24187	4528	2335	2193	18.72
11.	Porbandar	13039	2286	1187	1099	17.53
12.	Junagarh	55571	8009	4187	3822	14.41
13.	Amreli	7322	1493	787	706	20.39
14.	Bhavnagar	9110	1278	682	596	14.03
15.	Anand	24824	3634	1843	1791	14.64
16.	Kheda	40336	6046	3163	2883	14.99
17.	Panch Mahals	721604	130945	66968	63977	18.15
18.	Dahod	1580850	332872	170507	162365	21.06
19.	Vadodara	1149901	176876	90450	86426	15.38
20.	Narmada	481392	66651	34225	32426	13.85
21.	Bharuch	488194	62849	32154	30695	12.87
22.	The Dangs	216073	38957	19810	19147	18.03
23.	Navsari	639659	68156	34798	33358	10.66
24.	Valsad	902794	125711	63982	61729	13.92
25.	Surat	856952	101440	52007	49433	11.84
26.	Tapi	679320	74597	37919	36678	10.98
Gujarat		**8917174**	**1413312**	723667	**689645**	**15.85**

Source: Census 2011.

Tribal, Gujarat

Fig. 13   *Fig. 14*   *Fig. 15*

Fig. 13–15: Bhil, Pateila Tribes of Gujarat

Gujarat is home to 32 communities officially designated as Scheduled Tribes (STs). The scheduled tribe population in the state was estimated as 14,13,312 as per census 2011. The proportion of scheduled tribes to the total population of Gujarat stands at 15.85 percent. The tribal population in the Banas Kantha district of Gujarat is the highest at 23.56 percent of the total population in the district. Dahod stands second with respect to proportion of scheduled tribe in the total population (21.06). However the Navsari district of Gujarat has the least population of STs as proportion of the total population i.e. 10.66 percent. The Scheduled Tribe's population in Gujarat is considered socially and economically backward and marginalised. The Government of Gujarat has, over the years, made repeated efforts to boost the flow of funds to the tribal regions. The Tenth Five Year Plan had witnessed the highest financial allocation for Tribal Area Sub Plan, with an estimation amounting to ₹ 4977 crores. The latest—Eleventh Five Year Plan has received an allocation that has even surpassed all the previous allocations. The Eleventh Five Year Plan has allocated funds of ₹ 15,000 crore for Tribal Area Sub Plan. This new allocation has been backed by Vanbandhu Kalyan Yojana, an inspirational ten point programme focusing on a holistic, integrated an all-inclusive development of the tribal population. The ten point programme addresses the core segments important to the tribal communities, such as access to basic facilities, drinking water, health, livelihood, and housing, education, and irrigation facilities. The Tribal Area Sub Plan's approach and strategy for overall development of the tribal communities are implemented and formulated through various schemes and programmes in Gujarat under the sectorial development programmes for bridging the gap in the various levels of development.

Budget allocations, targets, and the number of beneficiaries are never the major considerations while monitoring the tribal development programmes in Gujarat. Instead, the impact on the living standards of the tribal communities, and the real outcomes with successful results are the decisive factors and parameters of observing the tribal development plans, pro-grammes, and schemes in Gujarat. Government officials in Gujarat are directed at different levels to make the best possible efforts to build a successful rapport with the local tribal to understand their views and perceptions on the various tribal development programmes, plans, and schemes brought out by the State Government. The government officials are en-couraged to maintain maximum transparency in their interactions and transactions with the tribal to enhance their participation and partnership in all the schemes, programmes, and plans undertaken by the Government of Gujarat for the welfare of the tribal.

Scheduled Tribes in Gujarat mostly live in the areas along the eastern border of the State. Dahod, Vadodara, Bharuch, Tapi, Narmada, Panchmahal, Surat, Navsari, Valsad, and some parts of Sabarkantha and Banaskantha districts fall under the tribal areas in Gujarat. Various GWRDC programmes and other different kinds of activities by the Government are carried out in the tribal zones of the state by GWRDC under the Tribal Area Sub Plan.

The Gujarat Government has undertaken various activities under the Tribal Area Sub Plan, including tube-wells being drilled by the Corporation in the several districts of tribal area. Lift Irrigation Scheme is the only alternative irrigation method that could have been adopted for giving irrigation facilities to the tribal farmers in the tribal zone. Lift Irrigation Schemes have been constructed in all such areas wherever the benefits of flow irrigation cannot be availed by river or canal owing to higher elevation. Several Mini Lift irrigation Schemes have been completed for irrigation facilities and have been handed over to various cooperative societies. A total of 713 hectares of land has been irrigated under this scheme. Numerous community wells have been built and put to use for irrigation facilities in the tribal zone. The community wells have covered 865 hectares of land. The Government of Gujarat has given super high priority to agricultural development in the tribal areas and plans to bring these areas at par with all other areas of the State. An expenditure of ₹ 50769.78 lakhs was incurred in 2011–12 under the irrigation and flood control fund.

The Government of Gujarat advocated several policies to ensure a better quality of life for the tribal population in Dahod and hence the expenditure has been increased by over 2.5 times in the last five years. The State Government has been constantly making conscious efforts to ensure to push the tribal people above BPL line, to improve the literacy levels and to create a reasonable infrastructure—on both social as well as civil level.

ECONOMIC INDICATORS OF DEVELOPMENT IN DAHOD

One of the main objectives of the state government is to achieve the sustainable development in the tribal regions, which would ensure that the economic development goes in synchronization with the natural resource conservation and environmental protection. It is a pre-requisite to plan specific schemes and programmes that have a direct bearing on the economic development of the tribal Gujarat. The schemes and programmes thus formulated need to be sent as proposals to the Ministry for examination, discussion and approval in advance. The Economic Development Corporation provides subsidy under various schemes against loan advanced by the nationalized banks. Several tribal families in Dahod have benefited by the arrangement of institutional finance with banks. The rate of literacy amongst the tribal has also improved. Some of the important economic development schemes brought out by the Government of Gujarat includes Manav Garima Yojana, tailoring classes for ST women, assistance to run training-cum-production centre for cottage industries, pre-exam training centre and short-hand typing classes, police constable training, financial assistance for agricultural tools for agricultural labourers, and financial assistance for competitive examination: such as IAS, IPS, etc.

Separately, Gujarat Women Economic Development Corporation has been working for the economic empowerment of women of all regions in Gujarat. The Corporation has been facilitating women to undertake income generating activities in order to achieve this objective of the Corporation. Gujarat Women Economic Development Corporation Ltd has been sponsoring loan applications of the women living below poverty line in order to enable them to undertake small business with the assistance of bank loan. Simultaneously, the Corporation is also providing subsidy to those women whose loan applications are getting sanctioned by the nationalised banks. An amount of ₹ 70.00 lakh has provided as subsidy for the year 2012–13. The Gujarat Pattern Funds, launched in the tribal areas, also aims at economic development and creation of local infrastructure. Gujarat Council on Science and Technology (GUJCOST) also promotes socio economic development in Gujarat by using science and technology. Various programmes and activities such as popularization of science and technology at grass root level, technology transfer, facilitation for registration of Intellectual Property Rights and carrying out various science and technology surveys of the state have been undertaken by GUJCOST.

Swarnim Krushi Mahotsav is an enlightened agriculture-extension initiative by the State Government to herald a revolution in agriculture sector. The project strategizes to improve the yield immensely by opening up bright avenues of progress and prosperity. The Krushi Mahotsav has been an exhaustive effort in agricultural extension organized by Government of Gujarat between the months of May and June, just before the onset of monsoon. The primary aim of this project is to increase agricultural income by promoting a scientific approach to farming. The project was conceived in such a manner that the farmers in tribal areas could receive immediate benefits and they can begin preparations for the next kharif season. Under the programme, the farmers have adopted innovations and modern technologies, learnt sustenance of agriculture and nurturing natural resources.

Krushi Rath, under the Swarnim Krushi Mahotsav, covers all 18000 villages, spreads awareness among farmers, provides know-how about how to select appropriate crop, proper insights about animal husbandry and latest technologies. Gujarat has simulated Krushi Mahotsav to find solutions to the various problems faced by farmers. Massive projects have been undertaken by the State under this programme, such as water-conservation drives by constructing Bori-Bandhs, Farm-ponds, check-dams and terrace-ponds. Under Krushi Rath, a team of horticulture, agriculture, animal husbandry and cooperation department's team members along with agricultural scientists travel with the Kisan Rath unit to every village.

Organic farming is also encouraged under the Swarnim Krushi Mahotsav programme. The Mahotsav has created a forum for the convergence of all major stakeholders. It has also facilitated doorstep availability of critical agricultural requirements such as seeds, fertilizers, pesticides and credit for the farmers.

EDUCATIONAL STATUS IN DAHOD

Since many schools in the tribal areas lack basic facilities like sanitation facilities, school furniture, benches, visual aids, school laboratories, and electricity, the Government proposed plans to improve such conditions and the educational status is much better today. The tribal students are supplied school textbooks at free of cost in order to achieve the goal of having 100% universalization of elementary education. It is estimated that all tribal area students are benefited under this scheme. An additional scheme of providing separate sanitation facilities for girl students studying in upper primary schools in the tribal zones has been sanctioned and provided by the Government. Almost all the primary schools falling in the tribal zone are provided with first aid facilities under a separate scheme brought out by Gujarat Government. The Education Department of Gujarat holds a future vision of 'Education for All' and plans of implementing the project using smart goals with several education and literacy policies inclined towards reducing dropout rates, promote literacy, health and sanitation, among various other initiatives. The Government's vision for Socio-Economic-Education growth has the major focus on continuous education, primary education, secondary education, higher education, literacy education, pharmacy education and technical education. It aims for universalization of primary education for children between the age group of 6 and 14 years with target setting and specific planning.

Several educational courses have been designed by the State Government to develop competence among students to take up any agricultural or allied activities profitably. Under these courses, the tribal in Dahod are trained to be useful in rural based agro industries. Various farm advisory services are offered to the tribal farmers, providing technical guidance in order to increase their agricultural productivity and allied services. These advisory services are provided at all the research centres in tribal area. Polytechnic in Agricultural Engineering at Dahod was started during 2008–09. Thirty students were admitted in the institute in 2009–10 while 35 students were admitted in 2010–11. A lot of progress has been made by Dahod under the Extensive Educational Programmes. For instance, the number of beneficiaries at the Tribal Training Centre at Dahod has been 1157, the number of beneficiaries at the Krushi Vigyan Kendra in Dahod has been 3308 and the number of beneficiaries at the Agro-Polytechnic in Dahod has been 8064.

LEADING ISSUES OF DELINEATION AND DEPRIVATION

Indian society is characterized by discrimination, deprivation, exploitation, subjugation and marginalization, particularly on the basis of caste and ethnicity. The Scheduled Tribes (STs) in India suffer from exclusion, neglect and under-development due to their geographical and cultural isolation and separation from the mainstream. The main roadblocks in equitable and sustainable Economic Development of Schedule Tribes are destruction of forests, illiteracy, indebtedness, lack of awareness about the schemes provided by the governments, strict adherence to traditions and customs, ineffective implementation of govt. schemes etc. Though there is a relative improvement in the conditions of Schedule Tribes, it has not been to the desired level.

Case for Preferential Treatment

A case for preferential treatment for Tribal has been advocated. Preferential Treatment implies assigning a certain advantage, weight or deference to certain individuals or collectives over others. A major reason for according such a preference is the disadvantage that the concerned individuals and groups suffer from through no fault of their own. The Constitution of India recognizes two important grounds for providing preferential treatment, namely, the principle of 'non-discrimination and equal opportunity', and the provision empowering the state to take steps to ensure equal opportunity. An initial step on behalf of the STs was the provision of reservations in employment and in legislative bodies. However, such preferences become meaningless when the tribal people are poorly educated. For this reason, education is envisaged as one of the most powerful instruments for the social and economic liberation of the STs. Starting with the creation of reserved seats in higher educational institutions and other schemes like scholarships, fee concessions, book grants, remedial coaching, special hostels, etc., there has resulted a five-fold increase in the levels of literacy of STs over the last five decades. Similarly preferences in services under Article 16(4) of the Constitution enable group advancement and security. Reservation of 7.5 percent of seats in the elected bodies at all levels of governance has brought about adequate representation of STs in the political arena, thereby strengthening democracy, security and the common good. *But their main travails lay in their land alienation and alienation of forest land and small forest products for their livelihood and last but not the least exclusiveness from the Social Sector—Education and Health.* Let us briefly see the extent of these issues leading to deprivation.

Tribal Land Alienation

Most Indian tribes are concentrated in heavily forested areas that combine inaccessibility with limited political or economic significance. Historically, the economy of most tribes was subsistence agriculture or hunting and gathering. Tribal members traded with outsiders for the few necessities they lacked, such as salt and iron. A few local Hindu craftsmen might have provided such items as cooking utensils. The twentieth century, however, has seen far-reaching changes in the relationship between tribal in India and the larger society and, by extension, traditional tribal economies. Improved transportation and communications have brought ever deeper intrusions into tribal lands; merchants and a variety of government policies have involved tribal peoples more thoroughly in the cash economy, although by no means on the most favourable of terms. Large areas fell into the hands of non-tribal around 1900, when many regions were opened by the government to homestead-style settlement. Immigrants received free land in return for cultivating it. Tribal people, too, could apply for land titles, although even title to the portion of land they happened to be planting that season could not guarantee their ability to continue shifting cultivation. More important, the notion of permanent, individual ownership of land was foreign to most tribal. Land, if seen in terms of ownership at all, was viewed as a communal resource, free to whoever needed it. By the time tribal accepted the necessity of obtaining formal land titles, they had lost the opportunity to lay claim to lands that might rightfully have been considered theirs. Generally, tribal were severely disadvantaged in dealing with government officials who granted land titles. The colonial regime realized the necessity of protecting tribal of India from the predations of outsiders and hence prohibited the sale of tribal lands. Although an important loophole in the form of land leases was left open, tribes made some gains in the mid-twentieth century. Despite considerable obstruction by local police and land officials, who were slow to delineate tribal holdings and slower still to offer police protection, some land was returned to tribal peoples.

Since land is the primary source of livelihood for the tribal, land-based livelihoods have assumed added importance with the depletion of Non-Timber Forest Produce (NTFP). Land alienation in its broad sense is among the major causes of impoverishment of tribal: Occupation by non-tribal; reduced access to forest-based livelihoods; reservation of forests and restrictions on shifting cultivation; land administration policies; and displacement by development projects.

Role of Non-Tribal in Land Alienation

Money lending is among the earliest routes through which tribal land has been alienated in Andhra Pradesh. Non-tribal settlers advance petty cash to tribal taking tribal land as collateral. The land would be in possession of the lender until the borrower repays the money completely. Because of income poverty most tribal default on their debts. This process of land occupation occurred on a larger scale in tribal tracts of coastal Andhra Pradesh. A study conducted in Saluru agency area of Srikakulam district found that the first outside trader entered this area about 45 years ago and began lending money at high interest rates. The debt burden could be reduced by tribal only by conceding their land. The trader acquired the first chunk of tribal land within 10 years after he had established his foothold. This process gained momentum as more and more outsiders followed suit. As a result only 11 percent of households retained land. In many tribal areas, the non-tribal men entered into marital relationships with the tribal women and purchased land in the names of tribal wives. Land alienation through polygyny has been found in Vishakha-patnam, East Godavari and West Godavari districts. The tribal of north coastal Andhra Pradesh have inherited a sacred social institution called 'nestam', i.e., the bond of friendship. The idea of this bond is to promote the well-being of the members. The non-tribal entered into these bonds of friendship and purchased land in the names of their tribal friends. In tribal tracts of East and West Godavari districts, many non-tribal farmers purchased land in the names of their tribal servants or attached labourers. Another means employed by non-tribal communities to occupy tribal land was to procure false scheduled tribe certificates. Armed with this status, the non-tribal migrants purchased tribal lands.

Post-Independence Initiatives Related to Tribal Land

Andhra Pradesh was formed in 1956 by merging the erstwhile Hyderabad and Andhra states. The new government enacted the first comprehensive legislation, Andhra Pradesh Scheduled Areas Land Transfer Regulation, 1959 (APSALTR 1959 or Regulation 1 of 1959) for the protection of tribal land. It came into effect in Andhra region in the same year and was extended to Telangana region through Regulation 2 in 1963. The Regulation 1 of 1959 provides that: (i) In the scheduled areas, transfer of immovable property by a member of scheduled tribe to non-tribal without permission from the competent authority shall be null and void; (ii) Where a transfer of immovable property is effected in favour of non-tribal, the designated official, on representation or suo moto may restore the property to the transferor. However, this legislation did not bar land transfer by non-tribal. Even in the case of transfer from tribal to non-tribal, it was only restrictive and not proscriptive. Moreover, the regulation remained largely unimplemented as the working rules were not framed for almost 10 years after its passage. Land alienation in scheduled areas continued in spite of this legislation. The government began moving in this direction after the tribal uprising in Srikakulam district in the 1960s by initiating more stringent measures in the form of Regulation 1 of 1970. The 1970 amendment prohibits transfer of immovable property in scheduled areas. It has a presumptive provision stating that any immovable property in the agency areas in the possession of non-tribal shall be deemed to have been acquired from a scheduled tribe. When this regulation was questioned, the high court of AP upheld the regulation with a directive that it would not have retrospective effect. Yet another amendment was effected to the above enactment in 1978 which prohibits registration of sale transactions in favour of non-tribal.

The tribal land policy took an interesting turn in 1979, following a lull in tribal tracts, when the state government directed the officials concerned not to evict non-tribal occupying up to five acres of wetland or 10 acres of dry-land in scheduled areas. The policy towards tribal land entered into another decisive phase in the 1990s. Attempts were made in the late 1990s and early 2000s by the reforms oriented by then Party regime—especially in the wake of Samata Judgment—to amend Regulation 1 of 1970 to allow land transfers between non-tribes. Both state and central governments began initiatives towards amendment of the Fifth Schedule following the Supreme Court verdict in Samata case.

It is thus evident from the above discussion that even prior to independence, tribal had lost their customary rights over land due to survey and settlement processes. With a view to raising revenue from natural resources, the colonial policies introduced new systems of land administration where estates were granted to influential non-tribal without conducting proper surveys. In some areas non-tribal were encouraged to bring as much land as they could under cultivation. In the post-independence period, tribal have lost their land rights through survey and settlement operations undertaken during the transition from the intermediary system to individual-based settlement. Land deprivation occurred on a massive scale owing to the lack of proper and regular survey and settlement practices. Most of the land in scheduled areas of AP was under feudatory systems of land tenure such as samindari, jagirdari, muttadari and mahaldari. Under these systems, the tribal tenant had no security and the intermediary had the right to evict the tenant at will. With a view to conferring 'patta' rights on tribal ryots and to putting in place proper land records after due survey and settlement operations, the government of Andhra Pradesh made the AP Mahals, AP Muttas, AP Scheduled Areas Ryotwari Settlement as discussed in the earlier chapter.

Under the above regulations, thousands of non-tribes were granted ryotwari pattas. Although the possession of land by a non-tribal for a period of eight years is subject to APSALTR, this provision was not understood in proper spirit by the implementing authorities. Further, the influential non-tribal managed to produce records showing that the lands were under their occupation at the time of the settlement. Haimendorf (1979), who studied the Gonds of Adilabad district, graphically chronicles the process of land alienation resulting from survey and settlement processes. The Gonds' inability to retain their land was due to a system of land tenure far too complicated for a region with an illiterate population. The right of ownership to land had to be formally recognised by the authorities and the name of the owner (pattadar) entered in the village registers before the ownership was regarded as valid. Most Gonds used to occupy land and pay revenue to the village accountant without insisting that they should be entered in the register as pattadars. Such tenure was called 'siwa-i-jamabandi' (without revenue settlement) and majority of Gonds cultivated lands in this way. Yet, anyone whose name did not appear in the register was liable to eviction. When pressure on the land grew and Gonds had to compete with non-tribal, this system was very much to their disadvantage. Non-tribal settlers' manoeuvred to get patta rights in siwa-i-jamabandi land held by Gonds on payment of a nominal sum. The Gond habit of giving up cultivation on a piece of land and occupation of vacant land of equal size on payment of the same revenue was also made use of by the immigrants. They turned the relinquished patta lands to government lands and got pattas in their own names. By the 1940s, the Gonds had already been ousted from many villages and large areas of land once held by their forefathers.

Forest Policies Alienating the Tribal

Laws governing forests have also contributed to large-scale land alienation in the scheduled areas. The concept of state ownership of forests came into conflict with the traditional rights and practices of tribal. In several locations, tribal lost access to their agricultural land and commons following the demarcation of forest boundaries. In north coastal districts of AP, in particular, tribal have lost large chunks of land that they had used for 'podu' (shifting cultivation). Around 65 percent of Andhra Pradesh forest area is spread over eight tribal districts in the northern part of the state. Historically, the relationship between tribal and the state agencies has been antagonistic which gave rise to several uprisings. The widespread commercialisation of forests during the colonial era, following the adoption of forest acts, restricted the traditional rights of tribal.

Although India has a long history of forest policy, the livelihoods of forest-dwellers have not been recognised in policy until recently. Predominantly tribal lands have been declared as state forests. The reservation of forests has been a historical process whereby the indigenous communities are pushed deeper into forests and tribal lands are appropriated by non-tribal. The state has appropriated large tracts of land without recognising customary rights, particularly of shifting cultivation. Much of the land classified as "encroached land" in AP is actually land under customary tribal podu forest fallows management. The case of Adilabad illustrates the process of alienation by forest policies. Until about 1900, the tribal of Adilabad had not been subject to any restrictions in the forest. While Kolams and Naikpods practised shifting cultivation, Gonds cultivated mainly the light soils of the hilltops, allowing long periods of fallow between periods of cultivation. When in the name of forest conservancy boundary lines were drawn round the villages where most of the land not actually under cultivation was notified as government forest. When the land Gonds had cultivated at the time of the demarcation became exhausted, and Gonds wanted to reoccupy the fallow lands, they came up against the claims of the forest department. When the forest lines were demarcated, the peculiarities of the tribal area were not taken into account. For instance, lands held by tribal under siva-i-jamabandi were included under reserve forest. Even in villages that were put in enclosures, the forest boundary ran so close to the villages that there was hardly any space left for future growth. And in violation of the principles of reservation, many fields held by Gonds on patta were included in the reserved forest. Owing to land alienation and population pressure, tribal in many locations had started cultivating land falling under the reserve forest. In several villages, there have been conflicts between tribal and forest officials over such "encroachments".

Government policies on forest reserves have affected tribal peoples profoundly. Wherever the state has chosen to exploit forests, it has seriously undermined the tribes' way of life. Government efforts to reserve forests have precipitated armed but futile resistance on the part of the tribal peoples involved. Intensive exploitation of forests has often meant allowing outsiders to cut large areas of trees (while the original tribal inhabitants were restricted from cutting), and ultimately replacing mixed forests capable of sustaining tribal life with single-product plantations. Where forests are reserved, non-tribal population have proved far more sophisticated than their forest counterparts at bribing the necessary local officials to secure effective (if extra-legal) use of forestlands. The system of bribing local officials charged with enforcing the reserves is so well established that the rates of bribery are reasonably fixed (by the number of ploughs a farmer uses or the amount of grain harvested). Tribal people often end up doing unpaid work for Hindus simply because a caste Hindu, who has paid the requisite bribe, can at least ensure a tribal member that he or she will not be evicted from forestlands. The final irony, notes von Fürer-Haimendorf, is that the shifting cultivation many tribes practiced had maintained South Asia's and India's forests, whereas the intensive cultivating and commercial interests that replaced the tribal way of life have destroyed the forests.

Dispossession in the Pretext of Development Projects

At the national level, tribal constitute at least 55 percent of the persons displaced by development projects such as irrigation systems, hydroelectric projects, mining operations, power generating units and mineral-based industries. In the name of development, tribal are displaced from their traditional habitat and are deprived of their livelihoods. The track record of governments on the resettlement and rehabilitation front leaves a lot to be desired. Even according to the official estimates, only 29 percent of the affected have been rehabilitated. In the recent past, some development projects in AP have become highly controversial due to their implications for tribal land and livelihoods. Mining is among the largest industries in India which has become contentious in the context of enforcing the safeguards enshrined in the Fifth Schedule. The recent pronouncements by the Supreme Court, following the interventions of Samata, on mining operations in the scheduled areas have set off a nationwide debate on tribal land issues. The discourse on mining activity should be set against the backdrop of the legal initiatives taken by Samata on the basis of their work in Vishakhapatnam district. Mining operations in Anantagiri area go back to the 1960s when mining leases were granted to private entities while tribal were denied title deeds to their lands. Samata moved the high court of Andhra Pradesh in 1993 against mining permissions arguing that the leases violated the land transfer regulations and the government was also a "person" (non-tribal) and hence does not have the power to grant leases to non-tribal. The court issued a stay order; but in 1995, the stay order was vacated and the case was dismissed. After hearing a special appeal by Samata, the Supreme Court delivered its landmark verdict in 1997. The judgment inter alia says:

1. Government lands, forest lands and tribal lands in the scheduled area cannot be leased out to non-tribal or to private industries.

2. Mining activity in scheduled areas can be undertaken only by the government or a society of tribal.

3. It would be appropriate to bring about a national legislation on mineral wealth in tribal areas.

4. At least 20 percent of the net profits from mining operations should be set aside for developing infrastructure in mining areas.

In the 1970s, the gains tribal peoples had made in earlier decades were eroded in many regions. Migration into tribal lands increased dramatically, and the deadly combination of constabulary and revenue officers uninterested in tribal welfare and sophisticated non-tribal willing and able to bribe local officials was sufficient to deprive many tribal of their landholdings. The means of subverting protective legislations were regional/local officials, who could be persuaded to ignore land acquisition by nontribal people, alter land registry records, lease plots of land for short periods and then simply refuse to relinquish them, or induce tribal members to become indebted and attach their lands. Whatever the means, the result was that many tribal members became landless labourers in the 1960s and 1970s, and regions that a few years earlier had been the exclusive domain of tribes had an increasingly heterogeneous population. Unlike previous eras in which tribal people were shunted into more remote forests, by the 1960s relatively little unoccupied land was available. Government efforts to evict nontribal members from illegal occupation have proceeded slowly; when evictions occur at all, those ejected are usually members of poor, lower castes. In a 1985 publication, anthropologist Christoph von Fürer-Haimendorf describes this process in Andhra Pradesh: on average only 25 to 33 percent of the tribal families in such villages had managed to keep even a portion of their holdings. Outsiders had paid about 5 percent of the market value of the lands they took.

Improved communications, roads with motorized traffic, and more frequent government intervention figured in the increased contact that tribal peoples had with outsiders. Tribes fared best where there was little to induce non-tribal to settle; cash crops and commercial highways frequently signalled the dismemberment of the tribes. Merchants have long been a link to the outside world, but in the past they were generally petty traders, and the contact they had with tribal people was transient. By the 1960s and 1970s, the resident nontribal shopkeeper was a permanent feature of many villages. Shop-keepers often sold liquor on credit, enticing tribal members into debt and into mortgaging their land. In the past, tribes made up shortages before harvest by foraging from the surrounding forest. More recently shopkeepers have offered ready credit—with the proviso that loans be repaid in kind with 50 to 100 percent interest after harvest. Repaying one bag of millet with two bags has set up a cycle of indebtedness from which many have been unable to break loose.

The possibility of cultivators growing a profitable cash crop, such as cotton or castor-oil plants, continues to draw merchants into tribal areas. Nontribal traders frequently establish an extensive network of relatives and associates as shopkeepers to serve as agents in a number of villages. Cultivators who grow a cash crop often sell to the same merchants, who provide consumption credit throughout the year. The credit carries a high-interest price tag, whereas the tribal peoples' crops are bought at a fraction of the market rate. Cash crops offer a further disadvantage in that they decrease the supply of available foodstuffs and increase tribal dependence on economic forces beyond their control. This transformation has meant a decline in both the tribes' security and their standard of living.

In previous generations, families might have purchased silver jewellery as a form of security; contemporary tribal people are more likely to buy minor consumer goods. Whereas jewellery could serve as collateral in critical emergencies, current purchases simply increase indebtedness. In areas where gathering forest products are remunerative, merchants exchange their products for tribal labour. Indebtedness is so extensive that although such transactions are illegal, traders sometimes "sell" their debtors to other merchants, much like indentured servants.

In some instances, tribes have managed to hold their own in contacts with outsiders. Some Chenchus, a hunting and gathering tribe of the central hill regions of Andhra Pradesh, have continued to specialize in collecting forest products for sale. Caste Hindus living among them rent land from the Chenchus and pay a portion of the harvest. The Chenchus themselves have responded unenthusiastically to government efforts to induce them to take up farming. Their relationship to nontribal people has been one of symbiosis, although there were indications in the early 1980s that other groups were beginning to compete with the Chenchus in gathering forest products. A large paper mill was cutting bamboo in their territory in a manner that did not allow regeneration, and two groups had begun to collect for sale the same products the Chenchus sell. Dalits settled among them with the help of the Chenchus and learned agriculture from them. The nomadic Banjara herders who graze their cattle in the forest also have been allotted land there. The Chenchus have a certain advantage in dealing with caste Hindus; because of their long association with Hindu hermits and their refusal to eat beef, they are considered an unpolluted caste. Other tribes, particularly in South India, have cultural practices that are offensive to Hindus and, when they are assimilated, are often considered Dalits.

The final blow for some tribes has come when non-tribal, through political jockeying, have managed to gain legal tribal status, that is, to be listed as a Scheduled Tribe. The Gonds of Andhra Pradesh effectively lost their only advantage in trying to protect their lands when the Banjaras, a group that had been settling in Gond territory, were classified as a Scheduled Tribe in 1977. Their newly acquired tribal status made the Banjaras eligible to acquire Gond land "legally" and to compete with Gonds for reserved political seats, places in education institutions, and other benefits. Because the Banjaras are not scheduled in neighbouring Maharashtra, there has been an influx of Banjara emigrants from that state into Andhra Pradesh in search of better opportunities.

Travails of Coffee Producers

(Findings are based on survey conducted in Paderu division in Vishakhapatnam)

India is the sixth largest producer of coffee in the world, with 4.2 percent of its share in world market, having 44.39 percent of area growing 'arabica' variety and the rest of 'robusta'. The average productivity of coffee in India is lower than world's average and especially lower than the productivity of major coffee producing countries like Brazil and Vietnam.

Fig. 2.15: Tribal Cultivators in Paderu Division

Though Indian Coffee constitutes only a small fraction of the world's production of coffee, it has an importance of its own as it is considered to be one of the best in the world. With a potential for high productivity levels on one side and growing urbanization inducing higher consumption of coffee on the other hand, there is a scope for large expansion of Indian coffee market. In Andhra Pradesh, coffee has made its impact since 1970s, having introduced only in one district i.e. Vishakhapatnam in its hilly areas of Eastern Ghats; grown at an attitude of about 900 meters. The area has increased from its initial 200 ha in 1975–85 to about 28,000 hectares as on now.

Fig. 2.16: Quality Coffee Beans Displayed at an Exhibition

Greatest advantage that coffee plantation has brought to this region of eastern Ghats is in regenerating the greenery of the already bared hills, with permanent shade trees under which coffee is grown, thus maintaining the ecological balance of this area. It is eye-catching in entire Paderu division, that wherever there are dense green patches on hill slopes, it is only due to silver oak, grown as shade tree for coffee.

The socio-economic profile of the sample households of coffee farmers and non-coffee farmers in Paderu division reveal that coffee cultivation is mostly done by males. Although female participation is quite low (2.5 percent) they are able to manage the farms very efficiently. In fact, where ever females are involved in coffee farming, productivity levels are higher and best quality coffee is produced. Moreover, their savings are productively utilized wherein they have invested in the construction of bigger houses for their families or by keeping their savings in bank deposits:

1. Tribe-wise analysis shows that coffee growing is more prevalent in the tribes of Bagatha, Konda Doras and Nooka Doras almost in proportion to their populations.

2. 84 percent of the coffee farmers are either small (34.0 percent) or marginal (50 percent) farmers, about 13 percent are medium farmers and the rest 2.9 percent belong to the category of big farmers who possess holdings of size 10 acres and above.

3. Nearly 58 percent of the tribal farmers are illiterate and 34 percent have education up to primary level. Even though the literacy levels of coffee farmers are low, general awareness levels of various aspects of coffee cultivation and marketing are very high. High awareness levels could be attributed to their 30 years of experience in coffee cultivation in this area.

4. 82 percent live in permanent or semi-permanent houses and only 14.1 percent of them still live in temporary

'kucha' structures indicating an elevation in their economic status.

5. Credit availed from financial institutions for coffee cultivation is negligible. Most of the finances received by the tribalis in the form of "Government Subsidies" and investment is mainly through their own contribution in the form of manual labour, coffee being a labour intensive crop.

6. Only 3.6% of the coffee farmers are borrowing money from money lenders, 9.5% from Commercial Banks, 3.1% from Cooperative Banks and just 0.4% from RRBs.

7. The outstanding debt in respect of coffee farmers is very low when compared to non-coffee farmers and those who are having outstanding debt above ₹ 10,000/- is just 1.1%.

8. Almost all Tribal Coffee growers feel that there is need to take up special capacity building programmes on issues like marketing, productivity and raising organic coffee to attain best quality coffee and to increase the productivity.

Problems of Market Access

'A community without roads does not have a way out'— Market access problems can affect areas owing to remoteness or lack of infrastructure, and groups such as the illiterate or poorly educated ethnic groups. Distance to markets and the lack of roads is a matter of concern for rural communities in the developing world. The rural poor need access to competitive markets not just for their produce but also for inputs, assets, technology, consumer goods and credit. A common problem of disadvantaged areas and disadvantaged groups is personal immobility. Remoteness and poverty both stand to reduce access to markets.

The perishable nature of agricultural produce, combined with lack of storage facilities and long distances to markets are impediments to get a good price to the coffee grown in non-traditional areas, especially the Eastern Ghats.

By 1996, Coffee Board's involvement in marketing was completely stopped and growers were free to market their crop as they choose. The tribal of Paderu area are adopted to sell their coffee beans in the local shandies. Some of the merchants directly approach the tribal coffee farmers in the respective villages and buy the coffee directly by making transport arrangements to the auction centres located at Vijayawada and Bangalore. This method has mostly benefited the middle men rather than the poor tribal coffee grower, who is illiterate and cannot organize together and invest to get better remunerative market price. Marketing of coffee may be handled by the professional management group.

Even though Self Help Groups have been formed in tribal villages under Kranthi Patham, these groups give mostly small loans to the members but not to the coffee growers. The community investment fund provided to these SHGs is not being used as credit facility to the tribal coffee in the region even if used it is only in small proportion as evident from the primary data.

Nandi Foundation an NGO, which started its activities in and around Araku valley, in association with 'ASSAV' (Adivasi Abhivrudhi Samskrithika Sangham, Araku Valley), which is a registered mutually aided co-operative society, assisted in funding for coffee programme since 2001. About 60 acres of coffee are under ASSAV's cultivation. Coffee roasting and grinding machines for retail coffee sales have been set up to ensure better price for their produce. They have model plantations in their demonstration farms for imparting knowledge to the tribal on organic farming and are done by expertise in organic farming.

Risk Management

Government of India is concerned with the problems faced by the small growers in the Coffee Plantation Sector, whose entire subsistence is dictated by the forces of nature. Yields differ from year to year and the period of busts faced by the coffee industry leaves much distress among the growers. With this background, Government of India had constituted a Task Force on 24th July, 2006 to examine particularly the problems faced by the smaller growers.

Today there is no credible alternative facility available to a grower to meet the risks of price movements and the price risk management is unknown to the small growers. To provide this, the Task Force recommended that an insurance cover may be provided to the small growers and the periodical premium may be shared between the beneficiary and the Government, roughly on 50-50 basis. The Task Force also feels that there is an urgent need to provide the personal accident cover to small growers. The Task Force felt that an innovative market literacy programme on trading in general and future trading in particular requires to be launched. This could be initiated at three levels (a) producers and processors (b) traders and (c) exporters and small corporates.

Research and Development

Research and development activities should be taken up in a big way. Wherever the traditional coffee is there, the bug attack comes in a very strange unexpected manner. The long attacks and many other pests attack the coffee plants and destroy coffee crop. Sufficient safe guards should be introduced to control the situation. To increase the overall productivity of Indian coffee on par with other coffee growing countries control of pests is primarily important as it is one of the factors that contribute to increased productivity. If the Indian farmer is not able to attain the productivity at least 75 percent of their counterparts in Brazil, Guatemala and Srilanka, it would be very difficult for India to survive in the international market.

Future vision for Coffee Producers

The total production of coffee in Paderu area of Vishakhapatnam district for the year 2010–11 is more than 4000 MTs, which is valued at about ₹ 30.00 crores that has contributed to the economy of this area. Seventy percent of the investment for this economy is by way of human labour, since coffee being a labour intensive crop. Average productivity of the coffee produced by tribal in the area is ranging between 175 kgs to 200 kgs per hectare, compared to 370 kgs by the APFDC and 650 Kgs of national average for 'arabica' variety. The Coffee Board in its demonstration farms in this region has achieved yields up to 625 kgs per hectare and hence there is a possibility to enhance the productivity of tribal coffee with some efforts. In traditional areas the productivity is on par with world averages in some areas producing the best in quality and yield. There is good scope for increasing the productivity of tribal coffee of Paderu area from its present yields to national averages, by resorting to latest coffee cultivation practices, and also upgrading the quality of coffee produced. Since Government of A.P. has already issued orders for conversion of conventional coffee to organic within a period of three years, this may be put into practice. This can happen only if proper support is given by deploying adequate number of liaison workers selected from the community as required and planned as per Project document and they are adequately trained and given required technical support. The economy of this entire area will see a sea change, if a two pronged approach is adopted, one by increasing the productivity, and the second by ensuring the quality. By doubling average coffee farm productivity of this region, one can immediately visualize the doubling of the average income of the farmer. This is possible by intensive efforts in coffee extension work and capacity building and will not cost much for the Government financially, since coffee being labour intensive crop.

ITDA, Paderu has proposed to expand coffee area by another 60,000 acres during the next five year period. While taking up the expansion programme, it is also essential to strengthen the existing coffee farms especially started during X Plan period to fill the gaps and lacunae which occurred mainly owing to inadequate flow of funds, which affect adversely on the overall productivity and sustenance of the programme. Hence it is desirable that in the XII plan coffee expansion project, there should be provision at least up to 30 percent of the Project cost, towards consolidation of coffee extension work in the villages of earlier years. Ministry of Commerce, Government of India should provide funds for consolidation of coffee of earlier years for the small tribal growers. Hence areas require consolidation of coffee planted in earlier years. In Paderu areas may be identified and simultaneous action may be taken to fill the gaps to increase production and productivity and quality of coffee. The Forest survey of India (2006) highlights how 60 percent of forest area was degraded between 1971 and 1979 in which millions of hectares of natural forest were cleared for industrial purpose and for plantation. Expansion of coffee plantation and its consolidation is the only hope that we can protect the green cover of Eastern Ghats, if the tribal of this region come to believe that coffee cultivation is their major economic activity, the forest cover and the ecological balance of Eastern Ghats is saved.

Coffee is a commercial crop with 80 percent of the produce being exported. Moreover, coffee grown in the agency areas (tribal tracts of Vishakhapatnam district) has been found to be one of the best varieties with an exotic flavour. However this best product has not entered the international markets at the expected levels due to non-availability of inputs, market imperfections and inadequate financial support to tribal. Hence if the efforts to expand the coffee in this tribal belt with increase in productivity and increase in production of qualitative coffee become successful, the scenario of the entire region of Eastern Ghats will change with a new thrust to its economy and thus contribute to the prosperity of the region and simultaneously reducing the poverty levels of tribal living in this region.

SOCIAL SECTOR: EDUCATION AND HEALTH

Deprivation in Terms of Quality Education and Delivery of Health Services

Quality Education

There were 16 million ST children (10.87 million of 6–11 years and 5.12 million of 11–14 years) as of March 2001, out of the total child population in India of about 193 million in the age group of 6 to 14 years *(Selected Educational Statistics— 2000–01, Government of India)*. Education of ST children is considered important, not only because of the Constitutional obligation but also as a crucial input for total development of tribal communities.

An important development in the policy towards education of tribal is the National Policy on Education (NPE), 1986, which specified, among other things, the following:

- Priority will be accorded to opening primary schools in tribal areas.
- There is need to develop curricula and devise instructional material in tribal languages at the initial stages with arrangements for switchover to regional languages.
- ST youths will be encouraged to take up teaching in tribal areas.
- *Ashram* schools/residential schools will be established on a large scale in tribal areas.
- Incentive schemes will be formulated for the STs, keeping in view their special needs and lifestyle.

The NPE, 1986 and the Programme of Action (POA), 1992, recognized the heterogeneity and diversity of the tribal areas while underlining the importance of instruction through the mother tongue and the need for preparing teaching/learning materials in the tribal languages. A working group on Elementary and Adult Education for the Xth Five Year Plan (2002-07) emphasized the need to improve the quality of education of tribal children and to ensure equity as well as further improving access.

The interventions being promoted in States under Janshala include:

- Schools, education guarantee centres and alternative schools in tribal habitations for non-enrolled and drop-out children.
- Textbooks in the mother tongue for children at the beginning of the primary education cycle, when they do not understand the regional language. Suitably adapted curriculum and the availability of locally relevant teaching and learning materials for tribal students.
- Special training for non-tribal teachers to work in tribal areas, including knowledge of tribal dialect.
- Special support to teachers as per need.
- Deploying community teachers.
- Bridge Language Inventory for use of teachers.
- School calendars in tribal areas appropriate to local requirements and festivals.
- Anganwadis and Balwadis or crèches in each school in tribal areas so that the girls are relieved from sibling care responsibilities.
- Special plan for nomadic and migrant workers.
- Engagement of community organizers from ST communities with a focus on schooling needs of children from specific households.
- Ensuring sense of ownership of school committees by ST communities through increasing representatives of STs in

VECs/PTAs, etc. Involving community leaders in school management.

• Monitoring attendance and retention of children.
• Providing context specific intervention e.g. Ashram school, hostel, incentives, etc.

Universalizing Access

Thus, one of the challenges in providing education to tribal children relates to setting up school facilities in small, scattered and remote tribal habitations. The majority of the Scheduled Tribes live in sparsely populated habitations in the interior and in inaccessible hilly and forest areas of the country. Nearly 22 percent of the tribal habitations have populations of less than 100 while more than 40% have population of 100 to 300. The rest have population of 300 to 500.

Relaxed Norm for Setting up Schools

One of the reasons for poor access to schooling in tribal areas before the 1980s was the high norm on population, number of children and distance for opening new schools. Most of the states have relaxed these norms to enable setting up school seven in small tribal hamlets. This, along with other measures has improved access intribal areas. For instance, Andhra Pradesh has relaxed norms to set up schools in habitations even with 20 school-age children. Some states have lowered the population size norm, especially for tribal areas. EGS centres can now be established even with 15 children. In remote tribal habitations in hilly areas of North Eastern states and Jammu and Kashmir, EGS schools can be opened with only 10 children.

The *Sixth All India Educational Survey (1993)* showed that 78 percent of the tribal population and 56 percent of tribal habitations have been provided primary schools within the habitation. In addition, 11 percent of the tribal population and 20 percent of tribal habitations have schools within less than1 km radius. About 65 percent of rural habitations covering 86 percent of the total rural population have primary schools within the habitation or within a distance of half a kilometre, as against 56 percent of tribal habitations with 79 percent of tribal population. Mizoram and Gujarat have the highest percentage of population and habitations covered by primary schools within the habitations. Up to 95 percent of the tribal population and 85 to 90 percent of the tribal habitations in the states are provided with schooling facilities within the habitation.

Quality Improvement

Development of Culturally Relevant Materials in Local Languages

Most of the states recognize the need to address issues related to teachers' attitudes, medium of instruction, textbooks and materials, curriculum and pedagogy and teaching-learning process in tribal areas.

An increasing number of researchers strongly advocate the use of the mother tongue or home language as medium of instruction in early stages of education. This assumes greater significance in the context of education of tribal children because their mother tongue is often quite distinct from the prominent languages in the state or regional languages. ST children face problems wherever teachers do not speak their dialect at all. From the perspective of language, it is desirable to have a local teacher from the same tribal community. However this may create future problems of higher education when children enter the mainstream. Local language can be used as a medium of instruction at initial stages.

Research evidence has demonstrated the positive consequences of bilingual or multilingual schooling on cognitive development and social interaction processes, tribal children would require special programs to be able to cope. The Constitution of India allows the use of tribal dialect (mother tongue) as the medium of instruction if the population of the tribe is more than 100,000.

Andhra Pradesh has developed bilingual dictionaries and teacher training has been organised in Warangal and Vizianagram districts. Research studies have also been undertaken on the issue of language and maths learning by tribal children. It has been decided to use the multi-level kits developed for tribal areas in Vishakapatnam district and also in other tribal areas.

Gujarat has developed dictionaries in Dangi and Bhili dialects. A local word glossary in Dangi has been prepared and distributed in schools for class I-IV in Dang district. Similarly a local word glossary in Adivasi dialect has been prepared for class I-IV in Banaskantha district and distributed inschools. The Vidyasahayaks were given training on the use of these dictionaries. Gujarat has also initiated extensive work for preparation of TLM in tribal languages. The TLM developed include flash cards for different languages and also cards for mathematics. These have been supplied to all schools in tribal areas. A Bridge Language Inventory has also been introduced in Ho and Mundari languages in Ranchi district of Jharkhand.

Two important aspects emerge from this. One is that the cognitive qualities of tribal children have to be viewed and evaluated taking into consideration their ecological and cultural contexts that place very different demands on day-to-day life. Because of differences in the demand of tribal ecology, the patterning of their cognitive abilities shows considerable variation from those of other groups. A related and more important aspect is that tribal children are neither culturally inferior nor cognitively less competent than the children of other groups. Instead many of their skills and abilities are highly developed and extremely sophisticated.

Thus the implications of these findings for schooling of tribal children are clear. A programme of schooling, which does not pay attention to the ecological, cultural and psychological characteristics of tribal children, is highly unlikely to make any significant impact. The educational system of the dominant non-tribal population is of very limited value in the tribal cultural milieu because it does not match with the lifestyle of individuals and the needs of the tribal community. Linking school education with life in general and the needs of the tribal communities in particular is a most important step that requires serious attention.

The evidences further suggest that tribal children do possess the basic cognitive abilities and psychological dispositions necessary for successful participation in school. Yet tribal children have very low levels of participation and success in school education programmes. This indicates our failure to develop a sensitive model of education, which is rooted in the psychological strengths of tribal children. Studies indicate that, in comparison to other groups, hunters and gatherers possess a high level of visual and tactual differentiation; they demonstrate capacity for fine judgment of shape and size of stimuli as well as spatial relations and they produce fine categorization of an array of objects. These abilities are required for success in science, art, music, dance, athletic activities, and vocations like carpentry, tailoring, wood and stone crafts. These skills need to be utilized not only for education of tribal children in schools, but also in the broader economic spheres of tribal life. Such attempts will be helpful in generating and promoting the sense of competence, self-efficacy, self-respect and positive self-image among tribal children in general.

Such attempts are also likely to provide tribal children with a culturally meaningful, ecologically valid and economically viable alternative to life by reinforcing the dignity of their culture and identity. Ever increasing contact of tribal with the outside world over the years has introduced several changes in their culture and life. These changes are reflected in their psychological characteristics also. Studies (e.g. Mishra *et al.,* 1996) indicate that their ways of perceiving the world, categorizing objects, interpreting pictures, and strategies of learning and memory become more similar to those with whom they interact and negotiate their life in these changed circumstances. This suggests that tribal children can acquire all those skills that the members of other groups of the society possess. What is important on our part is to develop a positive frame of mind about tribal children.

This is possible only through sensitivity to tribal culture and life, recognition of the cognitive strengths of tribal children, and appreciation of their personality qualities. Efforts in these directions will be very helpful in organizing the programme of tribal education as well as promoting economic and other aspects of tribal development (Gautam, 2003). Similarly a clear policy for language use in schools has to be developed. Research evidence suggests that significantly fewer students drop out of schools in which the language of tribal groups is used for instruction at the primary level. Development of primers in the tribal dialect involving content from the local context will go a long way in ensuring children's active participation in the learning process in school.

While there is a general need for improvement in physical facilities in all schools in remote tribalregions, change in perceptions and outlooks of teachers about tribal children are equally important. Teachers need to be sensitized to the cultural and behavioral strengths of tribal children and motivated to do their best for them in schools. Incentives should be initiated to attract effective teachers to work in tribal schools and to retain them there. Only such motivated teachers are likely to generate interest among tribal children towards schools education by attempting to link the contents of the curriculum with the existing realities of tribal communities through the use of innovative technologies.

Delivery of Health Services

Tribal development strategies need to be more human-centred with health at its centre. The conventional, bureaucratised approach of looking at health issues for tribal in a sectoral, compartmentalised manner can have little impact on achieving health goals. Strategies to reduce morbidities and mortality among tribal would need to contain specific directions for establishing interconnectivity between income, food security, female literacy and good health right down to the PHC level.

If financial allocations are indicative of policy intention, then it becomes clear that neither has adequate attention been paid to past experience nor full use made of the new insights gained from the facility survey. The Tribal Health Plan (THP), like most plan documents is full of sound-bytes—a statement of good intentions which, in the absence of a carefully worked out and tightly knit health delivery system, set within an integrated development framework will be a lot of effort with little utility. A serious shortcoming of the health policy for tribal is the reiteration of the routine compartmentalised approach. Besides not attempting the implementation of the national policy of having a multipurpose, integrated health care delivery system at the primary level, the Policy does not even deal adequately with the issues related to mother and child healthcare services. Implementation of these programmes has not been incorporated.

Surveys conducted on Health issues in Tribal areas have shown that, in view of the strong association of TB, malaria, AIDS, STD to reproductive health, the policy framework falls short in not assessing the operational inadequacies for improving the programme implementation of these public health programmes—for example, data shows that most malarial deaths are on account of delayed treatment. The average time taken in tribal areas for a blood slide to be examined and results informed is six weeks to six months. On account of inadequate budgets for travel allowances, workers tend to wait for 10–15 days till enough number of slides are collected before handing them in for testing by when the slides get spoilt and fixed. Likewise, the existing system of TB treatment requires patients to visit the district hospital, which on an average could be about 200 km away, obtain a referral and keep visiting the PHC for medication—a system that has been found to be expensive, time consuming and clearly unaffordable resulting in a significant increase in drop-out rates. Or worse still, on account of late release of budgets and sporadic supply drug resistance is on the increase. These are realities that need to be captured for reducing morbidity and mortality levels.

There is thus need for a new paradigm. Examined from the perspective of quality of life indicators, tribal development strategies will need to be more human-centred. This means bringing about a shift in the mind-set and a redefinition of the word 'development'; or measuring development by looking at outcomes such as the number of children or women saved from premature death: increasing literacy levels, reducing drop-outs and increasing retention in schools, etc. as contrary to focusing only on number of silver oak trees planted for coffee produced, houses constructed or buffalos distributed. This means having an agenda that consists of provisioning of basic education, basic health care and capacity building within the framework of a stable and sustainable land use policy:

where there is a basic inter-linkage of the individual activities. It also means better targeting so as to ensure an equitable development process, since the intra-tribal differentials are a major area of concern.

The development paradigm will need to make health centre stage in the overall development strategy. "Incomes depend exclusively on physical labour and have no savings to cushion the blow..It is impossible to recover with their human and financial capital intact". Therefore, any strategy for the development of tribal will need to not only protect income particularly during the lean periods, but also to realise that investments to reduce health risks among the poor and provision of insurance against catastrophic health care costs are important elements for reducing poverty (World Development Report, 1993).

The allocated issues within the health budget are critical for determining the quality of care. The WDR "Investing in Health" 1993, argued for low income countries such as India, to consider utilising available resources on provisioning of basic health services that, in the Indian context would consist of MCH services, treatment for TB, malaria, STDs. minor surgeries, trauma café and health education for preventive and which promotes health care.

In view of the financial crisis, increases in budgetary outlays for health would be increasingly difficult, as witnessed in each budget. It is in the context of affordability that more cost effective systems of health care need to be urgently examined. The indiscriminate propagation of modern medicine and high tech diagnostics through the proliferation of health centres and physicians trained in western medicine with treatment protocols that require repeated visits, etc. could be ruinous and unaffordable for the tribal in our country.

In China, where initial focus was to provide basic health care, cost effective options were adopted that broadly consisted of, educated youth, selected and paid for by the commune, provided six to nine months training in basic care and backed by small, neat and functional hospitals. The "bare foot" doctors were not only trained in anatomy and symptoms, cure of simple ailments, but also in traditional medicine, which was found to be acceptable, and proved over time, to be efficacious, affordable and easily acceptable.

In India, the blind adoption of the high cost western medicine system has resulted in the danger of destroying our own strengths, without having the money to sustain this new technology. In tribal areas, the Girijan Co-operative Corporation and the department of ayurveda have done commendable work in listing and identification of *herbal medicinal plants*—this research work should be fully utilised and exploited for the benefit of the tribal, as herbal medicine is acceptable, affordable, accessible and most importantly found to be capable of curing several ailments such as malarial fevers, STDs, etc. very effectively. Such an integration of systems of traditional medicine—nature cure, herbal cure, ayurveda, etc. which arc less dependent on the MBBS doctor and more familiar to the tribal needs to be consciously built into the package. But then the establishment of such a health system would require massive re-training of the health providers in traditional integrated medicine. Among the tribal, it is not only necessary for improving awareness but more importantly, carefully bringing about attitudinal development and behavioural changes for the promotion of good health values. Training would need to be not on health alone but related to empowerment of the community with the knowledge and understanding of interconnections between seemingly different activities, for example, linking of health goals to economic activities such as land use and development or implementation of employment generation programmes.

Scheduled Tribe in Vishakhapatnam and Warangal Districts of Andhra Pradesh
An Empirical Analysis

The population of Scheduled tribe in Warangal (14.10) as well as Vishakhapatnam (14.42) districts of Andhra Pradesh forms a considerable proportion of the total population of the district. The study was conducted on 100 respondents from the two above mentioned districts. Here we would analyse the socio-economic status of STs in the study area via primary survey, based on the parameters such as population, family size, educational status, medical and health conditions, employment status, consumption, area of land-holdings and the efficacy of various schemes issued for STs in the region. Scheduled questionnaire method of survey was used to draw information from the respondents.

A STATISTICAL ANALYSIS BASED ON DATA AND SURVEY CONDUCTED IN TRIBAL BELTS OF A.P. IN PARTICULAR THE TWO DISTRICTS UNDER STUDY

Before we analyse and make a comparative quantitative study of the data collected on field study at Vishakhapatnam and Warangal districts let us analyse the status of tribal in the districts under study based on the questionnaires and answers received from the respondents.

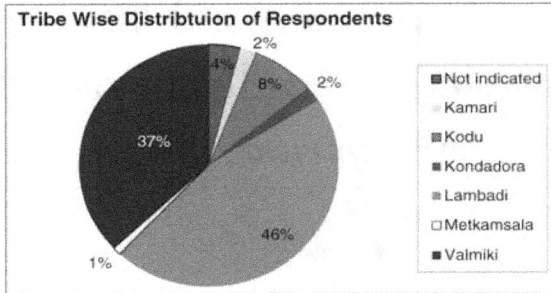

Fig. 3.1: Community: Sub-Caste

Source: Primary survey.

The Figure 3.1 shows that the entire tribal community is dominated by primarily two sub castes, the Lambadi's and the Valmiki's. The Lambadi sub caste constitutes the largest component of around 46 percent (46 of the 100 people sampled) of the entire tribal community in Andhra Pradesh, followed by the Valmiki sub caste, constituting around 37 percent (37 of the 100 people sampled) of the entire community. This makes up 83 percent of the population. Kodu, Kamari, Konda Dora sub castes make up 8 percent, 4 percent, 2 percent, and 2 percent respectively. The rarest sub caste is the Metkamsala's which constitute only 1 percent of the tribal community. 4 percent of the population does not belong to any sub caste.

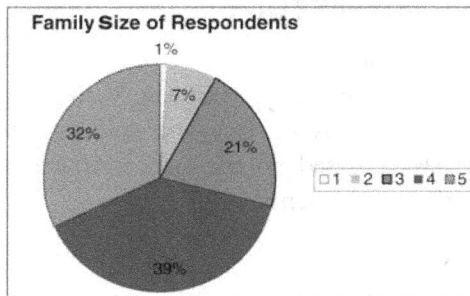

Fig. 3.2: Family Size Frequency

Source: Primary survey.

As shown in the above pie chart a family size of four has the highest frequency (39 out of every 100) followed by a family size of five (32 out of every 100), which has the second highest frequency. The above frequency distribution thus shows that 39 percent of the population has a family size of 4 and 32 percent has a family size of 5. 21 percent of the population has a family size of 3 and small percentages of 7 percent and 1 percent have a family size of 2 and 1 respectively. To conclude, majority of the families have 4 and 5 members.

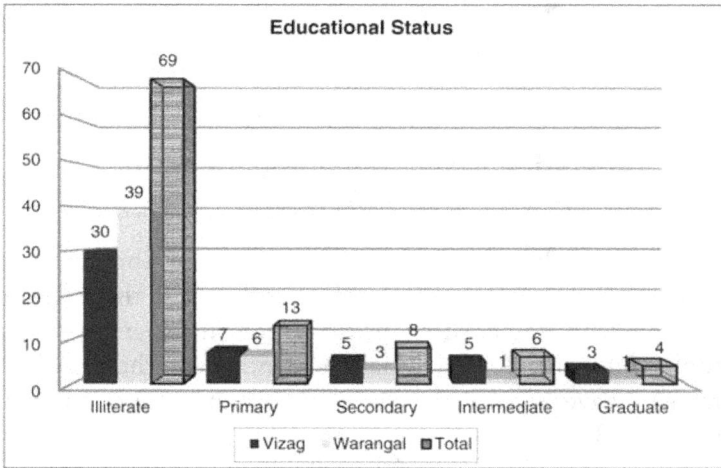

Fig. 3.3: District-Wise Educational Status

Source: Primary survey.

As per the study in Vishakhapatnam district, 60 percent respondents were illiterate, 14 percent had primary education, and 10 percent had up to secondary education, 10 percent passed intermediate and only 6 percent graduates. In Warangal district, 78 percent of the respondents were illiterate, 12 percent had primary education, 6 percent had secondary education, 2 percent had education up to intermediate and 2 percent of them were graduates. On the whole the illiteracy rate was a staggering 69 percent, 13 percent had undergone primary education, 8 percent had undergone secondary education, 6 percent had passed their intermediate and 4 percent were graduates.

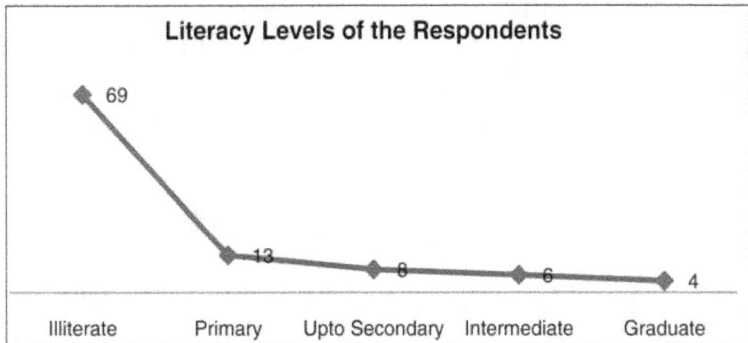

Fig. 3.4: Level of Literacy among Respondents

Source: Primary survey.

As shown in the above chart a majority of the tribal are illiterate (69 percent of the sampled tribe). Of the educated lot, a majority has ensured primary education and pre-high school education. A very small percentage of the tribal (10 percent) have invested in intermediate and graduate education. The primary survey thus brings out an alarming fact. 69 percent of the population is illiterate, only 13 percent have completed primary education and only 8 percent have completed up to secondary education. Only 6 percent of the population has intermediate level education and only a small percentage of 4 percent are graduate degree holders.

People Suffering from Various Diseases: In the study it was found that out of the 100 people sampled only one person was found to be physically disabled whereas the rest were found to be physically fit. None of the tribal people interviewed were found to be malnourished, which indicates that they have ensured proper nutrition among themselves.

Immunization of Children against Diseases: As per the survey 73 percent children were immunized and 19 percent children were not immunized.

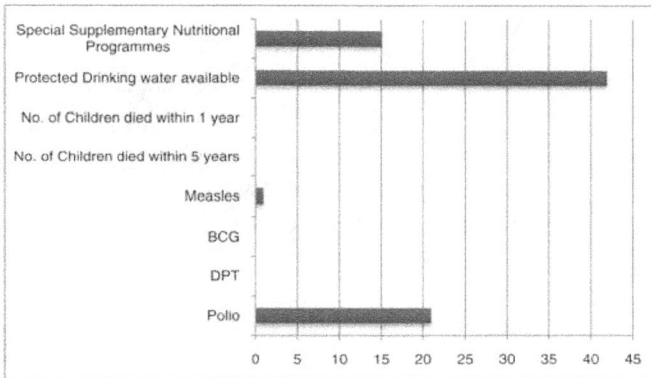

Fig. 3.5: Status of Immunization among Tribal Population

Source: Primary survey.

The infant mortality rate, surprisingly was found to be nil for the case of the 100 children sampled. The reason being, a large number of children (42 out of the 100 sampled) had access to protected drinking water, while 15 percent of the children were exposed to special supplementary nutritional programs, which ensured greater longevity for the children. 21 percent of the children were immunized from polio. Only one child was immunized from measles. None of the children were immunized from either DPT or BCG.

Employment/Occupational Status of the Tribal in the Organised/ Unorganized Sector: In Vishakhapatnam district, 94 percent are seasonal wage earners and only 4 percent earn wages throughout the year. In Warangal district, 82 percent of the respondents are seasonal wage earners and 12 percent of them earn wages round the year.

When we see all the respondents together, 88 percent of them are seasonal wage earners and 12 percent earn round the year.

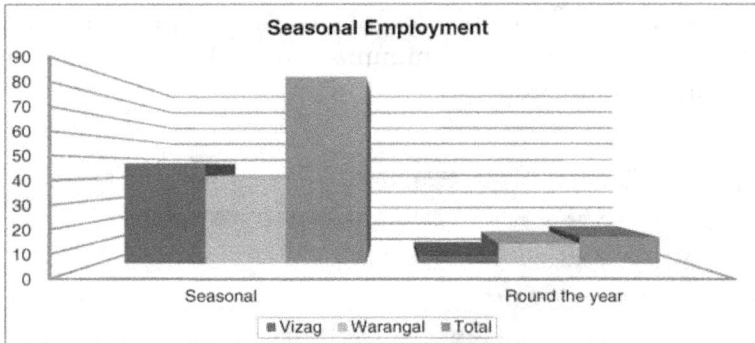

Fig. 3.6: Seasonal Employment among STs

Source: Primary survey.

As indicated from the study the tribal are primarily con-centrated in the agricultural sector for employment opportunity, either as a farmer or an agricultural labourer. Only two people were found to have an occupation as a government employee. None of the people were found to be unemployed while being educated. The survey also indicates that none of the tribal were employees in the public sector, private sector or industrial sector, neither were they employed as artisans. This indicates that these villagers are low risk takers and are traditionally stuck to the agricultural sector in their respective village.

Nature of Members Engaged in Family Occupation (Skilled/ Unskilled): The numbers of skilled family members engaged in family occupation are less than the number of unskilled family members engaged in family occupation.

Only 3 percent of the families consisted of one skilled member engaged in family occupation. A majority (53 percent) of the families consisted of two unskilled members engaged in family occupation. Around 18 percent of the families consisted of one unskilled member engaged in family occupation. Only 3 percent of the families had none of the unskilled family members engaged in family occupation.

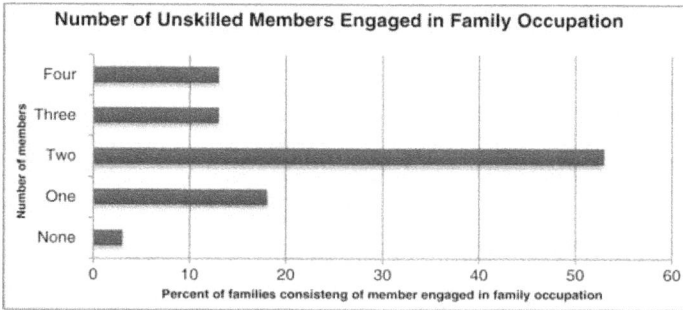

Fig. 3.7: Number of Unskilled Labour Employed in Family Occupation

Source: Primary survey.

It was also noticed that all members of families have no skilled nature of the skills processed. The work participation rates among the males or females are unknown. It is also not known if the children are employed.

Analysis

As shown in the below bar chart, the tribal in the Warangal district on an average consumes more food items than those in the Vishakhapatnam, except for vegetables wherein the tribal in both the districts consume approximately the same amount.

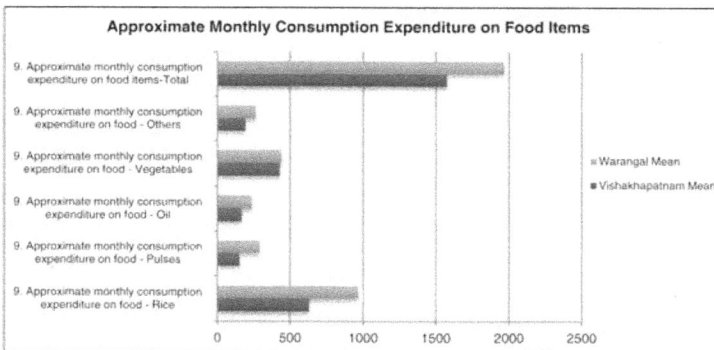

Fig. 3.8: Approximate Monthly Consumption Expenditure on Food Items

Source: Primary survey.

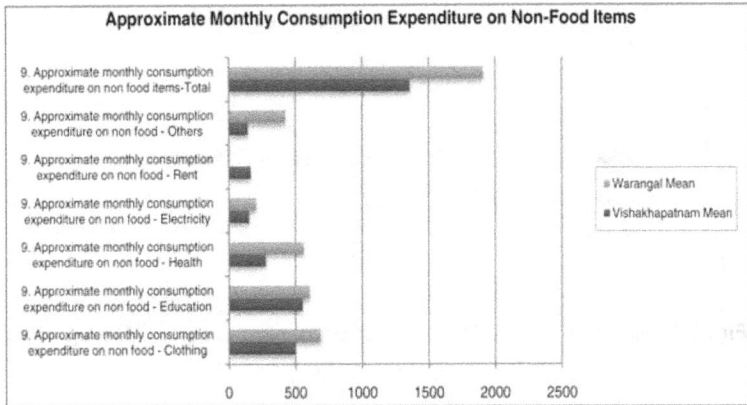

Fig. 3.9: Approximate Monthly Consumption
Expenditure on Non-Food Items

Source: Primary survey.

On an average, the tribal in the Warangal district consume more on non-food items than those in the Vishakhapatnam district on non-food items, except for electricity and education wherein the tribal in both the districts consume nearly the same amounts.

From the above Figures 3.8 and 3.9 we can analyse that in both the districts' expenditures on food items amounted to a larger percentage. (All amount in ₹)

- *Vishakhapatnam:* The mean expenditures on rice, pulses, oil, vegetables and other food items is 631.46, 152.60, 167.70, 429.38 and 193.00 respectively. The total is 1574.14.

- *Warangal:* The mean expenditures on rice, pulses, oil, vegetables and other food items is 963.54, 290.80, 236.20, 439.60 and 264.29 respectively. The total is 1967.14.

Therefore the total mean expenditures for both regions for rice, pulses, oil, vegetables and other food items is 797.50, 221.70, 201.95, 434.49, 201.75. The total mean is 1770.64.

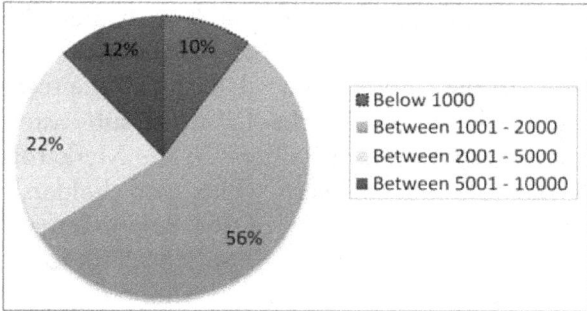

Fig. 3.10: Income Levels of the Family

Source: Primary survey.

As shown in the above diagram most of the families (56 percent) have income levels of ₹ 1001–2000, whereas only a few families i.e. 10 percent and 12 percent have incomes below ₹ 1000 or in between ₹ 5001–10000 respectively.

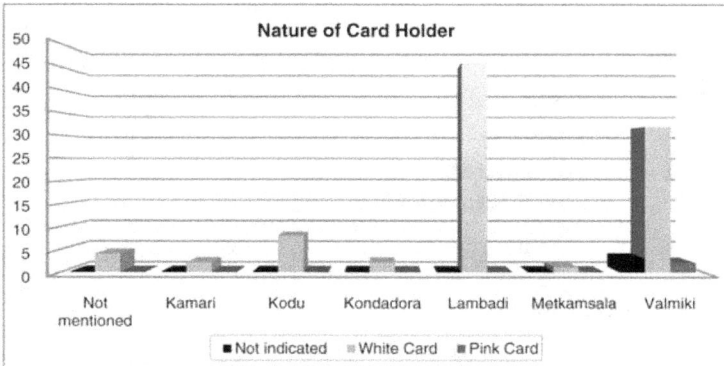

Fig. 3.11: Nature of the Ration Card Held by the Various Tribal

Source: Primary survey.

As shown in the above chart, white cardholders have the maximum frequency (94 of 100 people sampled) i.e. almost all the tribal prefer a white card as compared to a pink card, which is hardly preferred by anybody (2 of the 100 people sampled).

In the Kamari sub-caste, all respondents were white card holders. In the Kodu sub-caste, all the respondents were white card holders. In the Konda Dora sub-caste, all the respondents were white card holders. In the Lambadi sub-caste, all the respondents were white card holders. In the Metkamsala sub-caste, all the respondents were white card holders. In the Valmiki sub-caste, 8.1 percent of the respondents did not mention the type of cards they hold, 86.5 percent of the respondents were white card holders and 5.4 percent were pink card holders.

Nature of Land Holdings among Tribal Population: 51 percent of the people responded that they do not hold a land of their own, while 48 percent of the people responded that they hold a land of their own.

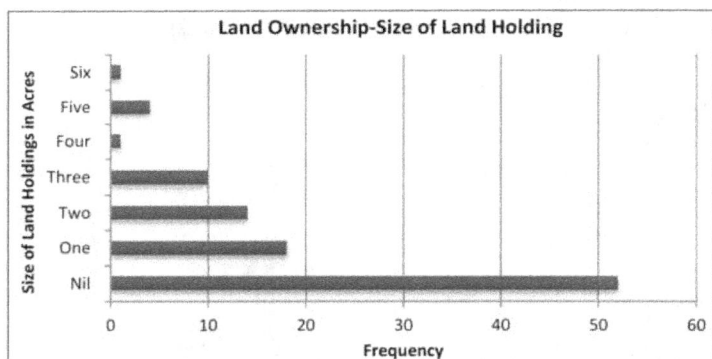

Fig. 3.12: Land Ownership—Size of Land Holdings in Acres

Source: Primary survey.

As shown in the above bar chart majority of the tribal either does not hold any land or holds a one-acre land. There was a higher concentration of people holding five-acre land than the people holding four or six acres. Almost 44 percent of tribe population surveyed hold no ownership over land. The ownership of tribe population over 1, 2 and 3 acres of land is 18 percent, 14 percent and 10 percent respectively.

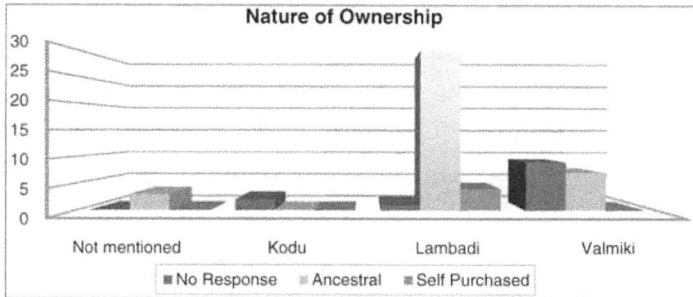

Fig. 3.13: Land Ownership—Nature of Ownership

Source: Primary survey.

The tribal have acquired land holding primarily through ancestral property (40 percent) while very a small fraction (4 percent) of the tribal have acquired land holdings through self- purchases. In the Kodu sub-caste, the respondents did not mention the nature of the ownership of the land under their possession. In the Lambadi sub-caste, 2.9 percent did not mention the nature of ownership, 85.7 percent owned ancestral land and 11.4 percent owned land which was purchased by them. In the Valmiki sub-caste, 56.3 percent of the respondents did not mention the nature of ownership and 43.7 percent owned ancestral property.

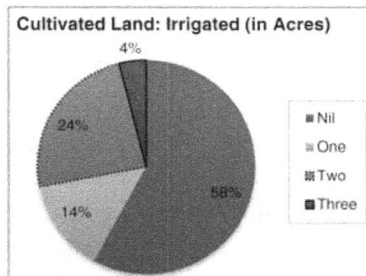

Fig. 3.14: Cultivated Land—Irrigated in Acres

Source: Primary survey.

As shown in the above bar chart, a vast share of land in these villages is uncultivated. Out of the hundred people sampled, there were 24 people who cultivated two acres of land but there were only 14 people who cultivated only one acre of land. 58 percent of the tribal population surveyed did not irrigate any land.

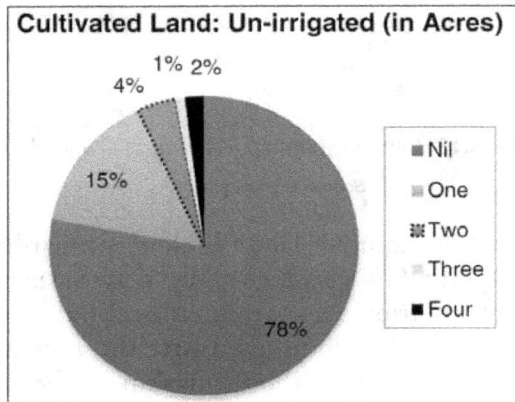

Fig. 3.15: Cultivated Land—Un-Irrigated in Acres

Source: Primary survey.

About thirty-four acres of land (22 percent) cultivated was left un-irrigated. There were seventy-eight people who had zero-acre of land left un-irrigated. As indicated in the above charts almost all (98 percent) the tribal have cultivated their land, which shows their high dependence on agriculture for livelihood and sustenance.

Land Actually in Possession of STs: According to the field study 97 out of every 100 tribal do not have any land held in their possession. Only 3 out of every 100 tribal actually have land held in their possession. In other words 97 out of every 100 people do not have any kind of a leased out land. 3 out of every 100 tribal have one-acre of leased out land.

Leased-in Land: The results of the survey indicate that 98 out of every 100 tribal do not have any leased-in land. Only 2 out of the 100 tribal sampled have three-acres of leased in land.

Pledged/Unpledged Land: A very high component of the tribal (96 percent) has not pledged their land as a guarantee. Only 3 percent of the people have pledged their land as a repayment during failure of debts.

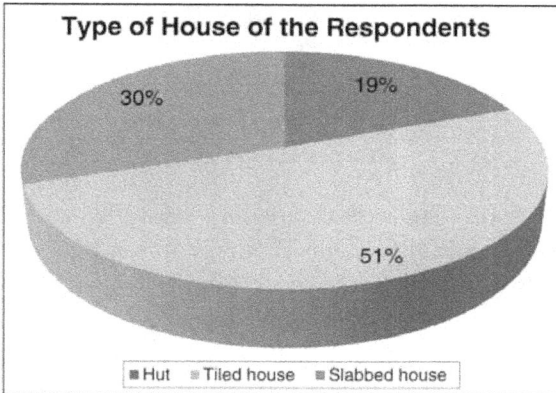

Fig. 3.16: House—Type of the House

Source: Primary survey.

During the survey 90 percent of the people replied that they own a permanent house whereas only 10 percent replied that they own a temporary house. The highest component of the tribal owns a tiled house (51 percent) as compared to owning a hut (18 percent). This shows that these people are better as compared to tribal in other states who primarily live in huts. In the Kamari sub-caste, all the respondents' families lived in tiled house. In the Kodu sub-caste, all the respondents' families lived in tiled house. In the Konda Dora sub-caste, all the respondents' families lived in tiled house. In the Lambadi sub-caste, 37 percent lived in huts, 8.7 percent lived in tiled house and 54.3 percent lived in slabbed house. In the Metkamsala sub-caste, all the respondents' families lived in huts. In the Valmiki sub-caste, 2.7 percent lived in huts, 91.9 percent lived in tiled house and 5.4 percent of the respondents' families lived in slabbed house.

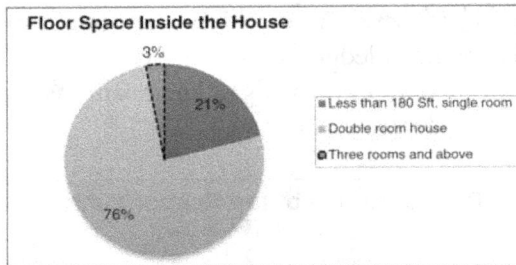

Fig. 3.17: House—Floor Space

Source: Primary survey.

A majority of the tribal live in double room houses (76 percent). Only 3 percent of the people sampled were able to afford a house which has more than two rooms. But at the same time there were a comparatively small fraction of people (21 percent) who live in less than 180 sq. ft. single room house.

Most of the tribal were allotted a house by the government (49 percent). A very small component of tribal sampled has inherited a house through ancestral property (15 percent). 28 percent of the respondents inherit self-built or purchased accommodations whereas 8 percent of them did not have any house allotted to them.

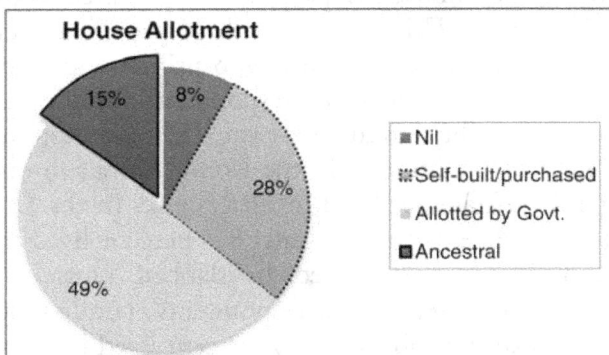

Fig. 3.18: Allotment of the Constructed House

Source: Primary survey.

Facilities Indide the Houses of Respondents (State Electricity and Sanitation): As shown in the above bar chart, around 77 people of the 100 sampled responded that they receive government electricity whereas only 2 people replied that they received proper sanitation facilities.

Awareness Regarding Government Schemes: Though 60 percent of the sampled tribal availed the IKP (Indra Kranthi Patham) pension and insurance scheme for SHG women, 40 percent of the tribal had availed no scheme at any time.

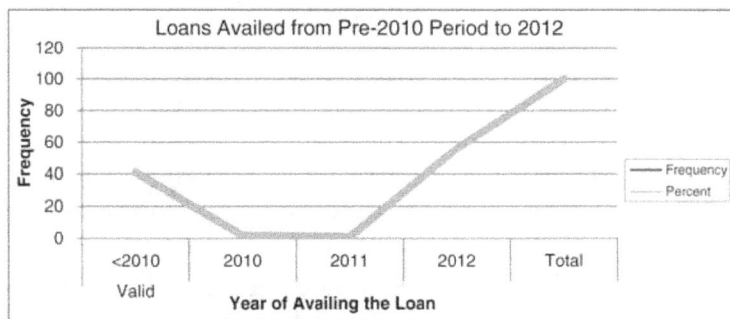

Fig. 3.19: Loans Availed in Various Years

Source: Primary survey.

As indicated by the study, 97 percent of people responded that the schemes used were satisfactorily functioning. Only 3 percent of the people felt that the scheme was non-functioning.

As shown in the frequency chart (Figure 3.19), maximum loans have been availed in the year 2012. There have been hardly any loans availed in the previous year or in the year before that.

On an average, the Warangal district tribal residents have a higher institutional indebtedness as compared to the Vishakhapatnam district tribal indebtedness. The above table tells us that (All amount in ₹):

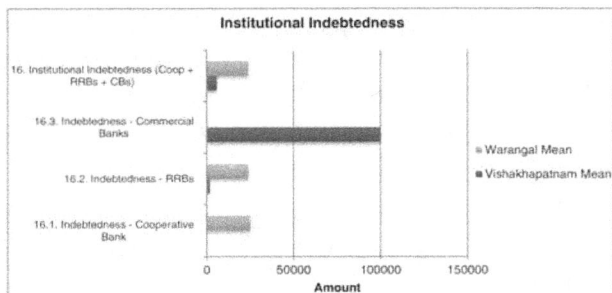

Fig. 3.20: Institutional Indebtedness (Coop + RRBs + CBs)

Source: Primary survey.

- *Vishakhapatnam:* The mean indebtedness to cooperative banks, RRB and commercial banks is 0.00, 1800.00, 100000.00 and respectively. The total mean is 5900.00.
- *Warangal:* The mean indebtedness to cooperative banks, RRB and commercial banks is 25000.00, 24035.71, 0.00 and respectively.
- Therefore the total mean indebtedness to cooperative banks, RRB and commercial banks is 25000.00, 22553.33, 100000.00 and respectively. The total mean is 22127.78.

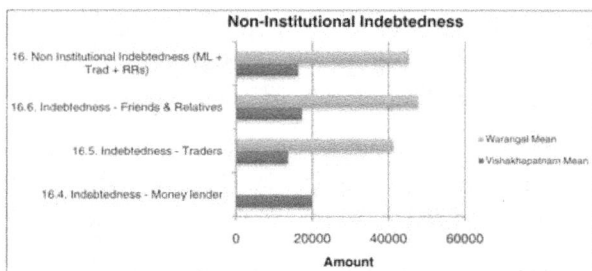

Fig. 3.21: Non-Institutional Indebtedness (ML + Trad + RRs)

Source: Primary survey.

On an average, the Warangal district tribal residents have a higher non-institutional indebtedness as compared to the Vishakhapatnam district tribal residents.

Of the 100 people sampled, 99 people replied that the unemployed family members are not interested in a self-employment venture. One person replied that he is interested in a self-employment venture.

98 percent of the people required no skills to run the schemes. 2 percent of the people required some amount to learn about the schemes.

Discrimination in Entry into Public Places or Participation in Social Events: 51 percent of the tribal sampled replied that there was no discrimination observed either in temple entry or in social functions. However, some felt uneasy and 49 percent of the tribal chose not to respond to this question.

A BRIEF SNAP-SHOT COMPARATIVE STUDY ON CERTAIN IMPORTANT PARAMETERS OF VISHAKHAPATNAM AND WARANGAL DISTRICTS

A comparative study of both the districts—Vishakhapatnam and Warangal based on bivariatetables have been prepared from the survey data collected from sample respondents.

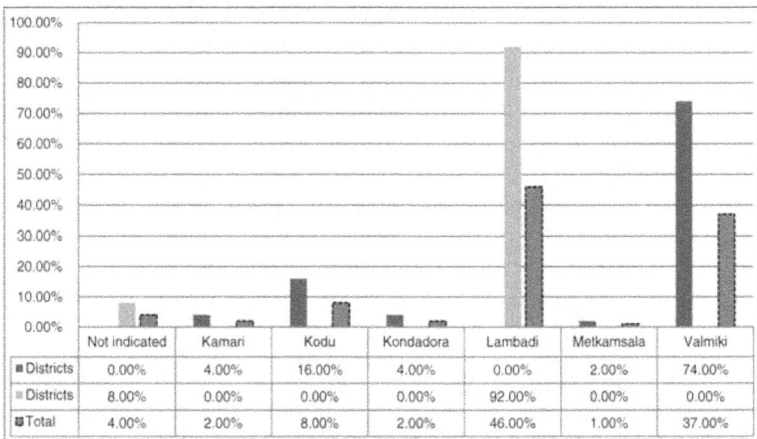

	Not indicated	Kamari	Kodu	Kondadora	Lambadi	Metkamsala	Valmiki
■ Districts	0.00%	4.00%	16.00%	4.00%	0.00%	2.00%	74.00%
▦ Districts	8.00%	0.00%	0.00%	0.00%	92.00%	0.00%	0.00%
▨ Total	4.00%	2.00%	8.00%	2.00%	46.00%	1.00%	37.00%

Fig. 3.22: Sub-Caste Wise Distribution of Respondents among the Districts

- Valmiki is the majority sub-caste in Vishakhapatnam.
- Lambadi is the majority sub-caste in Warangal.
- Metkamsala has relatively the weakest representation in Andhra Pradesh.
- Warangal lacks in caste diversity; Lambadi being the only prevalent caste.
- Vishakhapatnam has representation from a variety of castes.

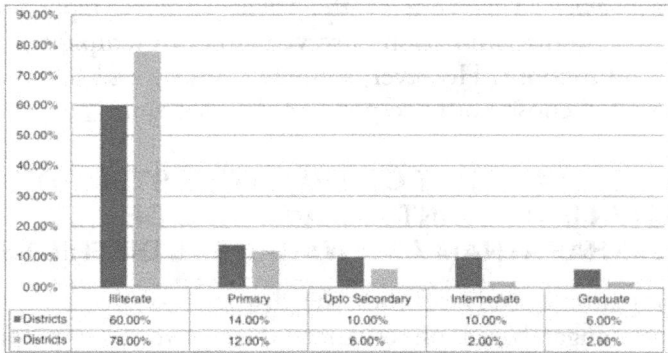

	Illiterate	Primary	Upto Secondary	Intermediate	Graduate
■ Districts	60.00%	14.00%	10.00%	10.00%	6.00%
▪ Districts	78.00%	12.00%	6.00%	2.00%	2.00%

Education wise Distribution of Respondents among the Districts

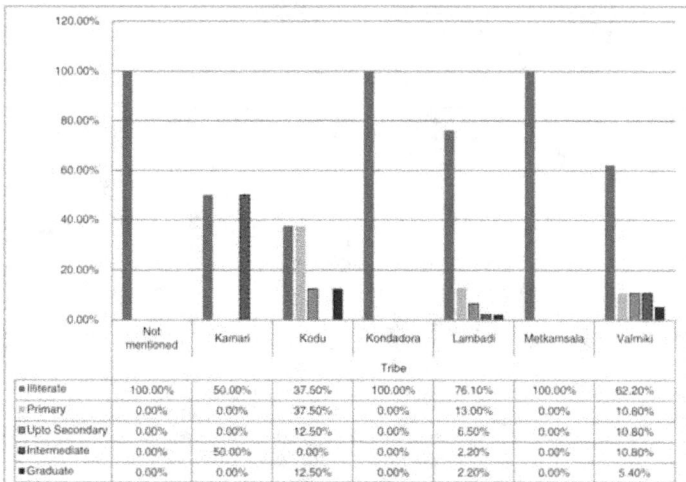

	Not mentioned	Kamari	Kodu	Kondadora	Lambadi	Metkamsala	Valmiki
■ Illiterate	100.00%	50.00%	37.50%	100.00%	76.10%	100.00%	62.20%
▫ Primary	0.00%	0.00%	37.50%	0.00%	13.00%	0.00%	10.80%
▪ Upto Secondary	0.00%	0.00%	12.50%	0.00%	6.50%	0.00%	10.80%
▪ Intermediate	0.00%	50.00%	0.00%	0.00%	2.20%	0.00%	10.80%
■ Graduate	0.00%	0.00%	12.50%	0.00%	2.20%	0.00%	5.40%

Fig. 3.23: Educational Status among the different Tribes

Illiteracy rate is evidently high; being approximately 69 percent:

- Vishakhapatnam is slightly better-off than Warangal with a difference of 18 points.
- Both the districts lack educational facilities.
- Konda Dora and Metkamsala castes suffer from highest illiteracy rate—100 percent.
- Major significance of education is witnessed only in Kodu and Valmiki castes

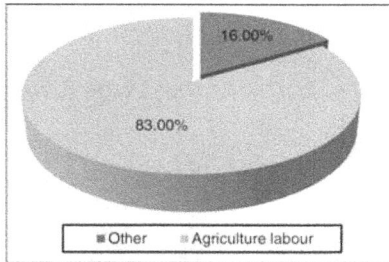

Fig. 3.24: Unorganised—Agriculture Labour among the Districts

- Both the districts depend majorly on agricultural activities (83 percent).
- Most of the production is used domestically.
- Other activities in the unorganized sector include dairy farming.

Tribes Still Depend on Orthodox Ways of Agriculture

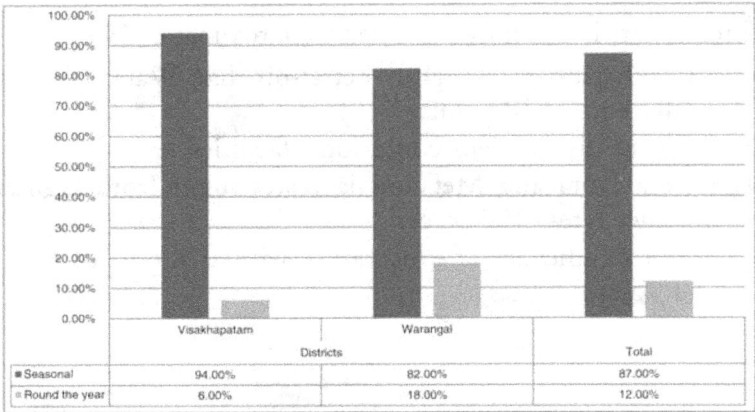

Fig. 3.25: District Wise Wage Earners

	Visakhapatam	Warangal	Total
Seasonal	94.00%	82.00%	87.00%
Round the year	6.00%	18.00%	12.00%

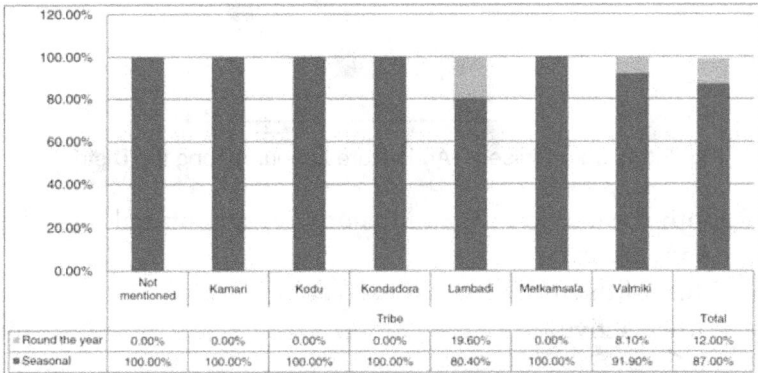

Fig. 3.26: Wage Earner among the Different Tribes

	Not mentioned	Kamari	Kodu	Kondadora	Lambadi	Metkamsala	Valmiki	Total
Round the year	0.00%	0.00%	0.00%	0.00%	19.60%	0.00%	8.10%	12.00%
Seasonal	100.00%	100.00%	100.00%	100.00%	80.40%	100.00%	91.90%	87.00%

- Most families in both the districts do not have a stable source of income; Round the year employment being only 6 percent in Vishakhapatnam and 18 percent in Warangal.
- In totality, about 87 percent of the families depend on seasonal occupations for household finances.
- Only Lambadi and Valmiki castes have a segment that is employed round the year, however, the percentage is very low.

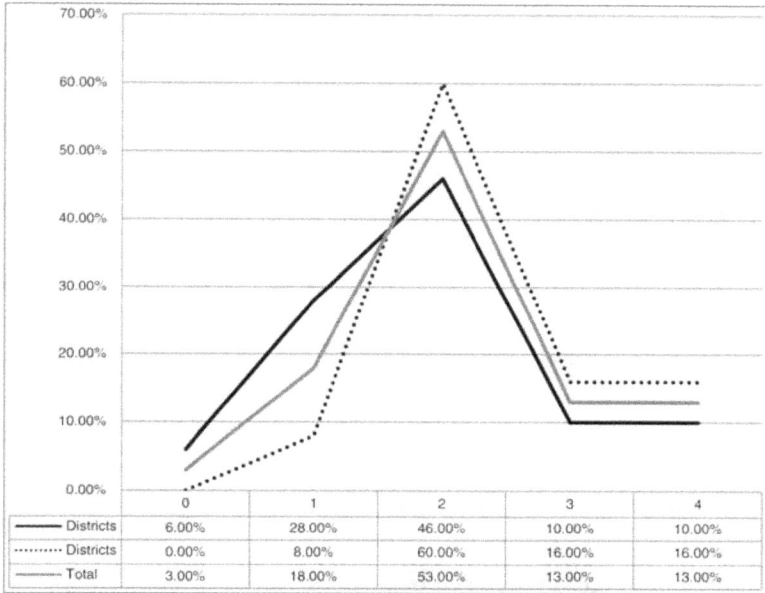

	0	1	2	3	4
——— Districts	6.00%	28.00%	46.00%	10.00%	10.00%
·········· Districts	0.00%	8.00%	60.00%	16.00%	16.00%
——— Total	3.00%	18.00%	53.00%	13.00%	13.00%

Fig. 3.27: Number of Family Members Engaged
in Occupation—Unskilled

- Households mostly depend on both father and mother financially.
- Few households (about 13 percent) also engage 1 or 2 children for added contribution to earnings.
- About 3 percent households still remain unemployed.

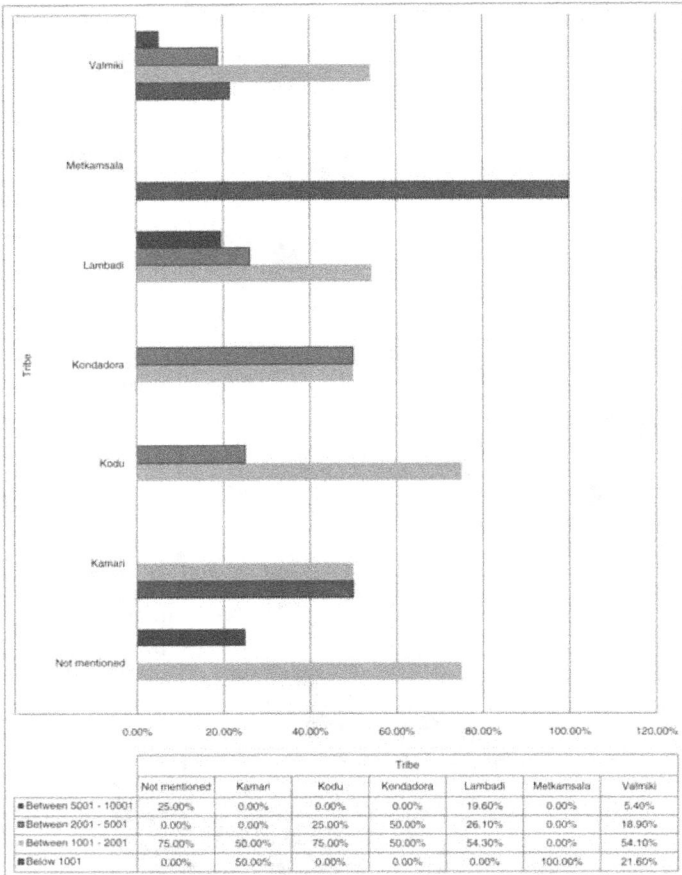

	Tribe						
	Not mentioned	Kamari	Kodu	Kondadora	Lambadi	Metkamsala	Valmiki
■ Between 5001 - 10001	25.00%	0.00%	0.00%	0.00%	19.60%	0.00%	5.40%
▩ Between 2001 - 5001	0.00%	0.00%	25.00%	50.00%	26.10%	0.00%	18.90%
▫ Between 1001 - 2001	75.00%	50.00%	75.00%	50.00%	54.30%	0.00%	54.10%
■ Below 1001	0.00%	50.00%	0.00%	0.00%	0.00%	100.00%	21.60%

Fig. 3.28: Income Levels of the Families among Tribes

- Most families earn ₹ 1001–2001 per month; poverty line being about ₹ 840 according to the Planning Commission.
- The percentage of families earning more than ₹ 5000 per month is only 12 percent.
- The majority income range is ₹ 1001 to ₹ 5001.
- Metkamsala caste lies below the poverty line.
- Only Valmiki and Lambadi castes enjoy decent incomes (between ₹ 5001 – ₹ 10001)

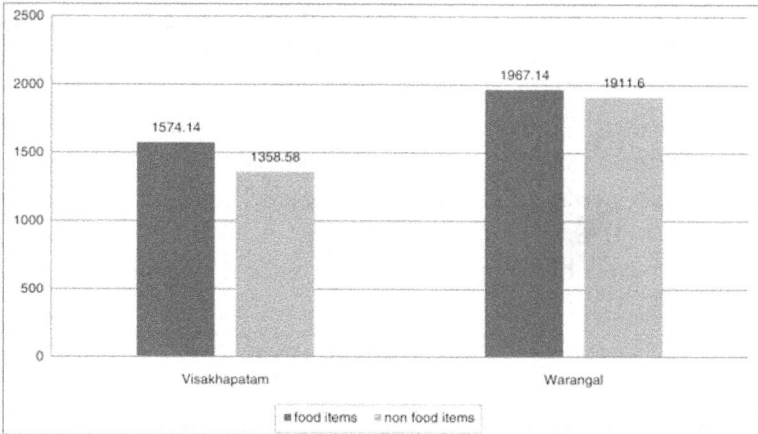

Fig. 3.29: Approximate Monthly Consumption Expenditure on Food and Non-Food Items

- Overall household expenditure is higher in Warangal than in Vishakhapatnam.
- Majority expenditure on food items—"Earn-to-Eat".
- Families prefer a low standard of living due to lack of adequate funds.

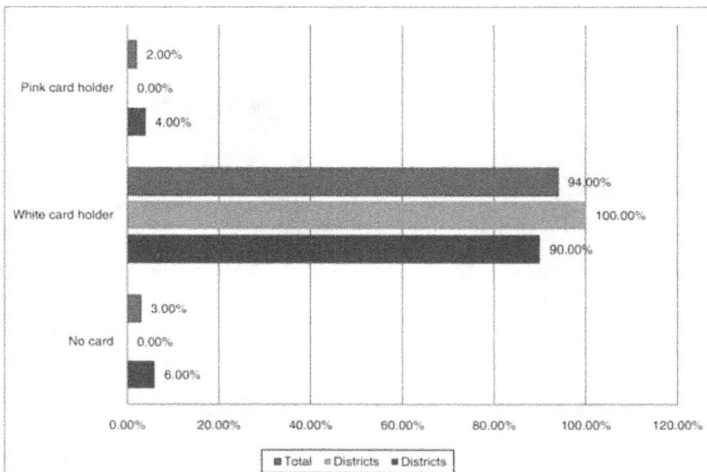

Fig. 3.30: Type of Nature of Ration Card in the Districts

- 100 percent families in Warangal are White-card holders (Income < 11,000); 90 percent belong to this category in Vishakhapatnam.
- In totality, 3 percent of the families still do not have access to ration cards.
- Only 4 percent families are Pink-card holders (Income > ₹ 11,000)
- Good availability of ration card service in Warangal.

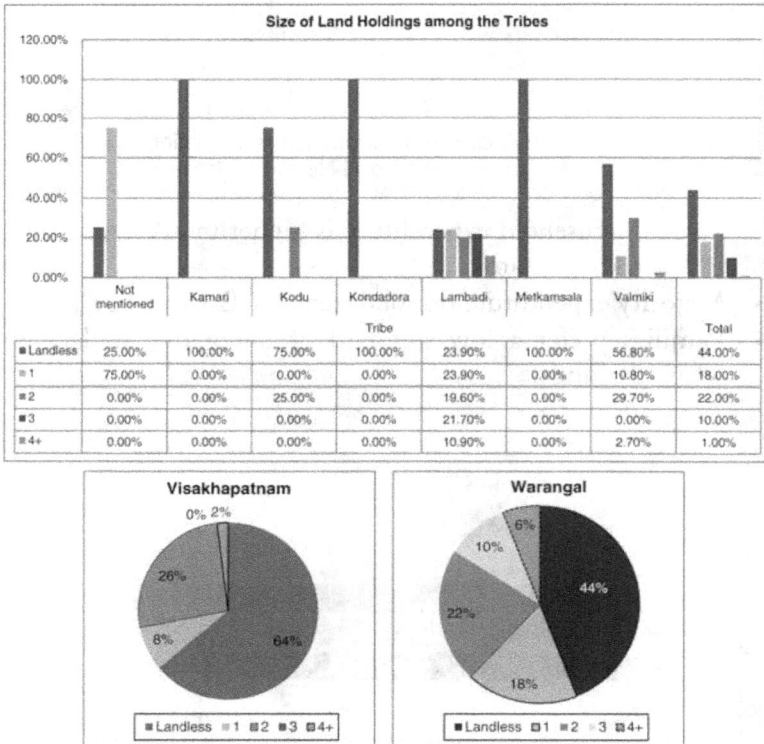

Size of Land Holdings among the Tribes

	Not mentioned	Kamari	Kodu	Kondadora	Lambadi	Metkamsala	Valmiki	Total
Landless	25.00%	100.00%	75.00%	100.00%	23.90%	100.00%	56.80%	44.00%
1	75.00%	0.00%	0.00%	0.00%	23.90%	0.00%	10.80%	18.00%
2	0.00%	0.00%	25.00%	0.00%	19.60%	0.00%	29.70%	22.00%
3	0.00%	0.00%	0.00%	0.00%	21.70%	0.00%	0.00%	10.00%
4+	0.00%	0.00%	0.00%	0.00%	10.90%	0.00%	2.70%	1.00%

Visakhapatnam

0% 2%
26%
8%
64%

Landless 1 2 3 4+

Warangal

6%
10%
44%
22%
18%

Landless 1 2 3 4+

Fig. 3.31

- Majority of the tribal population is landless.
- Kamari, Metkamsala and Konda Dora tribes have no land holdings.

- Few families belonging to Kodu, Lambadi and Valmiki tribes possess 1 to 2 acres of land.

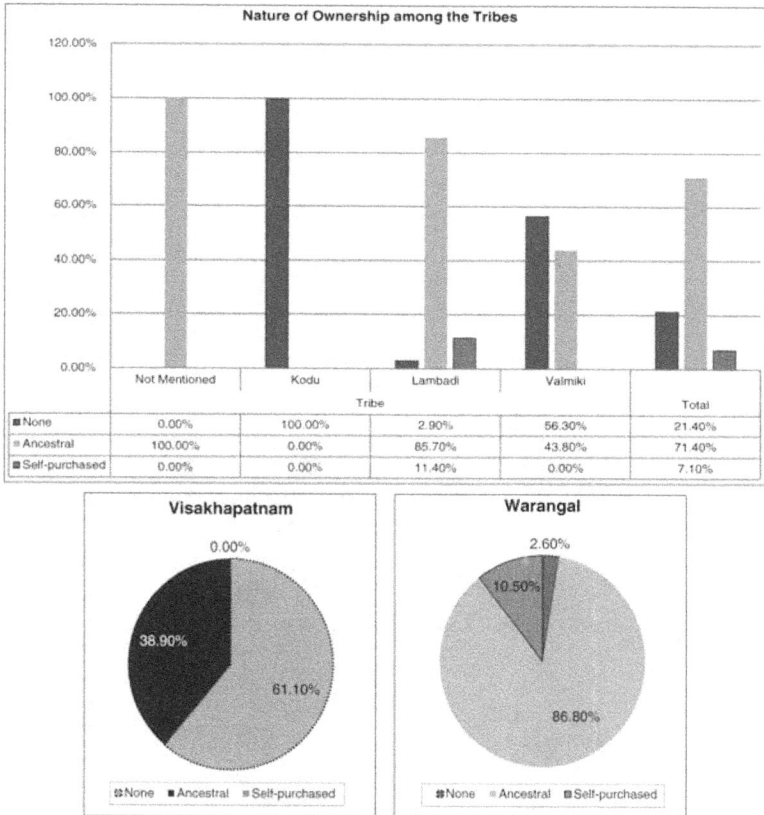

	Not Mentioned	Kodu	Lambadi	Valmiki	Total
▣ None	0.00%	100.00%	2.90%	56.30%	21.40%
▤ Ancestral	100.00%	0.00%	85.70%	43.80%	71.40%
▣ Self-purchased	0.00%	0.00%	11.40%	0.00%	7.10%

Fig. 3.32

- Majority ownership in Warangal is ancestral.
- Most tribes in Vishakhapatnam still do not have any kind of property possession.
- Majority of the Lambadi tribe enjoys ancestral property holdings.
- Kodu tribe lags with no land holdings what-so-ever.
- In totality, property among the tribes is mostly ancestral.

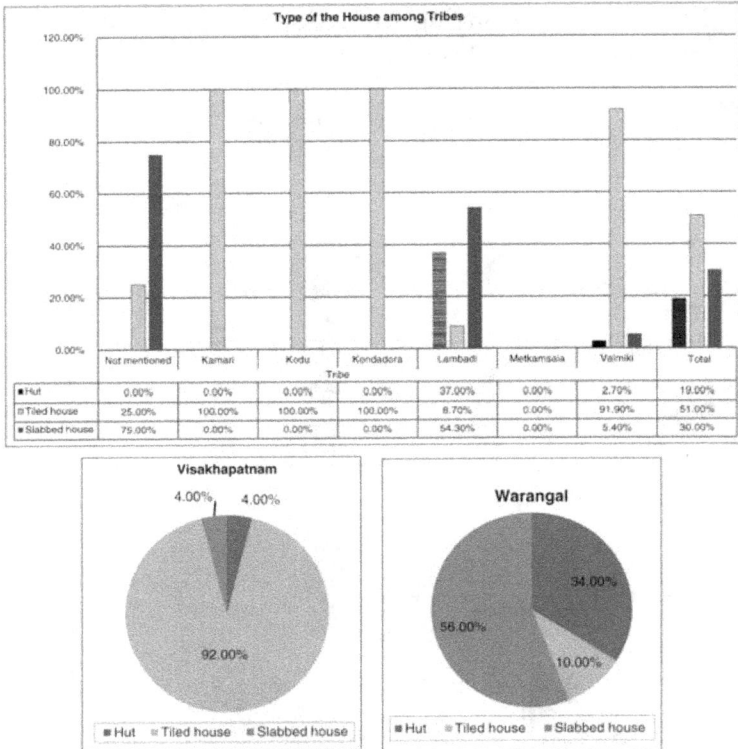

Type of the House among Tribes

Tribe	Not mentioned	Kamari	Kodu	Kondadora	Lambadi	Metkamsaia	Vaimiki	Total
■ Hut	0.00%	0.00%	0.00%	0.00%	37.00%	0.00%	2.70%	19.00%
▤ Tiled house	25.00%	100.00%	100.00%	100.00%	8.70%	0.00%	91.90%	51.00%
■ Slabbed house	75.00%	0.00%	0.00%	0.00%	54.30%	0.00%	5.40%	30.00%

Fig. 3.33

- Majority of the tribal families (about 51 percent) live in tiled houses.

- More than 90 percent of houses in Vishakhapatnam are tiled.
- Majority (about 56 percent) of the families in Warangal live in slabbed houses.
- About one-third of the Lambadi tribe still lives in huts.

Scheduled Tribe in
Dahod District in Gujarat
An Empirical Analysis

The research team visited Dahod district and selected five villages as sample study. Household questionnaires were prepared and personal interaction with the villagers gave us an insight to the problems faced by the tribal and the neglect by the authorities. The following are the findings from such interface from our sample study. Out of 150 respondents, 120 respondents belonged to the Bhil Tribe/Sub-caste, while 30 respondents belonged to Patelia Tribe/Sub-caste. The Patelia is known to be a much higher Tribe/Sub-caste than compared to Bhil. And hence there is huge discrimination and difference between both the Tribes/Sub-castes. They don't even allow cross marriages to take place within one another. All the respondents were selected randomly.

We selected five villages in Dahod District for our survey: Amba, Chilakota, Moti Handi, Nani Handi and Vislanga. Moti Handi and Nani Handi belong to Jhalod Taluka while Amba, Chilakota and Vislanga belong to Limkheda Taluka. We selected 20 percent of respondents out of each village. Dahod District has five Talukas, out of which we selected two Talukas—Jhalod and Limkheda. Out of them 40 percent of the respondents belong to Jhalod Taluka while 60 percent of the respondents belong to Limkheda district. Out of the 150 respondents, 88 (58.67 percent) respondents were male and 62 (41.33 percent) respondents were female.

The below chart (Figure 4.1) denotes the percentage of male and female respondents selected in each of the five villages. Nani Handihad maximum number of male respondents because females in that village were not able to talk or respond to our questions owing to their conventional and traditional constraints—because of the presence of senior male members around. We found the maximum number of female respondents in Vislanga village. The social strata of women in this village seemed much better than rest of the villages selected by us.

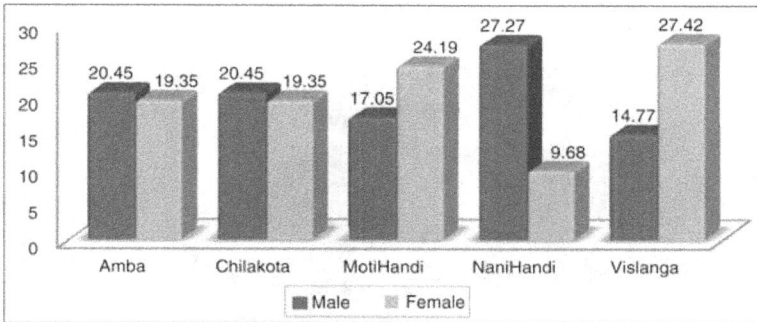

Fig. 4.1: Percentage of Male and Female
Respondents from Sample Villages

Source: Primary survey.

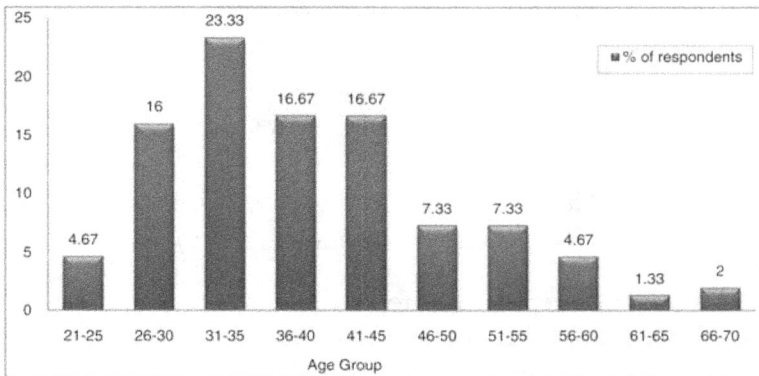

Fig. 4.2: Age Categorization of Respondents

Source: Primary survey.

This chart denotes the age of the respondents randomly selected by us. Maximum number of respondents belonged to the age group of 26–45 years. The number of respondents belonging to the age group of 26–45 years was 109 (72.67 percent). Respondents falling in the age group of 26–45 years appeared to be aware of few of the current Government policies. Respondents falling in the age group of 51–70 were mostly illiterate and had hardly any knowledge of the current Government policies.

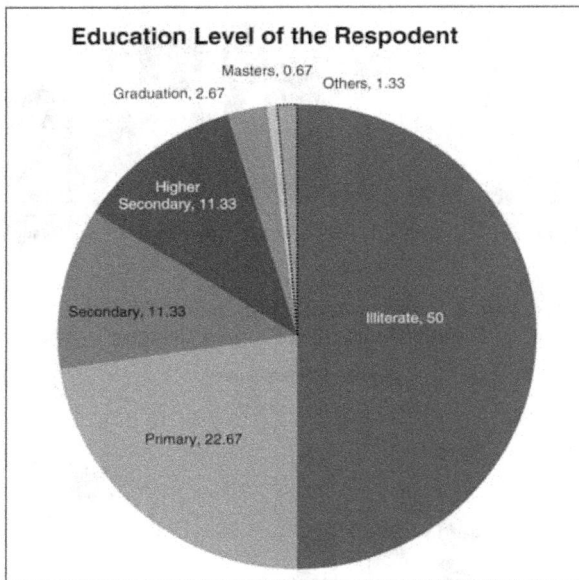

Fig. 4.3: Education Level of Respondent

Source: Primary Survey.

The above table depicts the literacy level of the respondents. It is sad to know that in spite of Gujarat being called a 'developed state', the tribal regions of Gujarat lacks even in basic education. Out of the 150 respondents, we found 50 percent of them illiterate. These results show drastic disparity within the state itself. Out the 150 respondents, 34 (22.67 percent) respondents have undergone primary education, 17 (11.33) respondents have undergone Secondary education,

17 (11.33) respondents have undergone Higher Secondary, while only seven of them pursued Graduation, Masters or other Technical Courses.

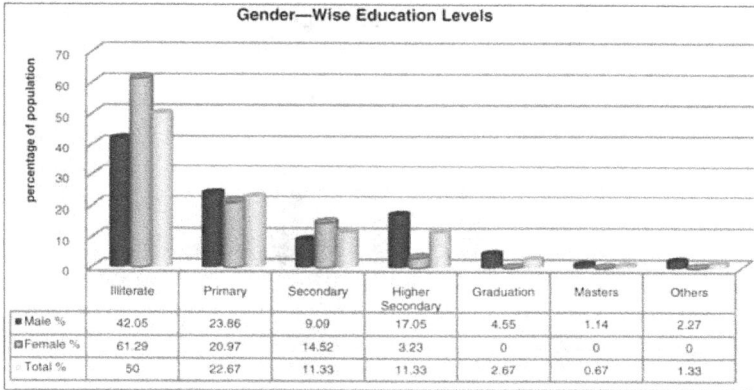

	Illiterate	Primary	Secondary	Higher Secondary	Graduation	Masters	Others
■ Male %	42.05	23.86	9.09	17.05	4.55	1.14	2.27
▣ Female %	61.29	20.97	14.52	3.23	0	0	0
Total %	50	22.67	11.33	11.33	2.67	0.67	1.33

Fig. 4.4: Gender Wise Segregation of Education Levels

Source: Primary Survey.

Above chart denotes the gender-wise segregation of education among the 150 respondents. Out of the 88 male respondents, 37 respondents (42.05 percent) were illiterate; while out of the 62 females, 38 (61.29 percent) were illiterate. 15 respondents of males (17.5 percent) have pursued Higher Secondary while only two respondents of females (3.23 percent) have pursued Higher Secondary. We found seven male respondents who had pursued Graduation, Masters or other Technical Courses, while there was no female respondent to have pursued Graduation, Masters or other Technical Courses.

There is no industry or factory in Dahod and hence all solely depend on agriculture as their source of income. The employment of most of the respondents in Dahod district was agriculture. All of the respondents were land owners. Out of the 150 respondents, 116 respondents (77.33 percent) were depended solely on agriculture. 14 (9.33 percent) of the respondents were those who worked in the field of agriculture (which was seasonal) and also had their income coming from Non Agricultural work, especially construction work. Nine of the respondents were self-employed; eight of them were government employed, while one of the respondents had a private job.

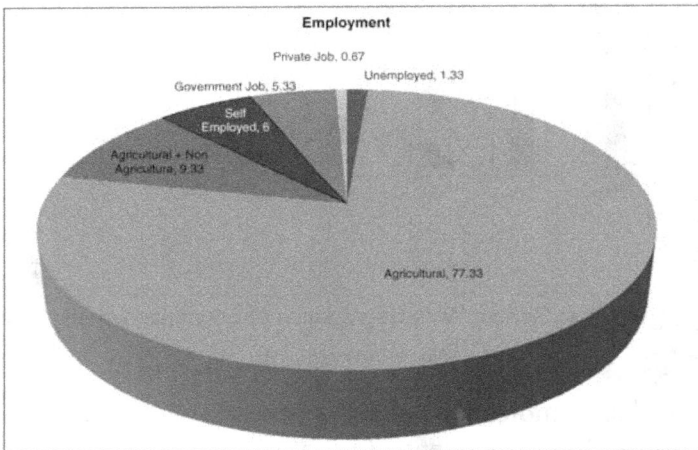

Fig. 4.5: Employment Levels

Source: Primary survey.

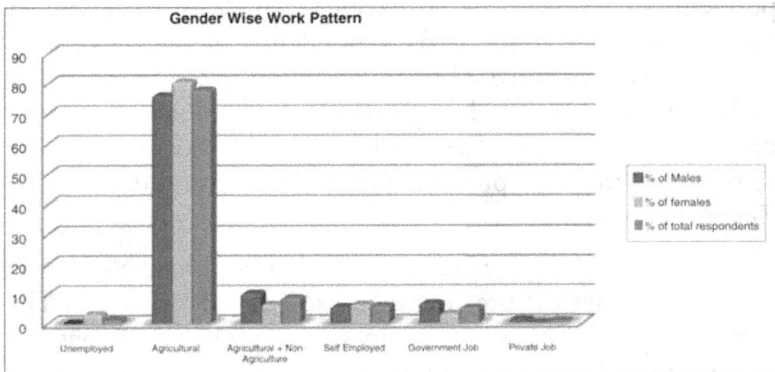

Fig. 4.6: Gender-Wise Work Pattern

Source: Primary survey.

This bar diagram segregates the work pattern of the respondents gender-wise. Out of total respondents two of the females were unemployed. They did not work because they were aged. Both males and females work in the field of agriculture because that is their main source of income. We also found that 67 (76.14 percent) of the male respondents and 50 (80.65 percent) of the female respondents worked solely in the field of agriculture. Nine (10.23 percent) of the males and four (3.23 percent) of the females had their income also coming from non-agricultural work, especially construction work. Five of the males were self-employed and owned electrical or provision or other kinds of shops. Four of the females were self-employed and were associated with Self-Help Group (SHG). The four females had received various kinds of training from SHG such as stitching, embroidery, etc. six of the males and two of the females had a government job. Two females were working in Anganwadi for children.

Disabilities among Scheduled Tribe: Out of the 150 respondents, two of the respondents were partially blind; three of them were handicapped, while one of the respondents was mentally challenged. It is heartening to note that a large percentage did not suffer from any such disabilities.

Immunization and Awareness about Polio, DPT, BCG, Measles: Out of the 150 respondents, 137 (91.33) of them were aware about immunization, while 13 (8.67) of them were not aware of it because they were old and illiterate.

Out of the 150 respondents, 137 (91.33) of them were aware about Polio, while 13 (8.67) of them were not aware of it. All the 137 respondents, who were aware of immunization, were all aware of Polio.

Out of the 150 respondents, very few of them were aware about DPT. Only 32 (21.33) of the respondents were aware about DPT, while 118 (78.67) of them were not aware of it.

Out of the 150 respondents, very few of them were aware about BCG. Only 22 (14.67) of the respondents were aware about BCG, while 128 (85.33) of them were not aware of it.

Out of the 150 sample respondents, very few of them were aware about Measles. Only 28(18.67 percent) of the respondents were aware about Measles, while 122 (81.33 percent) of them were not aware of it.

Child Mortality Rate: From the study it was apparent that out of 150 respondents, 12 of them were such whose child had died before the age of five and 8 of them were such whose child had died before the age of one.

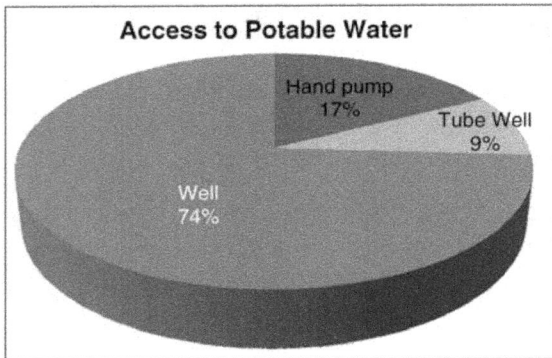

Fig. 4.7: Access to Potable Water

Source: Primary survey.

111 respondents out of the 150, still use well as their primary source for drinking water. 26 of the respondents use hand pump while 13 respondents use tube well.

Benefits of Nutrition Programmes: 96 respondents (64 percent) out of the respondents of the 150 have received the benefits of Nutrition Programmes, while 54 of the respondents (36 percent) have not received any benefits. This shows that the benefits of the nutrition programmes run by the government have not been fully utilized by the village people.

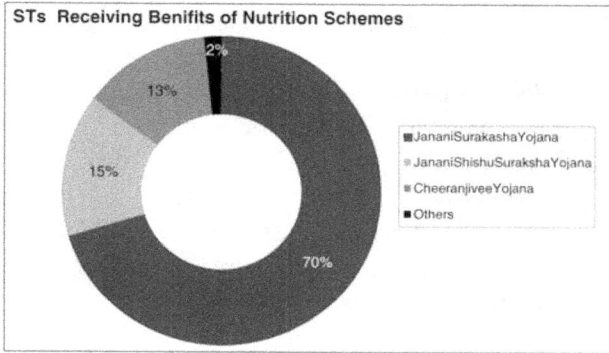

Fig. 4.8: Nutrition Schemes for Mother and Child

Source: Primary survey.

This chart depicts the various Nutrition Schemes for Mother and Child offered by the government. Majority of the respondents, i.e. 38 of them (70.37) have received the benefits of Janani Surakasha Yojana. Most of them are not aware that which Yojana provided them what benefit, however they were aware of the benefits received. Janani Surakasha Yojana fund is provided by National Rural Health Mission and is provided to people Below Poverty Line. Under this scheme, a pregnant lady is taken to the hospital in a 108 ambulance and is provided ₹ 700 cash after the delivery.

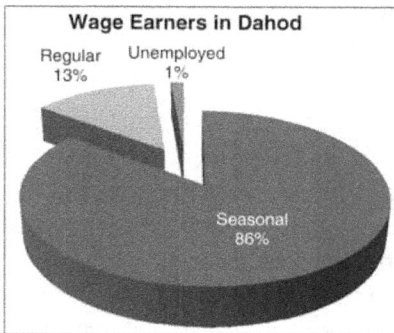

Fig. 4.9: Wage Earners in Dahod

Source: Primary survey.

Majority of the village people depend on agriculture for earning their wages and as agriculture is seasonal, 128 respondents (85.33 percent) fall under the category of earning seasonal wages. Majority of respondents, who pursued non-agricultural work along with agriculture, also fell in the category of seasonal wage earners because non-agricultural work like construction work is also seasonal. Those who are self-employed, have government jobs or private jobs, fall under the category of earning regular wages.

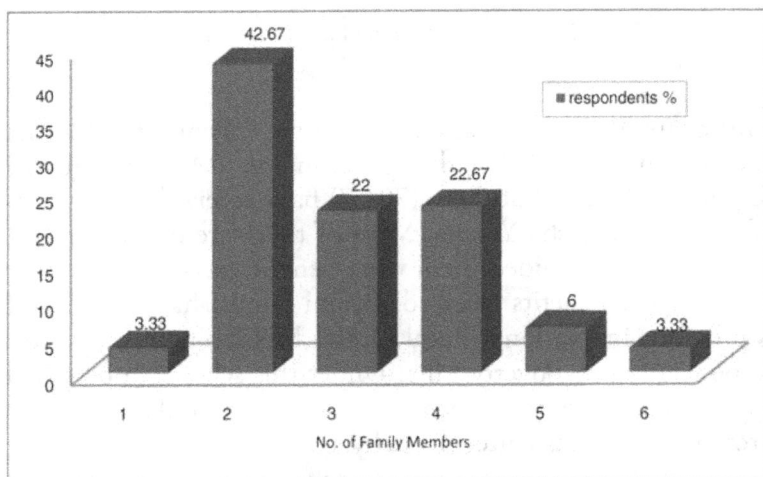

Fig. 4.10: Family Members in Various Occupations
Source: Primary survey.

Out of the 150 respondents, 64 respondents were such who had two members working in their family. 34 respondents had four members working in their family, 33 had three members working in their family, nine of them had five members working in their family, and five of them had six members working in their family. Rest five of the respondents had only one member working in their family. In the latter families, two of them were widows and stayed alone, while rest three stayed in nuclear families.

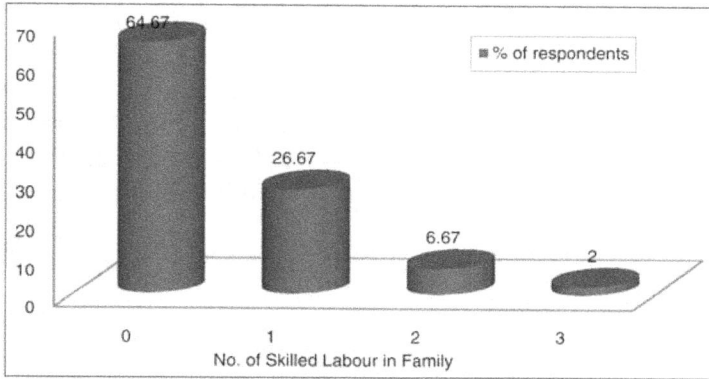

Fig. 4.11: Percentage of Skilled Labours
in the Family Engaged in Occupation

Source: Primary survey.

Out of the 150 respondents surveyed, 97 of them did not have any skilled workers in their families because they mostly depended only on agriculture. 40 of the respondents had one skilled worker in their family, while 10 of the respondents had two skilled workers in their family. There were very few such respondents who had three skilled workers in their families.

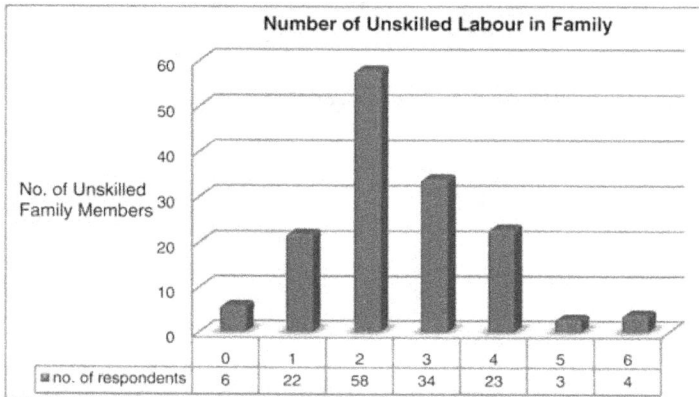

Fig. 4.12: Number of Unskilled Member in the
Family Engaged in Occupation

Source: Primary survey.

The above chart denotes the number of unskilled members in each family. Six of the respondents were such that they had no such family members who were engaged in occupation and yet were unskilled. 58 respondents were such who had at least two such family members who were engaged in occupation, but were unskilled. Most of them were occupied in agriculture.

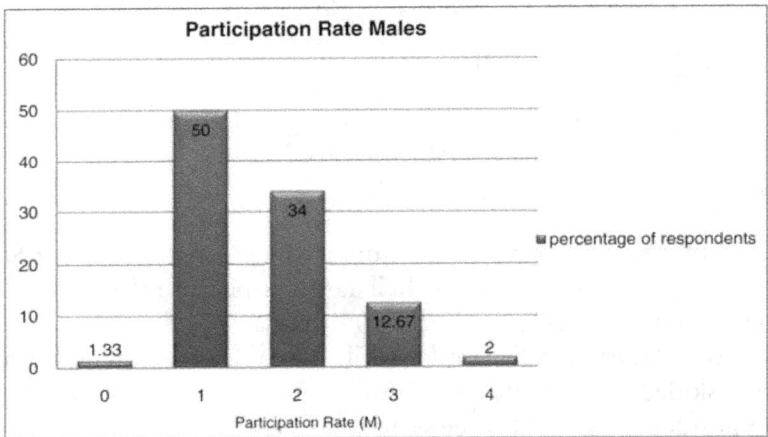

Fig. 4.13: Participation Rate Males

Source: Primary survey.

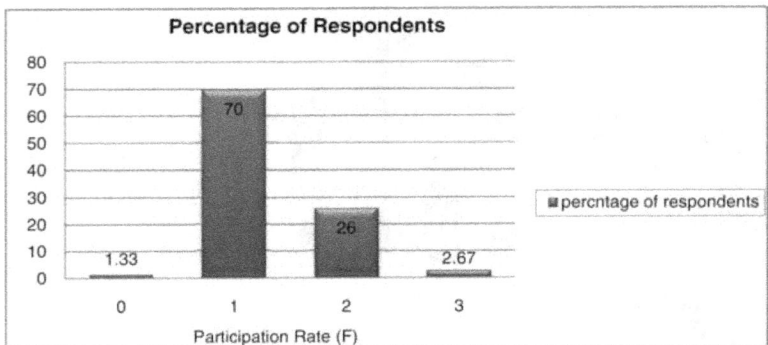

Fig. 4.14: Participation Rate Females

Source: Primary survey.

Out of our sample respondents, two of them had no male members working in their family since as mentioned earlier, these families had only widows. 75 of the respondents had one male working in their family, while 51 of the respondents had two males working in their family.

From the above chart two of the families had no females working in their family as these were widows and were not working at all but dependent on sons. 105 (70 percent) of the respondents had one female working in their family, mostly working in agriculture and construction. 39 of the respondents had two females working in their family, while four of the respondents had three female working members in their family.

Work Participation Rate among Children: The primary survey depicts the participation rate of children in occupation in the family. Out of the 150 respondents, only four of them had such children who had participated in occupation. These children accompanied their parents in construction work. The age of these children was between 11 and 14.

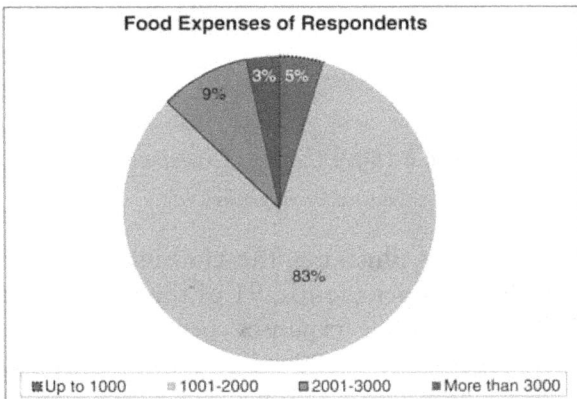

Food Expenses of Respondents

3% 5%
9%
83%

Up to 1000   1001-2000   2001-3000   More than 3000

Fig. 4.15(a): Food Expenses, Clothing, Education, Electricity, Health and Miscellaneous

Source: Primary survey.

We have divided the expenses of our respondents in six categories: Food, Clothing, Education, Electricity, Health, and other expenses. The above pie chart illustrates the food expenses of our respondents' families per month. 124 (82.67 percent) of the respondents spend ₹ 1001–2000 on food per year. Because of their main source of income being agriculture, quite a lot of food expense is reduced because they can use a lot of food items grown by themselves and do not even have to buy milk because they have cattle at their house. Only those respondents who have a higher income or who have a large joint family have an expenditure of more than ₹ 2000 and above per month.

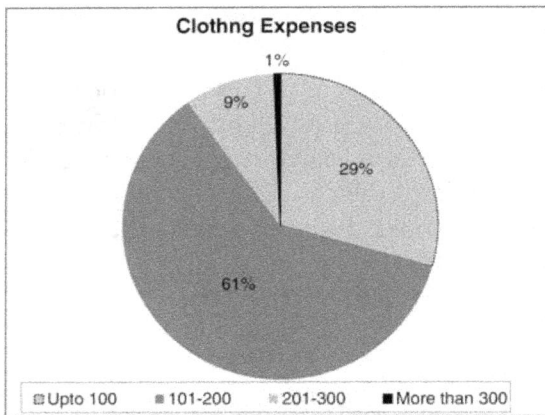

Fig. 4.15(b): Clothing Expenses

Source: Primary survey.

The above pie chart illustrates the clothing expenses of our respondents' families per month. 91 of the respondents spend ₹ 101–200 on clothing expenses per month. 44 of the respondents spend up to ₹ 100 on clothing per month. 14 of the respondents have larger families and hence spend around ₹ 201–300 per month as clothing expenses. One of the respondents, whose monthly income was high compared to others, spent more than ₹ 300.

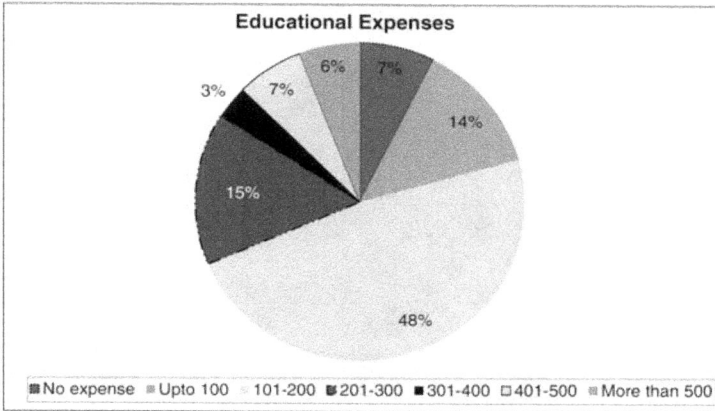

Fig. 4.15(c): Education Expenses

Source: Primary survey.

The above pie chart illustrates the education expenses of our respondents' families per month. 11 of the respondents had no one going to school and hence had no education expense. 72 of the respondents spent ₹ 101–200 as education expenses per month. 20 of the respondents spent up to ₹ 100, while 23 of the respondents spent ₹ 201–300 as education expense per month. Majority of the respondents falling in these categories have their children studying in primary and secondary classes and hence the expenditure is less. They also mostly study in government schools. 10 of the respondents spend ₹ 401–500 and five of the respondents spend ₹ 301–400. Both these categories have children studying either in higher secondary or college. Nine of the respondents have to spend more than ₹ 500 because their children also go for tuitions.

We found that education expenses are much higher than rest of the expenses, followed by food expense, because the village people today have become wiser and understand that if they allow their children study, it will help them to come above the vicious circle of poverty.

Electricity Expenses

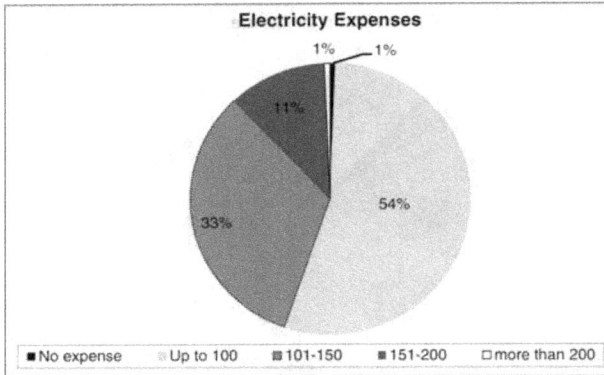

1%   1%

11%

33%   54%

■No expense   Up to 100   ■101-150   ■151-200   □more than 200

Fig. 4.15(d): Electricity Expenses

Source: Primary survey.

The above pie chart illustrates the electricity expenses of our respondents' families per month. One of the respondents, a widow, had no electricity in her house, and hence had no electricity expenses. 82 of the respondents spent up to ₹ 100 on electricity per month, while only one respondent spent more than ₹ 200 per month as electricity expense. Most of the villages face power cuts and do not have electricity all through the day.

Health Expenses

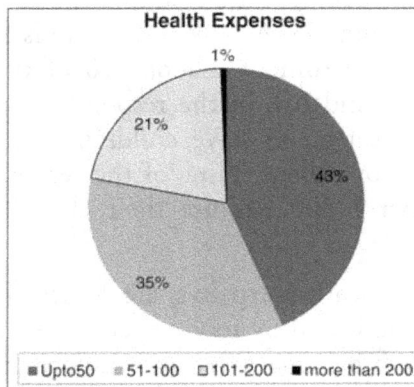

1%

21%

43%

35%

■Upto50   ■51-100   □101-200   ■more than 200

Fig. 4.15(e): Health

Source: Primary survey.

The (Figure 4.15(e)) pie diagram illustrates the heath expenses of our respondents' families. We have taken out an average of their yearly health expenses in order to find out the per month expense. 65 of the respondents spent up to ₹ 50 per month as health expense and most of them visit civil or government hospitals. 52 of the respondents spend ₹ 51–101, while only one respondent spends more than ₹ 200 as health expense per month.

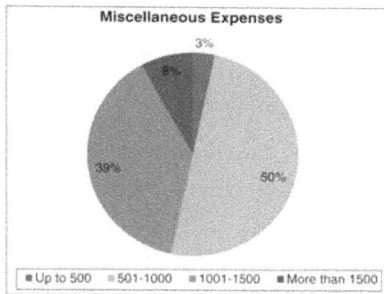

Fig. 4.15(f): Miscellaneous Expenses

Source: Primary survey.

The above figure illustrates the other miscellaneous expenses of our respondents' families, which includes transportation, social expense, mobile bills, entertainment expense, liquor, tobacco, etc. 75 (50 percent) of the respondents spend ₹ 501–1000 monthly on these expenses. 12 of the respondents have a higher income compared to others and hence spend more than ₹ 1500 monthly on other expense.

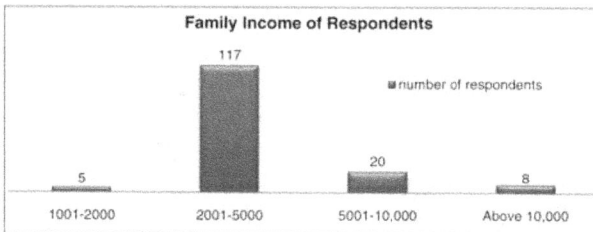

Fig. 4.16: Family Income

Source: Primary survey.

The bar diagram in Figure 4.16 illustrates the family income of our respondents. We have taken out an average of their yearly family income in order to find out the per month family income. Out of the 150 respondents, 117 fall under the category of income between ₹ 2001–5000 and most of them depend on agriculture as their primary source of income. Only five respondents have an income of ₹ 1000–2000. 20 respondents have an income of ₹ 5001–10,000 while eight of them have an income above ₹ 10,000. Most of the respondents having an income above ₹ 10,000 have a government job.

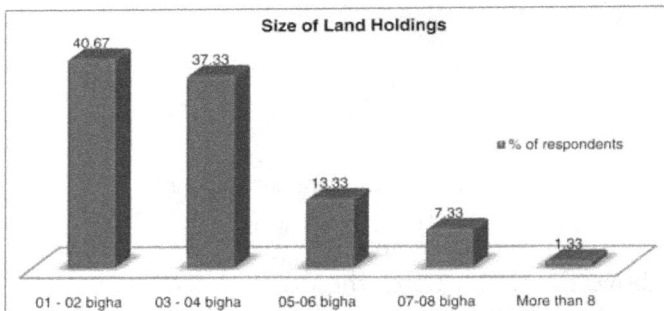

Fig. 4.17: Size of Land Holdings

Source: Primary survey.

Almost all the people residing in Dahod district have land of their own. 61 (40.67 percent) respondents out of the 150 respondents were those whose family had one to two Bighas of land. 56 (37.33 percent) of them had 3–4 Bighas of land, while only two had more than eight Bighas of land. This signifies that 117 respondents had one to four Bighas of land. The female respondents did not have lands on their names, and instead had lands on their husband's name because most of the lands are ancestral properties.

Nature of Land Ownership: None of the respondents had any self-purchased or government-provided properties. All the 150 respondents had ancestral properties which had been handed to them by legacy.

The above bar diagram shows that out of the 150 respondents, 78 of them had 1–2 Bigha of irrigated land. Whereas 56 respondents had 3–4 Bigha of irrigated land, 14 respondents had 5–6 Bigha of irrigated land. Only two of the respondents had a larger 7–8 Bigha of irrigated land. None of the respondents had more than eight Bigha of irrigated land.

Out of the 150 respondents, 45 of them had one to two Bigha of non-irrigated land, 10 of the respondents had three to four Bigha of non-irrigated land and two of the respondents had five to six Bigha of non-irrigated land. None of the respondents had seven or more than seven Bigha of non-irrigated land.

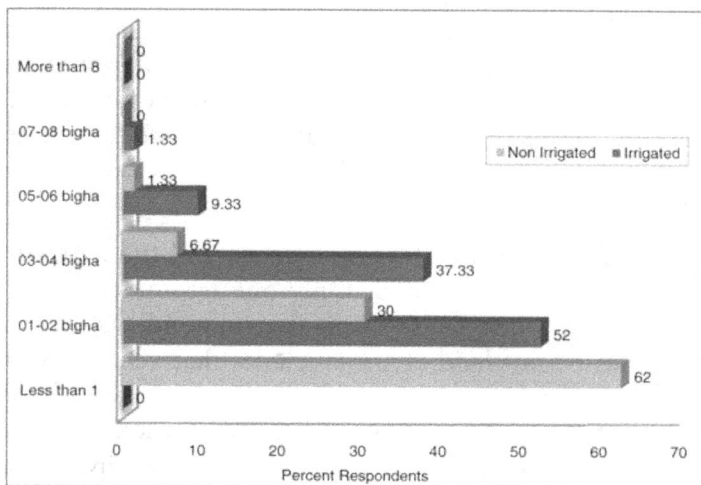

Fig. 4.18: Irrigated and Non-Irrigated Land

Source: Primary survey.

It is a positive indication shown by the above table which depicts that the respondents had more of irrigated land in comparison to non-irrigated land.

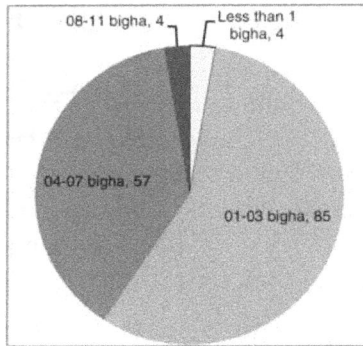

Fig. 4.19: Actual Land in Possession

Source: Primary Survey.

Out of the 150 respondents, 85 (56.67 percent) of them had one to three Bigha of actual land in possession, while 57 (38.00 percent) of the respondents had four to seven Bigha of actual land in possession. Four respondents had less than one Bigha of actual land in possession and rest four respondents had eight to eleven Bigha of actual land in possession. The actual land means the amount of land the respondents possess that they utilize for farming, which excludes leased out land and includes leased in land.

Leased out Land: Of the 150 respondents, 144 (96 percent) of them had no leased out land. Only one respondent had 0.5 Bigha of leased out land, while five respondents had one Bigha of leased out land. This concludes that very few of the tribal have any leased out land. Only those who have a government or private jobs are the ones who lease out their lands. They cultivate their own meagre land for their livelihood.

Leased in Land: From the primary survey it was found that out of the 150 respondents, 132 (88 percent) of them had no leased in land with them. 13 of the respondents had one Bigha of leased in land with them, one respondent had 0.5 Bigha of leased in land, while four of the respondents had two Bigha of leased in land with them.

Nature of Housing: Almost all the respondents had permanent houses, mostly inherited from their ancestors or made by them with funding received from government. Only one of the respondents lived in a temporary rented house. Out of the 150 respondents, 117 (78 percent) of them lived in a Kachcha (mud) houses, while 27 (18 percent) of them lived in a Pakka (bricks) house while 6 (4 percent) of the respondents lived in thatched huts.

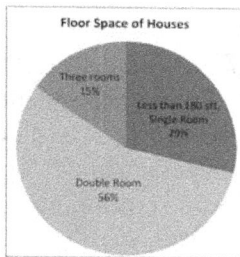

Fig. 4.20: Dimensions of the Houses

Source: Primary survey.

According to the primary survey 84 (56 percent) of the respondents lived in a double room house and 43 of the respondents lived in a single room house, measuring less than 180 sq. ft. 23 of the respondents lived in a house with three rooms. The dimensions reveal that accommodation is very small and little space for a large family. Most of the men sleep outside under the sky.

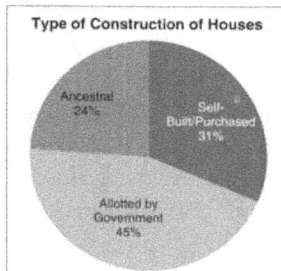

Fig. 4.21: House Construction

Source: Primary survey.

Out of the 150 respondents, 67 of the respondents had been allotted funds by government under the Indira Awas Yojna (IAY) and Sardar Patel Awas Yojana (SPAY) for house construction. 47 of the respondents had self-built houses reason being that today most of the respondents have separated and begun settling in as nuclear families. Hence they had the need to build a new house. 36 of the respondents still live in their ancestral properties.

Provision of Sanitation and Electricity: 122 (81.33 percent) of the respondents out of the 150 had toilet facility within their premises, however, 28 of the respondents did not have toilet facility within their premises. It is sad to know that these people still lack in having even the basic amenities.149 of the respondents out of the 150 respondents had electricity at their homes. Only one respondent, who is a widow and stays alone, did not have electricity at her home. The villages face power cuts and do not have electricity throughout the day.

Benefits from Government Policies: by the field survey we found that 87 respondents out of the 150 have received some form of economic benefit from government, while 63 of the respondents have not received any kind of economic benefit from government. This is still a very large number who are deprived from any economic inclusion from the efforts of the government.

Government Schemes and Programmes

The state government and central government both have brought out several schemes and programmes for the tribal, out of which three Yojanas have benefited most of the people of Dahod district: Indira Awas Yojana (IAY), Sardar Patel Awas Yojana (SPAY) and Vanbandhu Kalyan Yojana. However we found that none of the places surveyed by us for this project received any benefit out of the most recent schemes like the SJSRY, PMRY and NREGA.

Vandhanu Kalyan Yojana: Only 38 of the respondents out of the 150 respondents had received the benefits of Vanbandhu Kalyan Yojana, 112 of the respondents did not receive any benefits out of the Vanbandhu Kalyan Yojana. The respondents who received the benefits under the Vanbandhu Kalyan Yojana received facilities like: cycles, buffaloes, funding for agricultural equipment and machinery, seeds for agricultural farming, barbed wires for fencing, etc. The respondents knew about the Vanbandhu Kalyan Yojana as the Vaadi Yojana.

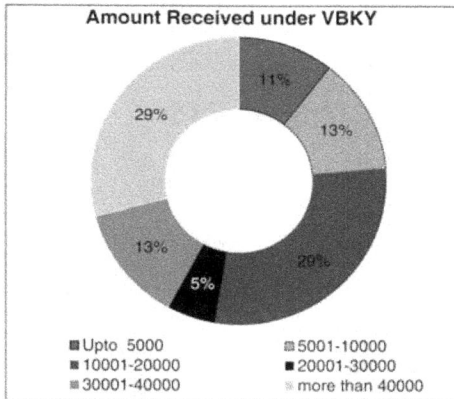

Fig. 4.22: Amount Received under Vanbandhu Kalyan Yojna

Source: Primary survey.

Under the Vanbandhu Kalyan Yojana, four out of the 38 respondents received benefits of up to ₹ 5000 and five of the respondents received benefits of ₹ 5001–10,000, which included cycle, seeds for farming and smaller equipment. 11 of the respondents received benefits of ₹ 10001–20000, while two of the respondents received benefits of ₹ 20001–30000— these benefits included subsidy for buying buffaloes and agricultural equipment. Five of the respondents received benefits of ₹ 30001–40000, while 11 of them received more than ₹ 40000—these benefits included funding for buying

barbed wires for fencing and subsidy for buying larger
agricultural equipment. All these facilities were received
between 2009–10 and 2011–12.

Indira Awas Yojana: Under the Indira Awas Yojana only 27
respondents received benefits. The benefits included funding
received for building houses. Only people living Below
Poverty Line receive the benefits of this scheme and a person
can receive this benefit once in a lifetime, that too only if he
or she has no property on his or her name till then. For a
scheme which claims to provide housing for all this is a very
small attempt.

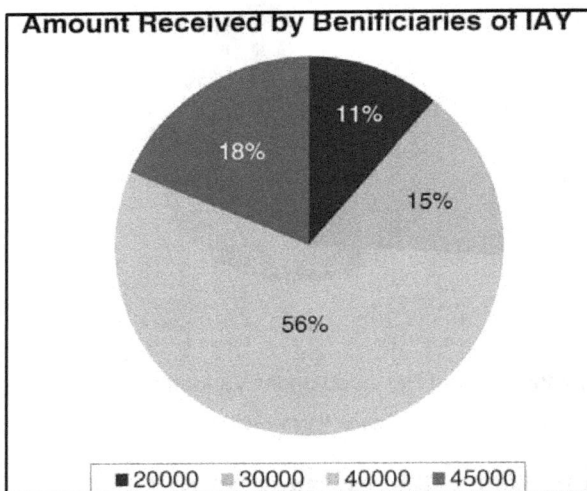

Fig. 4.23: Amount received by the Beneficiaries of Indira Awas Yojna

Source: Primary survey.

Three respondents received ₹ 20,000 under the Indira Awas
Yojana; 4 of the respondents received ₹ 30,000. People are
given ₹ 20,000 or ₹ 30,000 in the beginning in the first
round, the rest is given after inspection and confirmation that
the respondents have really begun construction. Rest of the
amount is given in the second/final round.

15 of the respondents received ₹ 40000 under the Indira Awas Yojana while five of the respondents received ₹ 45000. Those beneficiaries, who received ₹ 40000 or more, have received the entire amount and will not be eligible for any other amount further.

Sardar Patel Awas Yojana: From the survey it was apparent that 40 of the respondents out of the 150 sample respondents have received benefits under the Sardar Patel Awas Yojana. An amount of ₹ 45000 is given under this scheme and like Indira Awas Yojna, only those people living below Poverty Line receive the benefits of this scheme. It is heartening to note however, that there are several such people who were earlier Below Poverty Line cardholders when they had received this benefit, but most of them are now are better off and are above Poverty Line cardholders.

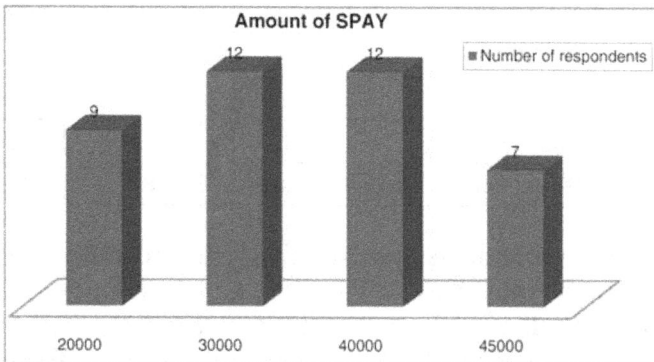

Fig. 4.24: Amount Received by Beneficiaries under this Scheme

Source: Primary survey.

Similar to earlier housing Schemes, while nine respondents received ₹ 20000 under the Sardar Patel Awas Yojana, 12 of the respondents received ₹ 30000. People are given ₹ 20000 or ₹ 30000 in the beginning in the first round, the rest is given after inspection and confirmation that the respondents have really begun construction. Rest of the amount is given in the second/final round. 12 of the respondents received ₹ 40000 under the Sardar Patel Awash Yojana while 7 of the respondents have received ₹ 45000. They have received the entire amount and will not be eligible for any other amount further.

All in all a total of 105 respondents have received the benefits of Indira Awas Yojana (IAY), Sardar Patel Awas Yojana (SPAY) and Vanbandhu Kalyan Yojana.

Table 4.1: Beneficiaries under the Various Government Housing Schemes

Category	Scheme	Respondents	Percent
A	VBKY	38	36.19
	SPAY	40	38.10
	IAY	27	25.71
	Total	105	100.00
B	VBKY + SPAY	13	72.00
	VBK + IAY	5	28.00
	Total	18	100.00
C = A–B	Grand Total Govt. Beneficiaries	87	100.00

13 of the respondents have received the benefits of both: Sardar Patel Awas Yojana (SPAY) and Vanbandhu Kalyan Yojana, while five of the respondents received the benefits of Indira Awas Yojana (IAY) and Vanbandhu Kalyan Yojana. A total of 18 respondents received the benefits of two of the schemes.

When we deduct the total number of people (18) who have received the benefits of two of the schemes from the total 105 respondents have received the benefits of at least one of the schemes, we receive the actual grand total number of respondents having received government scheme beneficiaries i.e. 87.

The Table 4.2 depicts the various other Schemes which have resulted in beneficiaries receiving benefits related to household expenditure. A total of 105 respondents had received some or the other benefits. While 22 of the respondents received agricultural related benefits, 14 respondents received animal related benefits, 67 of the respondents received house related benefits and 2 of the respondents received other benefits like bicycles and machines.

Table 4.2: Benefits from other Various Schemes

Category	Scheme	Respondents	Percent
A	Agriculture related benefit	22	20.95
	Animals	14	13.33
	House	67	63.81
	Others	2	1.90
	Total	105	100.00
B	Agriculture + House	18	100.00
C = A–B	Grand Total	87	100.00

Similar to the different housing schemes we observed that 18 of the respondents have received both agricultural and house related benefits. Hence when we deduct the total number of people (18) who have received the benefits of both agricultural and house related benefits from the total 105 respondents have received the benefits of at least one of the schemes, we receive the actual grand total number of respondents having received government scheme beneficiaries: 87.

Beneficiaries Possessing Assets under the Various Schemes: The study revealed that 76 out of the 87 respondents still have the assets under the schemes available with them. 11 out of the 87 respondents do not have the assets under the schemes now available with them. These include animals or agricultural related equipment. House related assets are available with all.

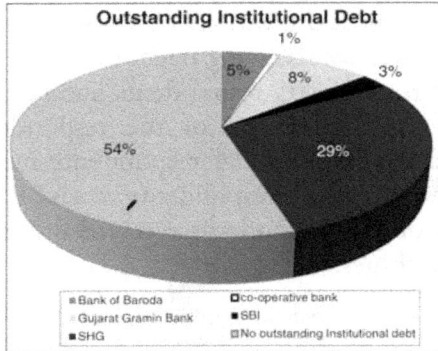

Fig. 4.25: Institutional Debts of the Respondents

Source: Primary survey.

From the above pie chart it appears that majority of the respondents were free from any debt from different institutions. 82 of the respondents out of the 150 respondents have no outstanding institutional debt. 32 of the respondents have outstanding institutional debts with them, out of which 43 numbers of respondents have taken loan from SHG. Those who are connected to government, NGOs or SHGs have received the loans from SHG—all of them being females.

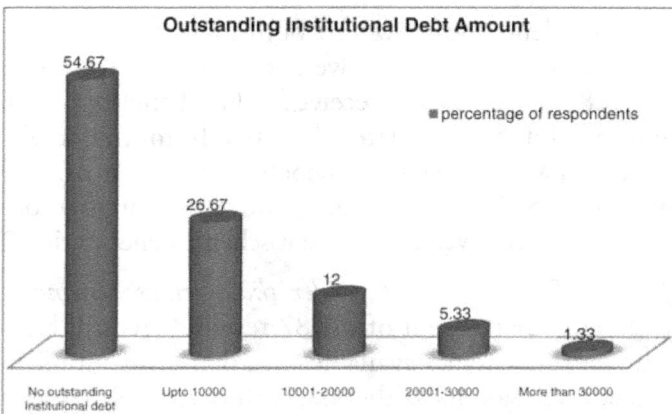

Fig. 4.26: Amounts of Institutional Debts of the Respondents

Source: Primary survey.

This signifies that in the five villages surveyed by us, SHG has been working very efficiently. 13 of the respondents have taken loans from Gujarat Gramin Bank, while very few of them have taken loans from other government banks. This is because the banks do not provide loans to the village people because they aren't able to be eligible as per the banks' criteria/rules. This also indicates that most of them are dependent and are in the clutches of private village moneylenders who charge exorbitant interest rates.

It is clear that the villagers do not receive a large amount of institutional loan from either – SHGs or the banking sectors. Majority of them receive a loan of up to ₹ 10000 to 20000. 40 of the respondents had received a loan of up to ₹ 10000, while 18 of the respondents had received a loan of ₹ 10000–20000. 10 of the respondents have received a loan of up to ₹ 20,001 and above and most of these loans have been received from the banking sector.

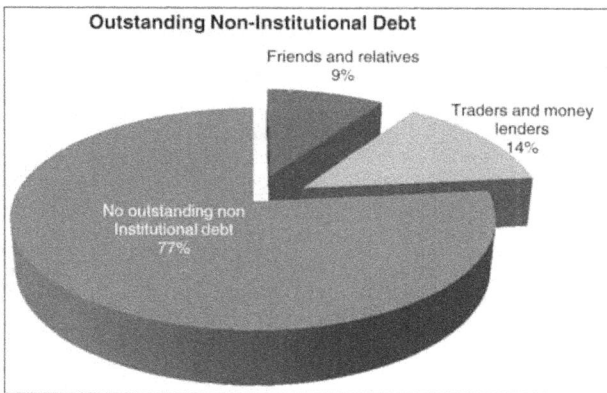

Fig. 4.27: Non-Institutional Debts

Source: Primary survey.

From ancient times villagers used to borrow money from their friends, relatives or even money lenders. However, owing to the benefits and facilities provided by the SHG, villagers have now begun lending money from the SHG. Still, in case of emergencies, when villagers do not get a loan from banks or are not associated to any NGO or SHG, they still tend money from friends, relatives, traders or money lenders. Out of the 150 respondents, 14 have taken loan from friends and relatives while a larger number 21 of them have taken loan from traders and money lenders.

Very few numbers of villagers receive a large amount of loan. The reason being that majority of the scheduled tribe do not have repayment capacity or any asset to mortgage or to provide security against any loan. Out of the 150 respondents, only five of them have received a loan of more than ₹ 10000. 17 of the respondents have received a loan between ₹ 3001 and 5000. The above table also denotes that villagers receive very less amount of loan from non-institutional loans in comparison to institutional loans.

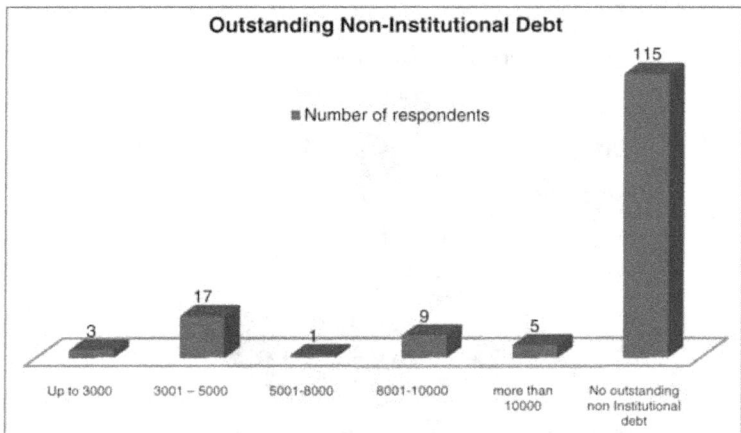

Fig. 4.28: Amount of Non-Institutional Debt

Source: Primary survey.

Social Discrimination against Scheduled Tribe: 127 of the respondents confirmed that they did not face any discrimination in social functions held because most of the people staying there are tribal and hence they feel no discrimination among themselves. They generally do not intermingle with non-tribal and hardly ever participate in their functions.

The same above reason holds true for temple discrimination. The tribal are a cohesive group and prefer to remain closely knit. They have their own temple where they go to worship hence do not face any confrontation with other communities. Thus, 118 of the respondents out of the 150 respondents confirmed that did not face any discrimination in temples because most of the people staying there are tribal and hence they feel no discrimination among themselves.

Schemes for Child Education: The primary survey revealed that 110 of the respondents were aware of the special scheme benefits given by the government for education of children. 40 of the respondents were not aware of it because they themselves were illiterate. The benefits of tribal scholarship for the tribal include ₹ 1600 per year in higher secondary and ₹ 700 for secondary. Every girl child going to school was given a cycle from the government.

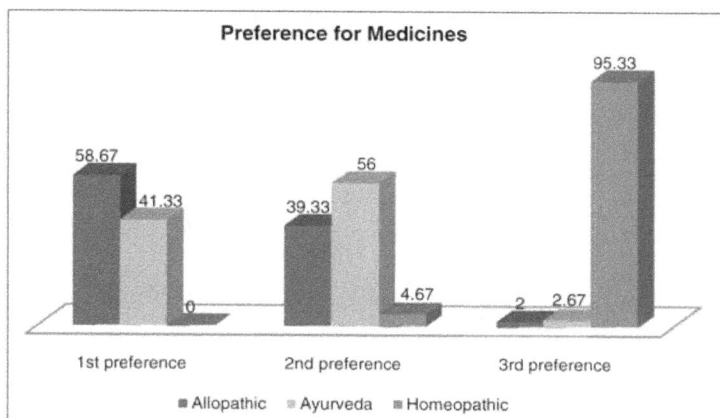

Fig. 4.29: Preference for Medicines Taken by Tribal

Source: Primary survey.

The above bar chart illustrates that maximum number of villagers give first preference to Allopathic medicine. 88 of the respondents gave first preference to Allopathic medicine while 62 of them still give first preference to Ayurvedic medicines. None of the respondents give first preference to Homeopathy because they are not aware of Allopath.

59 of the respondents give second preference to Allopathic medicine, while 84 of the respondents give second preference to Ayurvedic. Seven of the respondents give second preference to Homeopathic, which signifies that very few people give any preference to Homeopathy.

Three of the respondents were such who gave third preference to Allopathic medicine and four of the respondents gave third preference to Ayurvedic. Most of the respondents' third preference was Homeopathy.

Dahod being near to Ahmedabad the tribal are more exposed to basic amenities in health and do not totally rely on their traditional medicines of herbs and plants which other tribal in India who are inhabiting in real interior inaccessible to modern health facilities. Even access to Primary Health Centres in interior rural areas is not seen for the tribal.

Observations and Recommendations

Looking back in time tribal communities in India have thrived in a state of oblivion and deprivation. Poverty, illiteracy, bondage, indebtedness, exploitation, unemployment and disease have painted a very gloomy scenario for this marginalized community. Tribal population in India is mainly concentrated in the eastern states, Chhattisgarh, Madhya Pradesh and Odisha and also in some parts of Gujarat and Andhra Pradesh. Taking into account the gravity and multitude of the problems encountered by the tribal it is practically impossible to address these issues in a holistic manner. Piecemeal strategies adopted by states such as Gujarat and Andhra Pradesh have shown a beckon of light to do away with the existing gloomy situations of the tribal communities and help them drift towards a glorious future. Government policies focussed on bringing tribal communities in Andhra Pradesh and Gujarat in the mainstream of 'inclusive growth' as per the Twelfth Five Year Plan have shown a ray of hope in uplifting tribal from deep rooted poverty and solving their problems from grass root levels.

Government initiatives in Gujarat such as the Vanbandhu Kalyan Yojana, Integrated Tribal Development Projects, Tribal Area Sub-Plan, Swarnim Krushi Mahotsav along with health, housing and education schemes for tribal upliftment have shown positive outcomes in paving the way for a life of dignity and security for tribal in Gujarat. Nonetheless the State initiatives for tribal development in Andhra Pradesh which include interventions such as IFAD, Indira Kranthi Patham, Adivasi Mahila Sashaktikaran Yojana, Janshala Janashi Bhima Yojana, Employment Assurance Scheme, SGSY and other sectoral programs have played a vital role in setting benchmarks for tribal development in the region.

Despite eclectic measures taken by both the states to give tribal a better human face the fact remains that tribal people and tribal areas in Gujarat and Andhra Pradesh still lag pathetically behind other states or countries across the globe in terms of inclusive growth and sustainable development. Poverty, disease, hunger, unemployment and low standards of living all are the order of the day in the present tribal scenario of Gujarat and Andhra Pradesh. The story of female tribal is all the more pitiable and obscure. No doubt there are several special provisions for the promotion of economic and educational interests of STs in the Constitution of India. The constitution also endeavours to shield the STs from any form of exploitation and social injustice. As per the Fundamental Rights and Directive Principles of State Policy development of tribal population in India has been given special impetus. But the question that still lingers in front of three main players i.e. the government, the civil societies and the people themselves is that how can we shape policies into concrete actions and ensure a better sustainable future for the tribal. The much debated 'human development' has proposed a holistic approach to sustainability which includes upliftment of health, education, work and employment status and human security for all. But the grim fact remains, when talking about STs in Gujarat and Andhra Pradesh there has been no Human Development. 'Inclusive growth' and 'Sustainable Development' are two faces of the same coin. Hence if we dream of a glorious and sustainable future for the nation as a whole we have to leave no stone unturned to pull out the STs from the gloomy pits of underdevelopment, inequality and exploitation.

After examining in depth the various policies brought out by the Government of Andhra Pradesh and Gujarat and the situations and problems faced by the Government in implementing the policies particularly in reducing poverty levels of the tribal in the districts under study in both the statesit cannot be denied that Gujarat has fared better than Andhra Pradesh in some parameters, whereas Andhra has lagged behind.

The Vanbandhu Kalyan Yojana (VKY) has served as a bellwether for promoting 'sustainable and qualitative employment' opportunities for the tribes in Gujarat in particular and for the whole of India in general. This programme was launched in the year 2007 with an allocation of ₹ 15,000 crore for the upliftment of tribal population dwelling in the state. It is one of the most salient initiatives taken under the eleventh five year plan. The Chief Minister initiated the VKY with a vision of doubling the income of the 5 lakh under privileged tribal households in the state. The strategies adopted under this programme marked the dawn of a new era for the tribes in the face of enhancement of employment opportunities by improving agricultural productivity. Animal husbandry and dairy based activities got a boost by the VKY. Quality skill development of the tribal youth and preference to women-headed households are significant strategies laid by the Gujarat government. Moreover, emphasis was also laid on development of modern, scientific and technical amenities and also on making them accessible to the tribal youth in Gujarat. This has led to considerable augments in livelihood opportunities of the future generations of the tribes. The programme has also been carried forward in the twelfth plan period and has played a significant role in tribal development in the state of Gujarat.

The role of NGOs, SHGs, better financial inclusion and governance in Gujarat cannot be under-rated and Andhra has a lesson or two to learn from this. But the status and position of tribal in both the states are far from exemplary and needs priority concern from not only state authorities and machinery but from society as a whole. A public-private partnership model in the up-liftment and in mainstreaming the tribal in inclusive growth agenda is the call of the day.

Addressing the problems that we are facing in the tribal areas requires lot of understanding about the people, their culture and belief. Success in implementing in any schemes in the welfare of the tribal people and tribal area depends on how well it addresses the local needs than satisfying a political party or a leader for a short period.

Various community centres and training programmes should be there to bring the tribes to the mainstream of progress. Attention should be given to provide adequate education and health care and avenues for cultural activities to understand the tribes and ride away the fear in their mind about other people and communities they mingle in the development process. Programmes and schemes should be framed in such a way that it should create a sense of trust in the tribes that they are not deprived of from their right and freedom to live in their land with their culture and belief for ever.

The policies brought out by the State Government and the Central Government for the development of tribal regions has been based on a two dimensional approach—promotion of developmental policies and schemes through planned efforts; and protection of the interests of the Scheduled Tribes with administrative, legal, and constitutional support.

It is a fact that there are a few drawbacks in the process of implementing the government policies for the development of tribal. It would be a welcome step if State governments could make local arrangements in the tribal sub-plan areas to delegate Panchayat or Gram Sabha in such regions to enforce implementation and control of tribal sub-plan resources. The special policies, schemes and programmes formulated or proposed by the Government should necessarily reflect financial and physical targets with a specific time frame, in order to smooth the progress of monitoring in implementation of the same from time to time. The study concludes that during last two decades considerable attention has been given to the development of tribal areas in both the states. With separate administrative arrangements made by the State Governments and at the Centre for pursuing tribal development, it is to be hoped that the pace of development in tribal zones, would grow manifold and yield substantial benefits.

There is a lack of consensus regarding tribal development. Roy Burmanlong back had opined that: "there are four phases in the foci of tribal development planning in India. In the first phase, the emphasis was on providing immediate relief to the general mass of population, who were denied amenities of life during the colonial rule and at the same time to build up the productive infrastructure for the future growth. In the second phase, the emphasis was on resource mobilization and provision of social service infrastructure in the country side. In the third phase, the emphasis on educational level shifted to reduction of disparity and growth with justice. Simultaneously the commercialization of resources was stepped up. Fourth phase emphasizes programmes for meeting the basic needs of the population and poverty elevation had been stepped up. The Advantage of the tribal development of the first phase was mainly taken by the non-tribal living in tribal areas that were having more contact with those who have administrative power" (1989).

Repeatedly it has been argued that the question of tribal development has not yet received concentrated attention that it deserves, both in planning circles and in tribal studies. The real challenge of tribal development is to modernize the tribal economies and to integrate them with the larger national economy without at the same time disrupting their ecological existence, their socio-cultural systems and their traditions of socio-economic equity and innocence.

Thus, tribal in Andhra Pradesh have been badly served both by their exploiters and by their well-wishers. The latter also condone, if not support, tribaltaking to arms. Naxalite rebellion has brought the government to a virtual standstill in nearly half the country. Though it looks like success it is not, because the movement is strongly negative. Thus, the tribal become their own champions strangulating economic progress.

Recently, the Andhra Pradesh bureaucracy swung to the other extreme. It has decided that tribal children should be educated in their own dialect. Undoubtedly, these bureaucrats are sympathetic to tribal welfare but they are no less dictatorial. This new move isolates tribal children even further from the mainstream. It destroys what little chance of education and employment in future. The decision to change the medium of instruction to the tribal dialect may be well-intentioned but it is arbitrary, an act of high-handedness. The decision has been taken without consulting the affected people. As Prof. Amartya Sen has been saying "every individual can have—and should have—multiple identities".

The 73rd and 74th Amendments of the Constitution of 1992, which had introduced the three-tiered Panchayati Raj system in villages and urban settlements, had stopped short of the tribal areas listed in the Fifth Schedule of the Constitution. PESA was meant to extend the concept of devolution of power to areas notified for tribal. By earmarking areas containing predominant tribal populations and listing them in a Constitutional Schedule, the idea was to ensure that the land and natural resources were not alienated from the tribal communities.

The Supreme Court had upheld the protection of natural resources for tribal. In its July 1997 judgement on the petition filed by Samatha, an Andhra Pradesh-based NGO the Court said that granting of mining and prospecting leases to non-tribal in scheduled areas was void and impermissible. Though the case related only to Andhra Pradesh, the Court extended its jurisdiction to scheduled lands in other States.

You have requested "on-the-fly" machine translation of selected content from our databases. This functionality is provided solely for your convenience and is in no way intended to replace human translation. Show full disclaimer

Neither ProQuest nor its licensors make any representations or warranties with respect to the translations. The translations are automatically generated "AS IS" and "As available" and are not retained in our systems. ProQuest and its licensors specifically disclaim any and all express or implied warranties, including without limitation, any warranties for availability, accuracy, timeliness, completeness, non-infringment, merchantability or fitness for a particular purpose. Your use of the translations is subject to all use restrictions contained in your Electronic Products License Agreement and by using the translation functionality you agree to forgo any and all claims against ProQuest or its licensors for your use of the translation functionality and any output derived there from. Hide full disclaimer Translations powered by LEC.

When the tribal protested against being displaced from their land, given to mining companies, they were accused of stalling development by creating a social fuss. The fishermen at Gangavaram village are no exception to this. They were asked to leave the place where they have lived for generations. When they protested, they were beaten up. They are being evicted forcibly in the name of progress and development.

The emerging policy framework of today is a result of three major developments: a) Change in regimes in 2004 at the centre as well as in Andhra Pradesh and Gujarat; b) three national policy initiatives on triballand undertaken by the central government; c) and a more participatory and consultative policy-making process. Thus any policy initiative needs to cover three important areas of tribal land policy: A national policy on tribal; forest rights; and a national rehabilitation policy. These policies have to be given priority in keeping with the commitments made in its Common Minimum Programme (CMP).

The overall situation prevailing in AP today is one where the alienated land cannot be restored because of legal loopholes, non-retrospective land regulations, powerful outsiders and a continuing lack of political commitment to protecting tribal rights. Mostnon-tribal manages to hold on to their land by obtaining stay orders or producing false documents. Added to this is rampant rent-seeking among officials. Development projects are emerging as new sources of land alienation. In this context, tribal areas are used to attract private capital for exploiting mineral resources and tribal are forced to pay a far higher price in the case of irrigation projects as the lion's share of expected benefits would accrue to non-tribal. The track record of governments with respect to the resettlement and rehabilitation programmes is a classic case of too late and too little.

The tribal land problem in AP has assumed new dimensions in relation to the traditional rights over 'podu' and access to natural resources in general. The debate about shifting cultivation has been revived in the context of externally funded participatory forest management programmes such as JFM and CFM (joint/community forest management). Traditional rights and livelihood pattern of the forest-dependent tribal need to be respected while designing and implementing forest management programmes. At present the law seems to be harder on poor tribal than it is on more powerful and corrupt agents who are more damaging to forests than podu.

Tribal land issues are currently subjects of national debate thanks to the major policy initiatives taken by the centre. With respect to land alienation to non-tribal, the recommendations made by the NAC—particularly with regard to making the land administration system more transparent, participatory, accountable and tribal-friendly— could make a positive impact on the restoration process. Lessons could be learnt from other experiments such as the work on the right to information of the Mazdoor Kisan Shakti Sanghatan (MKSS) in Rajasthan. If training and capacity-building of tribal are given in land administration, survey and settlement and land transfer regulations, this will go some way towards empowering tribal. Imparting legal literacy to tribal should be an integral part of capacity-building approach. Interventions towards legal empowerment can draw upon some innovative initiatives adopted by NGOs such as SAKTI. Other complementary reforms such as plugging the loopholes in the protective laws and strengthening the quasi-judicial machinery that enforces these acts need immediate policy attention. The trained tribal would be able to assist the gram sabha expected to be further empowered by the proposed legislations. The gram sabha should be allowed to play a role in the adjudication of tribal land disputes. The survey and settlement process in the scheduled areas should be completed and this should recognise the customary rights to land. Customary rights need to be respected while drawing up boundaries under various forestry, wildlife and land programmes. The long overdue National Rehabilitation Policy needs to incorporate the special concerns related to tribal livelihoods. In this context, the suggestions made by the NAC are particularly relevant. The NAC's recommendations address the serious flaws of the policy and take into account the concerns voiced by civil society. Since indebtedness is a major vulnerability, there is a clear case for strengthening and expanding institutional credit in scheduled areas. The Self-Help Groups (SHGs) of women have great potential to meet the microcredit needs of the poor and address higher level needs and constraints. Empowerment of tribal women through SHGs has in several locations reduced the exploita-tion by vested interests.

Tribal development strategies, while respecting customary rights and tribal values, need to go beyond land-based activities. Human capital—education and health in particular—infrastructure, employment guarantee and food security are emerging as critical factors. Positive discrimination programmes have great potential to empower the STs. But Andhra Pradesh tribal are not homogeneous; upwardly mobile sections have already emerged. Some groups, notably the non-indigenous Lambadas or Banjaras, have been able to capture the lion's share of reservation benefits often at the expense of poorer and indigenous tribes. Policy and interventions need to take a more disaggregated view of tribal communities.

The Forest Rights Bill, despite its progressive spirit, has also attracted criticism from several quarters. The original bill had several ifs and buts that would have circumscribed the rights proposed to be conferred. The bill was tabled in the Parliament on December 13, 2005; it was then referred to a Joint Parliamentary Committee (JPC). The JPC has made several amendments to the bill and submitted its recommendations to the Parliament on May 23, 2006. The JPC has made several pro-tribal amendments to the bill so as to remove those hurdles and make it more progressive and comprehensive. In addition to the STs, the revised bill includes in its ambit "other traditional forest dwellers". The gram sabha is given more powers to hear and decide on the claims to forest land and other resources. The consent of the gram sabha is mandatory regarding land acquisition for development projects. More important are the changes relating to the cut-off date and the ceiling on the extent of land to be regularised. The revised draft extends the earlier cut-off date of 1980 to 2005 and removes the 2.5 ha upper limit. The bill makes it clear that it will prevail over other laws if the provisions of the latter contravene with those of the former. This is a welcome provision in that forest and wildlife laws have often been used against tribal. The amendments try to strike a balance between tribal rights and the state-induced deprivations caused by forest laws and development projects. So the pro-tribal tilt of the bill is understandable. A complementary policy initiative that is long overdue is related to land alienation to non-tribal. If protective laws are not strengthened and implemented effectively the forest rights contemplated by the above bill may not make a difference to tribal livelihoods.

The Forest Rights Bill also refers to the land rights of tribal displaced by development projects. The bill should have provisions to ensure that the land rights of the displaced tribal without documentary evidence to the ownership are also protected. Because the tribal lands remain unsettled; and unrestored in the case of alienation to non-tribal, this could result in non-tribal receiving compensation at the expense of tribal. More important, the policy should ensure that the resettled tribal do not lose their constitutional entitlements and the benefits of protective and developmental policies under the Fifth Schedule. Interestingly, the bill focusing on forest rights does not delineate the rights of tribal over mineral resources. Land alienation to non-tribal has also been a part of "historical injustice". But the state, instead of attempting to restore the alienated land to the tribal, seems to have opted the easy way out that is regularising the encroachments through the Forest Rights Bill.

Predominantly tribal villages that have remained outside the scheduled areas should be scheduled. Unfortunately, the centre is yet to act on the proposals, submitted by the Andhra Pradesh government two decades ago, to schedule 796 such villages in the state. Since the number of informal workers, including migrant labourers, among the STs is on the rise, providing them social security would go a long way towards reducing their vulnerability. The recently formulated bill, i e, the Unorganised Workers Social Security Bill 2006 seeks to provide minimum level of social security to the poor informal worker. Experience has shown that the *top-down tribal development policies* have largely failed to deliver on their promises resulting in a situation where the vast majority of indigenous tribal have remained at the receiving end. It is in this context that the suggestion of granting autonomy to the AP scheduled areas under the Sixth Schedule merits close consideration.

Moreover first proper living conditions, health and sanitation should be ensured, then education must be imparted and then the required skills to set up their own jobs. Action plans in different stages need to be made, implemented and followed in letter and spirit, this can also be achieved by joining hands with the local governments, NGOs, panchayats, etc. so that the actual needs of people come into light.

The International Fund for Agricultural Development (IFAD) works with poor rural people to enable them to grow and sell more food, increase their incomes and determine the direction of their own lives. Since 1978, IFAD has invested about US$ 13.2 billion in grants and low-interest loans to developing countries through projects empowering about 400 million people to break out of poverty, there by helping to create vibrant rural communities.

IFAD-initiated programmes focuses on building the capacity of poor rural people and their institutions, so that vulnerable groups, particularly women, can plan and manage their own development and negotiate improved entitlements. Key objectives include better access to and management of natural resources, improved access to financial services and markets and the development of non-farm enterprises. The programmes offer a wide range of options to meet diverse needs, including wage employment, microfinance services and short- and medium-term investments in agriculture and related activities, as well as a flexible fund for community infrastructure. As early as in 1999, IFAD had initiated an *Andhra Pradesh Participatory Tribal Development Project* with a total cost of US$ 50.3 million directly benefitting 76,810 households.

Suggestions

State Policy for Agricultural Development in Tribal Areas

The performance management can improve with fixing of accountability and with clear mandate and outcomes specified. It might serve therefore to bring in an Agriculture Policy for the State specifically for tribal areas. This is more so as poverty reduction is crucially dependent on agriculture and as state progress towards meeting MDGs will remain half achieved if the tribal areas does not become the focus of state agriculture policy. Balancing the policy focus on low productive areas and low productive population is important for promoting inclusive growth objectives of 12th Five Year Plan. Gender differential impacts can be defined in the state agriculture policy.

Equitable Investments, Positive Discrimination for Inclusive Growth

Tribal areas are resource poor areas. Tribal farmers are susceptible to socio-cultural, political, environmental and social factors of vulnerability (as highlighted by the study) thereby probability of a farmers falling back into poverty is much more evident in tribal areas than in non- tribal areas of the state. The principle of equity and higher allocations to TSP as tribal areas and farmers suffer from many disadvantages, which will require disproportionately higher public investments to improve tribal agriculture and economic well- being of tribal farmers dependent on agriculture for their livelihoods. It requires more commitment, flexibility and innovations to address agriculture and poverty link comprehensively, which can address currently skewed planning and budgetary allocations to a certain extent.

Impact Assessment of Agriculture Interventions in Tribal Areas

Clearly for poverty reduction outcomes investment needs in tribal areas requires to be differently understood and planned. Therefore the policy needs to look at agriculture investment in tribal areas differently than agriculture investments in other areas. Poverty reduction is possible in tribal areas but require an approach of agriculture and agri-allied focused livelihoods and watershed development. Such programme models exist within the tribal areas in Odisha and Madhya Pradesh. The Government agriculture set up in the states of Andhra Pradesh and Gujarat need to emulate these models and lead tribal agriculture on the path of sustained growth. The resource allocation decisions need to be based on schemes' reach and relevance. The decisions based on other considerations may not lead to desirable outcomes as is witnessed and presented by this study. The few resource allocations policy pointers can be as presented below:

- Micro minor irrigation needs to be promoted on a large scale with adequate allocations and appropriate targeting, the existing potential to increase cropping intensity can be realised. The overall budgets for these schemes should be based on local soil profile conditions. It is also advised that well recharging schemes are also promoted to maintain the water table.

- Kissan Mitra and Kisan Didi schemes are among the most relevant schemes in tribal areas as they follow the approach of community based extension. However the reach of these schemes is currently very limited which demand a detailed understanding of constraints facing Kisan Mitras and Kisan Didi to improve the implementation processes. Furthermore, the tribal areas need more RAEOs for the extension support, than the other areas. States needs to take a policy call on this aspect.

- The study results have also shown that the Seed Exchange scheme is not working in tribal area as tribaldueto their practices do not exchange own seed with seed from other sources. The tribal areas face the problem of availability of seeds at the right time and therefore Seed gram scheme is best suited intribal area.
- The relevance of crop insurance schemes for tribal farmers can never be over emphasised. Very limited awareness and benefit from crop insurance demand a policy intervention from the state.
- Soil and water conservation activities need higher allocation for tribal areas e.g. farm bundling and bunding schemes are very useful for the tribal areas with undulated topography requiring soil and water conservation work. Presently NREGS have provided opportunity to the farmers to work on their own land. SWC programme needs still lot of efforts by different implementation agencies in the tribal areas to improve land structure and moisture in the field.
- Tribal agriculture is close to the organic farming and this opportunity need to be leveraged by the state policy. The organic farming practices along with marketing support for organically grown crops will boost the organic practice in tribal areas of the state. This is more so true for coffee plantation in Paderu division in Andhra Pradesh.

Improving Relevance of Planning of Resources,
Interventions and Strategies

The process of planning should be strengthened in letter and spirit. The decentralization of planning with strong emphasis on robust district planning should become an urgent and critical priority of the department.

Necessary Push for Outcome based Budgets

Outcomes are the benefits drawn by the community of farmers and not limited to only delivery of activities. The policy therefore needs to strongly review the outcome based budgeting process and attainment of outcomes over a period of time.

Integrated Programme Models

The study results shows that integrated anti-poverty programmes in tribal areas are likely to generate the best outcomes/returns on public investments. One of the reasons is that these programmes can be most relevantly designed and intensively executed. Soil and water conservation, irrigation infrastructure will also significantly translate public investments in tribal areas.

Strengthening Institutional/Co-Operative Delivery of Agriculture Credit

Credit is an essential ingredient of agriculture investment for a farmer household in tribal areas. The credit delivery system is largely informal in the tribal areas. Unlike in other states, the co-operative societies are few and working for a very small percentage of the households in tribal areas. The model of co-operative societies providing agriculture, other investment and consumption credit can be strengthened though trying out linkages with Nationalised and other banks/MFIs. Banks will get access to large markets through correspondent model with co-operative societies providing the facilitation services as *'business correspondents'*. This may become a positive step towards financial inclusion.

Pushing Measures which Serve Environmental Cause

The agriculture interventions in the states especially in the tribal areas need to provide the necessary push to measures like soil and water conservation, organic farming, etc. which serve environmental cause while providing economic returns to low resource farmers.

Designing and Implementing Risk Management System

Agriculture especially tribal agriculture faces many risks. Managing these risks is crucial for a farmer in tribal areas to not fall back into the poverty trap. That continues to happen year after year for many tribal families. These can be prevented with a risk management strategy and fund for risk minimization.

Building the Agriculture Interventions on the Social Mobilization Base

Social mobilization is the pre-requisites for building the sustainable community mechanism that can become vehicle for agriculture development interventions in tribal areas. Extension requires social mobilization particularly to deal with the issues of information asymmetry.

Investing in Education Sector in Tribal Areas

Experiences from other states suggest that improvement in agriculture along with improvement in education attainment levels can lead to faster area development. Hence agriculture development requires investments in education (possibly higher investments and focus) in tribal areas. Tribal societies are changing for the better and getting into the mainstream of development. It may take another two decades to achieve envisaged growth and development in tribal areas. If education levels improve faster, tribal area agriculture and overall development can possibly be achieved in lesser time horizon.

Promoting Low Value Crops, Small Forest Products and Arts & Craft

Important traditional crops in the tribal areas need to be promoted. Such crops are mostly linked with the tribal life and its social, culture and health practices. The State Pro-poor strategy for supporting vulnerable community in the tribal areas can be strengthened with promotion of such minor crops. Food grain dependency on other cereals crops will reduce with increased traditional crop production as there are large potential for productivity improvement. It is therefore important that information reach which is limited needs to be provided to these small farmers.

Another most important aspect is the promotion of small forest products which is the livelihood of most tribal in the forest and hilly regions. Help in increased production, finance and marketing of these products will go a long way in making them self-reliant and financially better off. Small entrepreneur concepts need to be redefined. Private participation for processing and propagating benefits etc. of forest products need to be encouraged. Traditional medicines emanating and produced from small forest products requires promotion through marketing in exhibitions as well as export promotion.

Arts and crafts an expertise limited to Tribal needs to be exploited and promoted. Remote areas in Jharkhand and Chhattisgarh where these talents are latent and on extinct requires intense drive by state authorities, export promotion council and NGOs to help them retain this art.

Some Other Miscellaneous Interventions
- Establish Integrated farming system models.
- Agriculture product based value chain development/micro enterprise promotion.
- Markets facilitation for agriculture/forest commodities.
- NREGA led agriculture development.
- Promotion of organic agriculture in tribal areas.
- Developing markets for organic products.
- Private extension models up-scaled.
- Improvement in accountability and institutional delivery mechanism.

Periodic evaluation is required of agriculture/forest development and all State/Central schemes in tribal areas which may enable the necessary ideas on course corrections and improvement. The accountability will set in when performance is monitored and reflected upon in the spirit of improving agriculture for the cause of tribal development. For ensuring accountability of departmental investments, agriculture interventions, community based monitoring mechanism working with the Panchayats is the answer.

Improving Extension through Diverse Institutional Models

Extension being a basic essential service, can work through different solutions like privatization, PPP, NGO driven, convergence model, etc. as these solutions focus on collective-zetion and leadership development approaches. Tribal leadership, if developed can harness intent skills of tribal for agriculture/forest improvement in tribal areas.

Need to Impart Training

This is important in the context of tribal farm women and youth in various disciplines so that they can be motivated to start cottage industries and other income generating enterprises in their villages.

Self-Governance for Tribal

Another basic idea mooted by Tribal is that of self-governance. Schemes both State and Central are mostly lopsided and imposed on the Tribal without their consent and as to what their requirements are. Most often Schemes are decided at the top without grass-root interventions. There is need for greater autonomy and self- governance at their level for faster inclusive growth and development.

Thus we can conclude that multi-pronged efforts and concerted initiatives along with direct involvement of tribal for their betterment and development they can become part and parcel of mainstream economic activities. *Vision 2020 and Million Development Goals can be achieved and brought about by partnership of various stakeholders.* This distant dream then may not be far in the horizon.

Tribal people are always known as India's forgotten people. Official data of tribes reveal that all the indicators of development are worse off in terms of income, health, education, nutrition, infrastructure and governance. India has a vision for development which is much more inclusive and empowering but still today tribal people do not enjoy the fruits of socio-economic development in real terms. If we truly want to put the tribal population in equal platform we need to provide sustainable livelihood. Not only this for that we need a good governance. The Kuznets Curve will remain a mere fantasy if right programmes and policies are not followed properly. The much talked reforms are concentrating more on pro corporate side rather than on pro-poor the purpose if side. The rise of crony capitalism is a bar towards equity and justice. The popular schemes by the prime minister such as 'Skill India' and 'Make in India' will not serve the purpose if tribal at large are repeatedly ignored. We must development a new paradigm which follows a compassionate capitalism with more respect and dignity for the tribes. The situation of tribes in both Andhra Pradesh and Gujarat is no doubt gloomy but we have every hope that with sincere efforts of the government and the people tribes of both the states will march from '*gloom to glory*'.

Bibliography

A Baseline Survey Report (2004). Prepared by CESS, Hyderabad.

A Report on Census of Land Holdings (2000–01). Directorate of Economics and Statistics, Government of A.P., Hyderabad.

Anand Titus and Geeta N. Pereira (2007). "Shade Coffee at the Altar of Sacrifice—Indian Coffee and the World Market," www.ineedcoffee.com

Andhra Coffee one of the best, *Business Line*, Monday, May 12, 2003.

Andhra Pradesh—Claps for their Coffee, *The Hindu*, Sunday, May 14th 2006.

Andhra Pradesh—Data Highlights: The Scheduled Tribes, Census of India 2001.

Andhra Pradesh—Data Highlights: The Scheduled Tribes, Census of India 2001.

Andhra Pradesh—Forest Development Corporation launches Coffee export in *The Hindu*, Tuesday, July 13, 2004. Asha Krishna Kumar (2004), "A Brown Revolution", *Frontline*, July 17–30, 2004.

Census 2001 Government of A.P.

Center for Economic and Social Studies (Hyderabad) and Overseas Chaudhuri (ed.), Tribal Transformation in India, Vol. I, Inter-India.

Chengappa, P.G. (1981). "Growth Rates of Area, Production and Productivity of Coffee in India," in *Journal of Coffee Research*, 11(2), pp. 19–25.

Coffee Board, ITDA Plan to Boost Araku Brand, *Business Line*, 7th May 2007.

Coffee Regions of India—Araku Valley, *Indian Coffee*, January 2004.

Department Manual and Reports, Tribal Welfare Department, Gujarat Government.

Department Manual, Tribal Welfare Department, Government of Andhra Pradesh.

Development of 60,000 Acres of Coffee Plantations in the Agency Area of ITDA Paderu—A Report by Integrated Tribal Development Agency (ITDA), Paderu, Vishakhapatnam, 2003.

Development, Deprivation and Discontent: A Case of Dangs Tribals", in Development and Deprivation in Gujarat; Felicitation Volume for Professor Jan Breman; by Ghanshyam Shah, Mario Rutten and Hein Streefkerk (eds.) Sage, New Delhi, 2002.

Direct Export of Vizag coffee on the cards, *Business Line*, Tuesday, May 04, 2004.

District-Wise Socio Economic Indicators 2006, Directorate of Economics and Statistics, GoAP, Hyderabad.

Economic Survey, GOI, 2006–07.

Forest Rights Bill, 2005, available at: www.tribal.nic.in/billTA05.pdf.

Gopinath Reddy, M. and Madhusudan Bandhi, "Participatory Governance and Institutional Innovation—A Case of Andhra Pradesh Forest Project (JFM)."

Gopinath Reddy, M., Jayalakshmi, K. and Anne-Marie Goetz (2006). "Politics of Pro-poor Reform in the Health Sector: Primary Health care in Tribal Areas of Vishakhapatnam, *Economic and Political Weekly*, Vol. XLI, No. 5, pp. 419–426.

Guidelines for Production of Organic Coffee in India—Coffee Board 2003.

Hand Book of Statistics—Vishakhapatnam District (2004–05), Compiled and Published by The Chief Planning Officer.

http://encyclopedia2.thefreedictionary.com/Work+Participation+Rate

http://farm7.staticflickr.com/6064/6032472626_058908c0ab_z.jpg

http://nsct.nic.in

http://shodhganga.inflibnet.ac.in/bitstream/10603/1659/9/09_chapter%203.pdf

http://www.wikipedia.org

MahbubulHaq, 'Development Programing' A.P. Government, 2008.

Monitoring the Implementation of Social Security Schemes in Tribal Areas of Gujarat: with reference to Dangs District.", in a book on 'The Long Road to Social Security' by K.P. Kannan and Jan Breman (Eds.), Oxford University Press, New Delhi, 2013.

Nanda Gopal, J. (2002), "Branded Coffee from APFDC," *Business Line*, November 18.

Paderu Health Plan (2006). Tribal Welfare Department, A.P.

Prasad, R.R. and Sachchidananda (1998). "Encyclopaedic Profile of Indian tribes with maps and photographs", Discovery publishing house, New Delhi.

Qualitative and Sustainable Employment | Components of VKY | Vanbandhu Kalyan Yojana. (n.d.). Retrieved January 17, 2016, from http://vky.gujarat.gov.in/qualitative-and-sustain able-employment

Radhakrishnan, S. (2006). "Coffee Consumption in India-Perspectives and Prospects," Cover story, *Indian Coffee*.

Radhakrishnan, S. (2006). "Recent trends in Coffee Consumption in India," *Indian Coffee*, pp. 17–21.

Rajpramukh, K.E. and Palkumar, P.D.S. (2005). "Livelihood Challenges and Strategies: The Valmikis of Eastern Ghats," *Anthropologist*, 7(2), pp. 153–160.

Rao, Mohan K. (1999). Tribal Development in Andhra Pradesh: Problems, Recommendations on Tribal Welfare, available at: www.nac.nic.in.

Reddy, Ratna V. *et al.* (2004): Participatory Forest Management in Andhra.

Reddy, Subba N. (1988). 'Depriving Tribals of Land: Andhra Move to Amend.

Saxena, N.C. (2006). "The Resettlement and Rehabilitation Policy of India."

Scheduled Castes and Scheduled Tribes in Andhra Pradesh 1961 to 2001, Directorate of Economics and Statistics, GoAP, Hyderabad.

Scheduled Castes and Scheduled Tribes Literacy—Andhra Pradesh (2001). Directorate of Economic and Statistics, Government of A.P., Hyderabad.

State Five Year Plan Documents.

State, Development and discontent: People's Protest in Umbergaon, in *Economic and Political Weekly*, August 5, 2000, Vol. 35, No. 32.

Subrahmanyam, V. (2003). "Role of Government for the Enhancement of Education Status Among Tribes in the Integrated Tribal Development Agency Area of Paderu, Andhra Pradesh," *Stud. Tribes Tribals*, 1(2), pp. 155–161.

Subramanyachary, P. (2013). "Status of Scheduled Tribes in Andhra Pradesh", The Dawn Journal, Vol. 2, No. 1.

Sunita Reddy (2004). "Ecosystems Approach to Human Health: A Case of KondaReddi Tribes and Women's Health," *Journal of Human Ecology*, 16(4), pp. 271–282.

Sustainable Tribal Empowerment Project (STEP) CARE-Vishakhapatnam, T W Department, Government of Andhra.

Tribals, Missionaries and Sadhus: Understanding Violence in the Dangs, in *Economic and Political Weekly*, September 11, 1999, Vol. 34, No. 37.

Uma Devi, K., Pandurangarao, A. and Raju, V.T. and Shareef, S.M. (2003). "Constraints in Production and Marketing of Coffee: A Case Study in Vishakhapatnam District," *The Andhra Agricultural Journal*, No. 50 (3&4), pp. 322–326.

World Development Report (1993). 'Investing in Human Development'.

www.ingramcontent.com/pod-product-compliance
Lightning Source LLC
Chambersburg PA
CBHW061722270326
41928CB00011B/2074